ARABIA FELIX
FROM THE TIME OF
THE QUEEN OF SHEBA

ARABIA FELIX FROM THE TIME OF THE QUEEN OF SHEBA

Eighth Century B.C. to First Century A.D.

Jean-François Breton

Translated from the French by Albert LaFarge

University of Notre Dame Press
Notre Dame, Indiana

Manufactured in the United States of America

Translated by Albert LaFarge from the French *L'Arabie heureuse au temps de la reine de Saba: Viii^e–Ier siècles avant J.-C.*, published by Hachette Littératures, 74, rue Bonaparte, 75006 Paris, France.

The publisher is grateful to
THE FRENCH MINISTRY OF CULTURE
for support of the costs of translation.

© Hachette Littératures 1998

Library of Congress Cataloging-in-Publication Data

Breton, Jean-François.
    [Arabie heureuse au temps de la reine de Saba⸴. English]
    Arabia Felix from the time of the Queen of Sheba : eighth century
B.C. to first century A.D. / Jean-François Breton ; translated from the
French by Albert LaFarge.
        p. cm.
    Includes bibliographical references (p.) and index.
    ISBN 0-268-02002-7 (alk. paper)
    ISBN 0-268-02004-3 (pbk. : alk. paper)
        1. Arabia, Southern—Civilization. I. Title.

    DS247.A144B7513 2000
    953'.02—dc21   99-043002

Then she gave the king a hundred and twenty talents of gold, and a very great quantity of spices, and precious stones; never again came such an abundance of spices as these which the queen of Sheba gave to King Solomon.

1 Kings 10:10

CONTENTS

Introduction   1

The Queen of Sheba: Myths and Legends — The Myth
of Arabia Felix — In Pursuit of Myths?

1. The Gardens of Saba   9

The Roof of Arabia — A Land of Monsoons — Down
the Wadi Dhana — Mastering the Floods — A "Hydraulic" Society? — The Two Gardens — Crops and Forests
— The City of Maʾrib — The Temples outside the City
Walls — Words Carved in Stone

2. The Caravan Kingdoms   29

The Sources — What Is Saba? — The First Mukarribs
— The Reign of Mukarrib Karibʾîl Watar — The
Sabaean Peace — Reasons for the Success of the
Sabaeans — Saba: Kingdom without a Queen? — The
Decline of the Sabaean Empire — The Rise of Qatabân
— Maʿîn and the Minaeans — Hadramawt — More
Than One Arabia Felix?

3. Fragrances of Arabia   53

Theophrastus's *Natural History* — Myrrh — Frankincense — Two Harvests a Year — Other Spices — Unknown Quantities — Frankincense Routes through

South Arabia — From Arabia to the Mediterranean —
Some Prices — Organization of the Caravans — Maritime Routes

4. Cities and Villages   75

A Sparsely Populated Land — Fortified Cities — A Distinctive Urbanism — A Visit to Shabwa — Wooden
Houses — Tower-Houses — A Wealthy Man's Home —
Austere Dwellings — Functions of the House — The Villages — Farmhouses

5. Economy and Society   93

A Unique Society — Tribal Organization — A Hierarchical Society — The Place of Women — The Peasants —
Animal Husbandry — The Rural Economy — The Urban Economy — The Fragility of the Urban Economies
— The Builders — Scribes and Clerks — The Steppes
and the Deserts

6. The Gods and Their Temples   117

Fragmentary Sources — The God ꜥAthtar — The God
Almaqah — Hawbas — Principal South Arabian Divini-
ties — Other Divinities — Gods without Human
Forms? — The Economy of Temples — Peculiar Rites —
Some Ceremonial Costumes — Sanctuaries of the Ar-
chaic Period — Temples of Jawf and Hadramawt

7. The World of the Dead   143

The Heritage of the Past — Cavern-Tombs — Mausole-
ums — Images of the Dead — A Final Dwelling Place —
Burial of the Dead in the Silt — The Tombs of Camels
— Later Burial Practices

8. Toward New Horizons   159

The Rise of Himyar — The Royal Tribe of Saba — The
Arrival of the Nomads — The Roman Army in South
Arabia — New Horizons beyond the Sea — The
Periplus of the Red Sea — A Hybrid Art

Conclusion   177

Glossary   181

Notes   185

References   197

Index   207

Arabia Felix

Ancient Names
in italics
(read West to East)

Yalá/*Hafari*
Ma'rib/*Maryab*
Hajar Ibn Humayd/*dhū-Ghayl*
Hajar Kulhān/*Tamna'*
Nisāb/*Abadān*
Shabwa/*Shabwat*
al-'Abr/*'Abrān*
Hurayda/*Madhāb*
Raybūn/*Raybūn*
Bi'r 'Alī/*Qāni'*
Shibām/*Shibām*
Say'ūn/*Say'ūn*
Tarīm/*Tarīm*

Shibām-al-Ghirās/*Shibām*
al-Haqqa/*Damhān*
Zafār/*Zafār*
al-Baydā/*Nashq*
Kamna/*Kaminahū*
Aden/*Dhu 'Adan*
Ma'īn/*Qarnaw*
Barāqish/*Yathill*
Sirwāh/*Sirwāh*
al-Asāhil/*Ararāt*

GULF OF ADEN

AL-JAWL

HADRAMAWT

RAMLAT AS-SAB'ATAYN

AL-JAWF

TIHĀMA

RED SEA

Makaynūn
Tarīm
Mashgha
Say'ūn
Shibām
al-'Ulayb
Balas
al-Mukallā

Raybūn
Hurayda
Shabwa
Bi'r 'Alī

al-'Abr
al-'Uqm
al-'Uqla

Nisāb
Hajar Ibn Humayd
Hayd Ibn-'Aqil
Hajar Kulhān
Hajar Arra
Hajar al-Barqa
Hajar adh-Dhaybiyya
Hajar Tālib

Jabal Makhniq
Kamna
Ma'īn
Barāqish
al-Asāhil
Sirwāh
al-Baydā
ash-Shaqab
Rayda
Amrān
Shibām
al-Ghirās
al-Haqqa
Shibām-Kawkabān
San'ā'
Yalá
al-Jūba
al-Masājid
Harib
Hinū az-Zurayr
Ma'rib

Kharibat al-Ajhar
Zafār
Shuka'
Ibb
al-Baydā'
Sabr
Aden

Sa'da

al-Hudayda
Île Kamarān
al-Makhā'
Bāb al-Mandab

100 km

w. al-Masīla
w. Hadramawt

▲

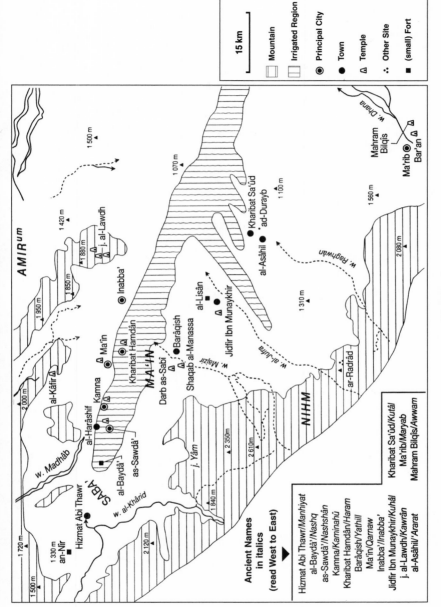

The Jawf

Legend:

15 km

Mountain
Irrigated Region
⊙ Principal City
● Town
△ Temple
∴ Other Site
■ (small) Fort

AMIR^um

j. al-Lawdh

1 500 m

1 420 m

1 880 m

850 m

1 950 m

1 070 m

⊙ Inabba'

△ al-Kāfir

2 000 m

Ma'īn △
Kharibat Hamdān △

Kamna

al-Harāshif

w. Madhāb

as-Sawdā' △

al-Baydā' ■

w. al-Khārid

Hizmat Abi Thawr ●

1 330 m
an-Nīr ■

1 720 m

1 500 m

MA'ĪN

Barāqish ●

Darb as-Sabī

Shaqab al-Manassa

j. Yām

2 120 m

1 840 m

2 350 m

2 610 m

al-Lisān ■
△

Jidfir Ibn Munaykhir

w. Majzir

NIHM

ar-Radrād ∴

1 310 m

w. al-Jufra

Kharibat Sa'ūd
ad-Durayb ●

1 100 m

al-Asāhil ●

w. Raghwān

1 560 m

2 080 m

Ma'rib ⊙
Bar'an △

Mahram Bilqis △

w. Dhana

**Ancient Names
in italics
(read West to East)** ▶

Hizmat Abi Thawr/*Manhiyat*
al-Baydā'/*Nashq*
as-Sawdā'/*Nashshān*
Kamna/*Kaminahū*
Kharibat Hamdān/*Haram*
Barāqish/*Yathill*
Ma'īn/*Qarnaw*
Inabba'/*Inabba'*
Jidfir Ibn Munaykhir/*Kuhāl*
j. al-Lawdh/*Kawrān*
al-Asāhil/*Ararat*

Kharibat Sa'ūd/*Kutāl*
Ma'rib/*Maryab*
Mahram Bilqis/*Awwam*

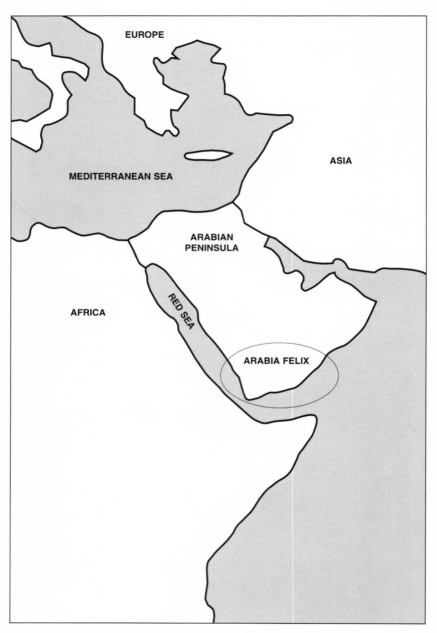

Arabia Felix and surrounding regions

INTRODUCTION

Arabia Felix was the name the ancient Romans gave to a fertile and prosperous land blessed with rare fragrances—and shrouded in mystery. This name, a Latin translation of the Greek Arabia Eudaimōn, would eventually make its way into English as Araby the Blest. This exotic landscape, thought to be located at the southern edge of the inhabited world, was said to disappear regularly under thick fog and violent monsoon rains. After a storm, its soil would exude a fragrance strong enough to roil the senses. The pleasure of myrrh was considered divine; frankincense subverted the body's equilibrium, producing a sublime stupor. Arabia Felix was fabled for its luxuriant fields, fragrant date palms, inexhaustible gold mines, and countless flocks and herds. High mountains barred access from the north, but traders brought reports of boundless luxury and palaces studded with gems, where precious cinnamon was burned like kindling. Decadence and inertia were said to sap the strength of the men, who renounced all earthly pleasures in favor of the fountain of immortality. The richest of these fabled tribes were the Sabaeans, who possessed all the fruits of the earth and the riches of Asia and Europe. Fortune was evidently an unjust goddess: She had imparted all good things in abundance to the Sabaeans.[1]

Those who could see past the mirage were appropriately cynical. Pliny the Younger derided the misnomer of Arabia *so-called* Felix as ungrateful to the gods: The country's "felicity" brought a luxury that carried men to their graves, and incense created for the gods was instead burned in lavish funeral ceremonies. Moreover, the country's bounty aroused a covetousness that spurred men to the greatest of dangers. How many sailors had succumbed to the inde-

scribable scent of spices wafted by the breezes off these shores—
only to drown in a sudden storm on the Red Sea or suffer ship-
wreck while attempting to pass the Gate of Tears?[2] The Roman
legions, ever disdainful of a foe unpracticed in the art of war, alleg-
edly inflicted heavy casualties on the Sabaeans. But how many soldiers were lost in forests so dense that the hapless men might as
well have been marching in the dark? And for greedy traders, the
sole measure of Arabia's "felicity" was the millions of sesterces that
poured in every year from the Empire. Pliny described the South
Arabian nations as "the richest in the world; the treasuries of the
Romans and Parthians flow there. They don't sell the products
of their seas or forests, and they purchase nothing from abroad."
Greek and Roman historians could at least distinguish Arabia Felix
from its stony and inhospitable neighbor to the north, aptly known
as Arabia Deserta. But even as the geography of South Arabia came
to be defined with increasing precision, the land of aromatic spices
remained beyond the reach of the Roman armies which had penetrated to the very heart of the realm.

Knowledge of South Arabia grew out of the quest for aromatic
plants, and the region's fortunes depended on commerce with
Assyria and the eastern Mediterranean. The camel came to be used
for transportation as early as the ninth century B.C. (its earlier use
was primarily as a food source), and crossings became increasingly common in the early eighth century B.C. Assyrians, Hebrews,
and Phoenicians all imported frankincense in their turn, at great
expense, from South Arabia. Frankincense comes chiefly from
Hadramawt (in modern-day Yemen), where the caravans gathered.
But it was the merchants of Saba who controlled the commerce.

It was in this capacity that Saba, or the biblical Sheba, emerged
in the Orient. The name Sheba arises in the genealogies of Genesis,
in the First Book of Kings, and in the Books of the Prophets, as a
country that sold spices, precious stones, and gold, and was active
in the caravan trade. Job 6:19 establishes a link between the caravans of Tema in North Arabia and the merchant trains of Sheba.
The precise location of Sheba remains uncertain, but its frequent
mention in association with frankincense lends credence to its having been in South Arabia.

The Queen of Sheba: Myths and Legends

The visit of a queen of Sheba to Jerusalem is briefly recounted in the First Book of Kings, in the context of an idealizing panegyric to the wisdom of Solomon. The queen had learned of the king's great reputation and set off to find him, bringing with her an imposing retinue including camels loaded with spices, gold, and precious gems. She was stunned by his greatness. "Blessed be the Lord your God, who has delighted in you and set you on the throne of Israel! Because the Lord loved Israel for ever, he has made you king, that you may execute justice and righteousness" (1 Kings 10:5–9).[3]

Is this passage historically reliable? Its date of composition is relatively late—doubtless no earlier than the eighth century B.C.— but nonetheless retains traces of an ancient legend of caravans arriving from a mysterious country, laden with exotic goods. This account gave rise to an extraordinary range of religious tracts, and its origin is extremely ancient. The Evangelists took up the story in their turn, referring to the Queen of Sheba as the "queen of the South" familiar to Judaism. Thus the Book of Luke predicts the Last Judgment, when "the queen of the South will rise at the judgment with the men of this generation and condemn them; for she came from the ends of the earth to hear the wisdom of Solomon; and behold, something greater than Solomon is here" (Luke 11:31). But the impression she left on Jewish memory is mainly the negative one of a sorceress. In the Book of Esther, compiled toward the end of the seventh century B.C., the author, relying on eastern sources, gives free rein to the imagination. Solomon, king of the beasts of the field, the birds, and the demons, meets a hoopoe bird which has just returned from a long voyage: "I observed certain countries whose capital city is called Kitor in the Orient," the bird said, "where the earth is rich with gold and silver is spread like dust along the roadsides. . . . And I saw a certain woman who reigned there, whom they call the Queen of Sheba." The hoopoe carried a message of invitation to the queen and begged her to go and bow before Solomon, warning her that failure to do so would result in the destruction of Sheba. The queen promptly set out on her route with her vessels full of precious wood and pearls. Solomon awaited her in a crystal palace. The queen, thinking she saw a basin of water before her, tucked up her gown, revealing her hairy legs. "Her beauty is that of a woman, but her hair is that of a man!" exclaimed Solomon, alarmed at how this woman's role reversal had upset the natural order of the universe.

The tale of this royal encounter survived to fire the medieval imagination.[4] Like the story of the Three Wise Men, the visit of the Queen of Sheba prefigured the Church of the gentiles coming to hear the words of the Savior, a theme illustrated notably in Hohenbourg's *Garden of Earthly Delights,* a virtual catalogue of twelfth-century iconography. In this work the queen pays homage to Solomon in a reinterpretation of the arrival of the Three Wise Men who, like the ancient queen, arrived in Jerusalem laden with gold, gems, and spices. In the scene of the crowning of the Virgin, she is seated at the side of Solomon along with Mary and Christ.

The Muslim tradition changed the name of the Queen of Sheba while otherwise appropriating the biblical tradition. In the Koran, Solomon (or Sulaiman), in his great wisdom, recruited his armies from among men, jinns, and birds. The inevitable hoopoe brought word of strange news from Sheba: "Surely I found a woman ruling among them, and she has been given abundance and she has a mighty throne: I found her and her people adoring the sun instead of Allah, and the Shaitan has made their deeds fair-seeming to them and thus turned them from the way, so they do not go aright." Solomon then dispatches the hoopoe to deliver his invitation, and at length the queen arrives with a request to meet him. "Alter her throne for her," the king commands; "we will see whether she follows the right way or is of those who do not go aright." When the queen is before him, he asks her, "Is your throne like this?" "It is as it were the same," she replies, "and we were given the knowledge before it, and we were submissive." She was turned away because she worshiped another besides Allah and lived among a nation of unbelievers. As she entered the palace, the queen mistook it for a body of water, and as she pulled up her robe, she revealed her calves. Solomon said: "Surely it is a palace made smooth with glass." "My Lord! surely I have been unjust to myself," she replied, "and I submit with Sulaiman to Allah, Lord of the worlds." (Surah XXVII [The Ant]:22–44) The Koran describes an impious queen and her subsequent conversion to monotheism.[5]

Yemeni historians regard Bilqîs as one of the three Himyarite queens known through their genealogies and their husbands. Bilqîs, daughter of a Himyarite king, was unable to decide upon a husband, as none of the eligible princes seemed to behave in a way befitting marriage. Consequently she summoned a group of noble officers and made the journey to visit Solomon. Having first complimented his wisdom and grace, she opened up her heart to him. Solomon advised her to choose a nobleman from the tribe of Bataʾ. She followed his advice and ruled Yemen through her husband, whose royal status gained through her favor. Solomon sent a group of jinns to build her a palace, but one day the artisans returned bearing news of her death; history suggests that Bilqîs and Dhû-Bataʾ left no royal heirs. These legends were succeeded by the accounts of authors from the classic period.

The Myth of Arabia Felix

At the beginning of the seventh century B.C., Egyptians, Assyrians, and Persians in the large cities of the eastern Mediterranean encountered caravans of aromatic products coming from South Arabia. The Assyrians used frankincense and myrrh in religious rituals, and the Hebrews soon adopted the practice; a proliferation of small altar boxes used for burning frankincense attests to the widespread diffusion of this precious spice. The Greek words for myrrh, saffron, and cassia from the Orient are first attested in the poetry of Sappho (probably dating to the late seventh century B.C.). During the so-called archaic period of Greek literature, an entire olfactory vocabulary developed as exotic fragrances made their way to the Mediterranean in increasing quantities to satisfy the demands of this new fashion.[6]

Around 450 B.C., Herodotus arrived in Babylon and was astounded by the profusion of frankincense reserved for ceremonial purposes by local cults: he noted several fantastic stories about the spice's origins and uses. He explained that the Arabian land exuded "a most marvelous sweet smell" (3.113), inviting comparison with the ashes of incense from which the mythical Phoenix rose. The area that is now modern Yemen was for Herodotus a mythical land whose only plants were frankincense, cinnamon, and gum-labdanum; nonetheless, he and other classical authors remain our principal source of knowledge on this subject. Theophrastus, a geographer of the third century B.C., heard that frankincense trees were said to grow in Saba, Hadramawt, Qatabân, and Maʿîn: the political geography was determined by the distribution of aromatic spices. Wild rumors circulated of nations endowed with natural bounty in prodigious measure, inviting the covetousness of others. After all, it had been Alexander's ultimate dream to conquer this marvelous land—a dream left unfulfilled at his death in 323 B.C. The Roman Emperor Augustus later attempted to lay his hands on this idyllic land, wishing to break the commercial monopoly on aromatic resins and take possession of the regions that produced them. The overland expedition of 26–25 B.C. was withdrawn a few months later, having achieved nothing more than a slightly improved knowledge of Arabia. But the Romans had already begun exploring maritime routes with the goal of gaining direct access to the ports of Hadramawt and controlling the sea routes of the Red Sea and the Indian Ocean. The local caravan traders never recovered from the development of sea routes. Deprived of all sources of wealth, the Arabian desert tribes slowly but surely settled into the vast territory of the Highlands, which eventually became the independent principality of Himyar.

In Pursuit of Myths?

Where did the Queen of Sheba come from, and what was her kingdom? How could the legend of Arabia Felix have arisen in such an arid country, with such a torrid climate and limited resources? The outside world had to wait until the modern era before the first light was shed on these questions. Beginning with a Danish expedition in 1762, scientists have attempted to make copies of certain inscriptions thought to date back to the Himyarites. In the nineteenth century, French botanist Paul-Emile Botta succeeded in collecting numerous plant specimens, and his countryman Théodore Arnaud managed to find his way to Maʾrib and Sirwâh.[7] In 1869, the Académie du Inscriptions et Belles-Lettres sent Joseph Halévy to Yemen, where he made 686 copies of inscriptions; his successful efforts in the face of difficult conditions yielded a decisive advance in our knowledge. He was followed several years later by Eduard Glaser, who returned with four stone inscriptions for the Louvre. In 1880, Alfred Bardey set up an office in Aden and enlisted his own brother, Pierre, along with the poet Arthur Rimbaud, to manage a workshop in Harar, across the Gulf of Aden in Africa. After Rimbaud's death in 1891, Pierre was drawn to the antiquities in Yemen and made regular contributions of South Arabian objects to the Louvre.

Archaeological research did not begin in Yemen until well after World War I. The first digs were undertaken by German scientists Carl Rathjens and Hermann von Wissmann, who discovered the small shrine of al-Huqqa, northwest of Sana, in 1928. Taking advantage of Britain's dominant position in Aden, the British established an archaeological presence in the southern part of the country. A team of women led by Gertrude Caton-Thomson opened up the temple of al-Huraydha, which they dated back to the six–fifth centuries B.C., as well as its necropolis and a neighboring building. In 1950, the American Foundation for the Study of Man sent an expedition to excavate the site at Hajar Ibn Humayd, at Tamnaᶜ, and its necropolis, Hayd Ibn ᶜAqîl, in the ancient kingdom of Qatabân. The following year, the expedition moved to Maʾrib, where it remained for only a short while.[8] More than two decades passed before digging resumed in Yemen. It was not until 1974 that the Yemen Arab Republic finally allowed a French group to excavate Shabwa, the ancient capital of the Hadramitic Kingdom.[9] These workers gradually extended their researches into the wadis Hadramawt, Dura, and Bayhân, and into the Jawf valley. Other teams from Germany, Italy, Russia, and Yemen have since contributed to a spate of new archaeological discoveries in South Arabia.

The image of so-called Araby the Blest (or Happy Arabia, as it was also known to earlier English speakers) that will emerge from this work is that of a country whose unique geography has forged a remarkably original culture. The mountains of Yemen rise as high as 3,700 meters, and their brutal descent on each side—westward into the Red Sea and eastward into the desert—frames an inexhaustible water supply. Monsoon rains and the flash-floods that follow were channeled through ancient irrigation works into the oases bordering the desert below. These techniques, and the socioeconomic models associated with them, had the effect of consolidating the culture of ancient South Arabia. The foundations of this common culture had been solidly established by the end of the second millennium B.C. In the period between the eighth century B.C. and the first century A.D., the region's cultural unity manifested itself in the development of a new form of writing known as Epigraphic South Arabian, the emergence of a common pantheon and iconography, and the development of a material culture of great homogeneity that transcended the different regions. This culture remained relatively unaffected by the outside world despite regular contact with the regions of the Fertile Crescent through the caravan trade. The uniqueness of South Arabian culture was largely born of this isolation.

Our picture of ancient Arabia remains incomplete; though several thousands of inscriptions have so far been found, they do not reveal all sides of its history. Literary, religious, and funerary texts are not sufficient to re-create the mental world of the South Arabians, nor can their economic activities be clearly reconstructed through surviving documents. Curiously, classical authors remain our principal source of information on crops and commerce in aromatic products. Archaeological digs are currently underway in several parts of Yemen, but our understanding of daily life progresses slowly. In our efforts to reconstruct the essential elements of their material culture, we continue to rely on our limited knowledge of their agricultural techniques, living quarters, funerary customs, and coinage. The scope of this study is necessarily constrained by the many gaps that limit all research in this field.

1. THE GARDENS OF SABA

Agatharchides, famed grammarian to Alexander the Great, described Saba and its territory in the following manner:

> The Sabaeans are the most important people of Arabia and possess all possible opulence. Their land is every bit as productive as our own, and the people exhibit the most remarkable characteristics. They have livestock in abundance. Visitors arriving at their ports are greeted with a divinely pleasurable fragrance from the many balsam and cassia trees that grow near the seashore and which are unspeakably lovely to behold.[1]

This fanciful description reflects a picture of the East that was typical among Greek geographers who had rarely ventured farther than the eastern shore of the Mediterranean or perhaps the Nile Valley; the stony desert of Arabia Petraea was certainly unfamiliar to them. It was mainly traders with Arabia Felix who brought back stories of the strange mountains of Yemen, which soared higher than any others in the Near East.

The Roof of Arabia

The topography of South Arabia is indeed dramatic. A wall of rock runs a thousand kilometers along a north-south axis parallel to the Red Sea, forming one of the major rifts of the Arabian-African plate. Its summits soar more than three kilometers above sea level, culminating in a peak at 3,760 meters not far from Sana in the Jabal Nabī Shuᵓayb. The mountains have been deeply contoured by

erosion, and valley walls often rise precipitously above the high
mesa to form veritable fortresses such as that of Jabal Haraz. Beyond these ridges, the high central plateaus are one of the most
bizarre features of the geography of Yemen. Here, at an altitude of
more than two kilometers above sea level, floodplains carpeted with
fertile deposits alternate with desert shelves, the former corresponding with volcanic deposits and the latter with eroded rock. A
succession of plains are strung in a line northward from Yarîm (at
2,300–2,500 meters above sea level) to Dhamar, Sana (2,300 meters), Amrân, Harf Sufiân, and Saada (about 1,800 meters).

> This immense plateau is protected from all sides by sharp mountain
> peaks, each of which is ringed by fortified towns which act as sentinels
> of the Imam (Sana). There is an unbroken ring protecting the plateau
> from all sides—seaward and landward, from the north, south, east, and
> west. It is as if a mysterious, all-powerful hand had thrown up these
> rocks high above the clouds to serve as a permanent bastion against all
> external forces.
>
> Nothing changes on the plateau, whose soil is composed of gray
> stones and whose mountain slopes of dark rock are eternal. The water
> has forever fixed the locations of villages and houses, gardens, orchards,
> and the old capital city. The caravans have traced strong and unchang-
> ing trails. Black camels advance slowly from the mountain passes,
> forming a line as long as the centuries.[2]

This mountain range dominates the low plain of Tihâma to the
west, one of the least habitable regions in Yemen. It is a coastal
desert region almost entirely devoid of water and with only sparse
vegetation, mainly date palms and locust trees. Just to the north is
the High Tihâma, which is greener due to irrigation from the great
wadis that flow from the Highlands. The mountains in eastern
Yemen rise gently from the desert of Ramlat as-Sabʾatayn, the
southern extension of the Rubc al-Khâli. This desert, with its rows
of dunes oriented along a north-south axis, stretches eastward all
the way to the edge of the plateaus of Hadramawt and is drained
by a single river basin combining the wadis Jawf and Hadramawt,
which then runs down the Wadi Masilah to the Indian Ocean.

A Land of Monsoons

The mountains of Yemen are the greenest part of the Arabian peninsula. Receiving the full brunt of powerful monsoons from the
southwest, the mountain bastion, and especially its southern extension, benefits from annual rainfall often in excess of 500 millimeters. Certain regions, like that around Ibb, receive as much as 900
millimeters of rain a year.[3] This is the region known as Green
Yemen, in the heart of Arabia Felix. The year is basically divided
into a rainy season from March through August, marked by heavy
downpours in the late afternoon, and a dry season in winter.
March and April receive heavy rains, but the heaviest rainfall tends
to come in the months of July and August. The ancients, who were
keenly aware of seasonal patterns of rainfall, referred to the July-
August rainy season as *kharaf* (autumn), in distinction from the
April-May season, which they called *datha* (spring). In the Highlands, where the seasons are more pronounced, the soil is yellowish and swept by sandstorms throughout the winter season; the
land becomes green again after the April rains.

These mountains trap great volumes of water which is then distributed to the areas below. The great basins to the east form a watershed that flows down the wadis toward the eastern desert. The
largest of these is the Wadi Dhana, with an area estimated at 8,000
square kilometers; at its eastern extremity lies the Sabaean capital
of Ma'rib.

Down the Wadi Dhana

On the high plateaus southeast of Sana, fertile floodplains are
hemmed in on all sides by mountains, and volcanic formations are
surrounded by recent lava flows. On the plains, river terraces run
alongside fields rimmed by high walls of rock that form natural basins for rainwater and topsoil. The valley walls have been remarkably adapted to terrace cultivation. The fields are brown or ochre in
winter but turn green in the rainy season; crops of sorghum and

durum wheat can be harvested twice a year with sufficient rainfall. It is a land of small-scale, intensive farming.

Agriculture is an ancient practice here. Archaeologists have discovered terrace walls and evidence of animal husbandry dating back to the Neolithic period, when climatic conditions supported relatively dense settlement in these regions. In the Bronze Age, such sites proliferated along the routes connecting the Red Sea and the desert. The largest of these settlements sprawled over an area of more than 10,000 square meters, dwarfing the smaller farming villages that dotted the area. These communities tended to support themselves with cereal crops such as sorghum and barley, as well as with goats and sheep. Donkeys were probably used as beasts of burden to carry pottery, semiprecious stones, and obsidian through the villages.

In these Highland territories, small settlements tended to be composed of linked adjacent units arrayed around a central space; larger settlements tended to have several units of this type. The houses generally contained two adjoining, oval-shaped rooms that opened onto a central courtyard.[4]

Certain units were distinguished by large entryways, many rooms, and prominent location. The ringed formation was a defensive measure to protect the settlement from external threats; each village therefore was an isolated and independent entity whose communal activities took place in its central area. The drawback of the circular plan was that it limited growth within the community in succeeding generations, and eventually these communities faced problems of population pressure. But the roots of urbanism in South Arabia date back to these Bronze Age settlements and run deep in the culture of this region.

The ravines that form the high terraces gradually deepen in their long descent into an increasingly dense network of valleys along the mountain's main rifts, often in a linear course. From the high plateaus, these deep valleys open up a path down through limestone (forming what is known as the Amran rifts) and volcanic rock to a granite base at an elevation of approximately 1,500 meters above sea level. Here the valleys merge into the Wadi Dhana, itself an aggregation of many smaller tributaries, and wide enough to carry the sudden surges of their combined floods.

In the Pleistocene era, the mouth of the Wadi Dhana was located at what later became the mouth of the Wadi Qawqah, roughly forty miles upstream of Maʾrib, well south of the city. Several kilometers farther on, the Wadi Dhana enters into the great volcanic complex of Sirwâh, whose lava flows extend all the way to the gates of Maʾrib. Though not farmed intensively today, the Sirwâh basin was dominated by an ancient city of the same name. An important Sabaean city, Sirwâh was protected by a massive wall, and there are still remnants of the remarkable temple to Almaqah. One of the most important historical texts of the Sabaeans was found inside this partly oval-shaped temple.

Not far from the temple is the site of the Sabaean city of al-Qarn, perched on a rocky hilltop that is now surrounded by water from a recent dam. This modest settlement, which probably dates back to the eighth–seventh centuries B.C., consists of an array of several similarly designed homes adjoined to form a vast oval, perhaps originally enclosing a sanctuary.[5] Atop another hill stands the temple of Wadd dhû-Masmaʾim, a modest structure with three *cellae,* and an edifice known as "Samsara," or the caravansery. The latter structure consists of a group of rooms around a small altar. The rooms contained ceramic objects, an inscribed incense altar, and several containers filled with frankincense.[6]

Ten kilometers upstream of Maʾrib, the Wadi Dhana reaches the gorge of Jabal Balaq which, though barely 600 meters wide, is dominated by steep slopes with no growth of any kind. At the bottom of this gorge, the wadi opens onto the immense plain of Maʾrib, on the edge of the Sabʾatayn desert, at an elevation of approximately 1,200 meters above sea level.

Mastering the Floods

The plain of Maʾrib is a dramatically different landscape from that of the sources of the Wadi Dhana only 150 kilometers distant. The environment is extremely dry, with annual rainfall of less than 100 millimeters; in exceptionally dry years, such as 1985, precipitation levels can be as low as 20 millimeters. The summers are extremely hot, with average temperatures of 31 to 32 degrees Celsius and a recorded high of 43 degrees. Evaporation is therefore very rapid. The region's rare rain usually falls in July and August, but the main water source is the hinterlands of the Yemen Highlands. When rain does arrive, it comes in a torrent, carrying along earth and pebbles in its mighty surge down the stark limestone mountainscape and into the granite defiles that end in that of Jabal Balaq, which serves as a funnel. These flash floods (or *sayl* in Arabic) come two or three times a year.

There are certain signs that announce the impending arrival of flash floods on the desert's edge. Clouds begin forming for several days until they block the horizon; then, just before the showers begin, violent gusts begin to blow. The flood is preceded by a dull roar that can be heard for miles around. When the water first arrives it is moving slowly, brimming with a white scum that contrasts with the sun-baked pebbles. Then comes a yellowish tide of silt and the odd plant snatched up by the current upstream. If the flood were to begin around, say, 3 P.M., it might rise as high as 1.4 meters by 4 P.M.; then slowly subside until around 5 P.M.; then surge rapidly until 6 P.M., when it would reach a height of 2.4 meters before subsiding just as rapidly a half-hour later, falling to about 1.3 meters around 9 P.M., then down to half a meter by midnight; and it would all be over by 6 A.M. the next morning.[7] The floods sweep away trees, carve out river banks (along with their earth and stones, even boulders), destroy levees, and carry away any fodder stored in nearby fields. No buildings near the river banks can hold up long against the current; any stray animals or unwary peasants busy in the fields are borne off as well. Any fields not protected by dikes suffer erosion along their edges. In the course of a flood of normal size, some 400 cubic meters of water per second come rushing down, and in a truly exceptional flood—about every twenty-five years—the volume can be as high as 1,500 cubic meters per second. Even in modern times the regions along the edge of the desert are alarmingly desolate after a violent flood.

The genius of the ancient Arabian peasants lay in their ability to harness the power of these floods. Over the course of several millennia, they gradually began to use simple dikes to hold some of the water, perhaps originally experimenting with the secondary wadis where the volume of the floods was no more than a few cubic meters per second. They became familiar with the areas where the slope was gentle and the water slowed, and where the terrain showed promise for irrigation, with its meandering streams where water could be captured. They learned how to direct the water through sluices built out of wood or stone toward collecting areas prepared in advance. Eventually they were able to direct most of the rainfall toward irrigation zones where the fine sediments suspended in the water would settle, bringing excellent nourishment to the soil. The long process of experimentation probably began as early as the fourth millennium B.C., and by the end of the third millennium the peasants had begun to tame more powerful torrents and thus irrigate a relatively wide area. Mastery of the wadis Dhana and Markha probably came some time in the third millennium B.C. An undertaking of this scale and sophistication required tight organization and precise management of the flood waters that passed onto the irrigated fields.[8]

The skill of the Sabaeans allowed them to irrigate the fields every year—more than once a year if possible—without major destruction. The challenge was to channel a sudden gush of water into a large bed that remained dry for most of the year, and only stonework could hold up to the water's power. Therefore they started with stone bulwarks to break the initial onset of the water, and below these were long channels of stone (or earthwork) that directed the water toward a precise destination. In Ma'rib, monumental hydraulic works have recently been discovered in the very riverbed of the Wadi Dhana. The most ancient of these was a lock dating back to the latter half of the third millennium B.C., located approximately two kilometers southwest of the mouth of the wadi. Another lock was built upstream in the early second millennium B.C.. The two structures are similar in design, with three or four long breakwaters built out of stone and aligned in parallel formation three to four meters apart. The upstream ends of these long masonry bulwarks were smoothly rounded to withstand the impact of flood-waters; the downstream sides fed into large stone sills with regularly spaced lateral grooves designed to support a wooden sluice.[9] The earthwork levees to which they were joined have long since eroded under subsequent flooding, but the masonry that remains is of stunning quality, with stones of huge dimensions artfully hewn and meticulously assembled in a mortise-and-tenon technique or with interlocking convex and concave surfaces. If the dating of these works is correct, they can be viewed as stunning exemplars of construction techniques in the early history of South Arabia.

After flowing through these monumental structures, the water was then distributed through a series of earthwork canals, each measuring between seven and eight meters wide. These fed into large stone sluices fitted with grooves which supported a superstructure of wooden beams. Farther downstream, narrower canals led into structures designed to distribute the water in different directions. The current had to be slowed somewhat as the water approached the fields, in order to limit erosion of the earthen levees, but had to travel fast enough to hold the fine sediments in suspension until the water reached the fields. Side trenches branched out from the central path of each channel into the borders of rectangular (often square) fields whose size was determined by the amount of water available to the area.[10]

Similar systems were in place for most of the wadis that periodically brought water down from the Highlands. The growth of the cities of Tamnaᶜ in the Wadi Bayhân, Hajar Yahir in the Wadi Markha, Shabwa in the Wadi ᶜIrma, and Raybûn in the Wadi Dawʾân can be attributed to similar irrigation networks. In all these cities, the basic principal was the same: guiding a portion of the brief but violent floodwaters into fields prepared in advance. The irrigation works were generally similar in design, with large stone breakwaters leading into canals.

Sediment carried down by the water enriched the soil but also posed technical challenges as great volumes of sand and silt accumulated in the fields over time. The rate of siltation is thought to have been approximately 0.7 centimeters per year, or 0.7 meters per century. (This is a theoretical average, since floods occur with a certain randomness, and the floodwaters were not dispersed equally over all areas.) Over time, the entire area around Ma'rib rose inexorably by some thirty meters, while other areas suffered a rise of as much as fifty meters.[11] The first and easiest solution to this long-term problem was to dredge the canals periodically, but this was only feasible for the first several hundred meters of their trajectory, and dumping the silt outside the canal banks had the unwanted side effect of reducing the area of the surrounding fields proportionately. Clearing the fields was a task of an entirely different order of magnitude, though such projects are thought to have been undertaken in more recent (and undoubtedly more prosperous) times in certain areas around Shabwa.

In Ma'rib, the hydraulic works mentioned above were eventually abandoned in favor of others higher up the river, along the banks of the Jabal Balaq al-Awsat, as is evident from the traces of a lock whose foundations survive as deep trenches cut into the rock. Farther upriver are remains of other works including a canal carved into the rock.[12] It is unclear whether this canal was ever part of a structure that included a dike, but if so, such a dike would have been designed to dam up the entire valley and would therefore have represented a last-ditch effort to direct water to the highest fields below.

Several traces remain of ancient efforts to cope with the problem of ongoing siltation in the valley. Ma'rib waged a long struggle against this phenomenon. Its western rampart, which faced the dike, had to be raised several times, despite the presence of an outer "protective wall." The Temple of Bar'an, built some time in the ninth century B.C., was slowly surrounded by sediment, and its forecourt was in particular jeopardy. The gates were raised but were eventually covered over. Around the third century B.C., a three-meter-thick brick wall was built to the north and west and subsequently reinforced with three rectangular towers. The sanctuary of Mahram Bilqîs faced the same menace, and its oval wall was repeatedly raised. Down in the oasis, isolated hamlets and farms gradually sank beneath the silt; recent archaeological samples have revealed brick walls popping up here and there from under the silt.

In the Wadi Bayhân, the entire village of al-Haraja was covered over; the recent return of erosion in the area has revealed pottery and even entire multistory houses dating back to the fourth century B.C.

A "Hydraulic" Society?

An oasis like that of Maʾrib must have supported thousands of small-scale peasant farmers. But agricultural productivity depended on a form of collective organization. Farmers must have come to an arrangement whereby water was distributed equitably, with the fields closest to the breakwaters receiving roughly the same amount of water as those at the farthest ends of the canals. Such an arrangement implies a coherent system of land ownership and a pact of mutual agreement among the various tribes. The situation was unstable over the long term, since more influential tribes would have enlarged their domains or taken possession of the fields closest to the canal heads, which "drank" the most water. The violence of modern-day rivalries over the land around Maʾrib suggests, if imprecisely, similar ancient conflicts.

The orderly functioning of an oasis like that of Maʾrib is thus the clearest indicator we have of the existence of social union and community in ancient times; sadly, the details of this community remain blurry. They chose a "master of the waters" who was responsible for directing the operation of sharing out the floodwater, overseeing the distribution of allotments by volume or by time, and arbitrating the invitable conflicts. While surviving inscriptions are essentially mute on this subject, they do mention a *madarr* whose function evidently had something to do with irrigation.

The Two Gardens

Let us pause briefly in the oasis of Maʾrib, the largest in South Arabia at approximately 9,500 hectares. It is a difficult challenge for modern scholars to reconstruct the original appearance of this area.

The building of a dam across the gorges of the Jabal Balaq in 1986 resulted in the destruction of the majority of canals and hydraulic works below. Moreover, the peasants have put the ancient fields back under cultivation, except along the borders of the main works situated to the west.

One of the most effective tools in understanding the appearance of the ancient oasis remains the aerial photographs taken in 1973. These clearly show the Dhana valley, at the mouth of its gorges, some 700 meters wide. Each of its slopes shows traces of lateral canals that once carried the floodwaters. On the southern end, a huge trench is visible, cut into the rock in the shape of a Y; this trench, which dates back to the sixth century B.C., fed into a canal that irrigated the oasis all the way to the village of al-Arqâ some 15 kilometers to the south. On the other side of the Dhana is the southern breakwater, an impressive structure, though of later date. A jumble of inscriptions have been found there. This floodgate leads into a gently curved canal with stone banks that terminates in a large distributor with thirteen gates arrayed in a semicircle.[13] From there, the entire northern area of the oasis is covered in a dense network of six major canals, three of which carry the water on to Maʾrib and thence to the village of Husn al-Jadîda beyond. The aerial photographs clearly show a checkerboard pattern of ancient rectangular fields over an area of dozens of square kilometers. This northern oasis, covering some 5,700 hectares, also received the floodwaters of the Wadi Sayla, and an irrigated zone flanks the course of the Wadi Jufayna, whose flow was controlled by a giant lock. The southern oasis was limited by its topography to an area of about 3,750 hectares. On either side of the Wadi Dhana were the "two gardens" known to Yemeni writers from the Islamic era as the land of the Sabaeans.

All of these hydraulic works belonged to the late centuries of the history of Maʾrib, the time of the celebrated dike. In its final form, around the fifth–sixth centuries A.D., this dike consisted of an earthen wall fortified with stonework, twenty meters high and running some 650 meters, that dammed the course of the Wadi Dhana between the two great breakwaters to the north and south. Even this massive structure was vulnerable against the force of the most violent floods, and it was washed away several times. In 549 A.D., Abraha, an Ethiopian king of Yemen, had inscribed on a large stela a description of the repair work required on more than one occasion and on a grand scale, because of this plague.[14] The dike was finally washed away for good in 580 A.D. The Koran described its destruction in terms of divine retribution:

> Certainly there was a sign for Saba in their abode; two gardens on the right and the left; eat of the sustenance of your Lord and give thanks to Him: a good land and a Forgiving Lord!
>
> But they turned aside, so We sent upon them a torrent of which the rush could not be withstood, and in place of their two gardens We gave to them two gardens yielding bitter fruit and (growing) tamarisk and a few lote-trees.
>
> This We requited them with because they disbelieved; and We do not punish any but the ungrateful. (Surah XXXIV[Saba]:15–17)

Even if the final ruin of the dike can be dated with precision, it is difficult to know about its origins.

Some suppose the dike dates back to the sixth century B.C.—making it the oldest known structure of its kind in the world—though there is no conclusive proof for such an assertion. The two inscriptions carved into the canal mention no such dike, saying only, "Rahbum [or Habâbid] has carved into the limestone the Rahbum water source to feed Yasrân."[15] Others conjecture that earthen dikes built to dam the riverbed at least partially have existed since the third millennium B.C., and that this type of bulwark was gradually enlarged in later times. Others doubt the very premise of a full dam, arguing that such a structure could not have withstood the force of the floods; they theorize instead that the entire river was once canalized by stone walls over a course of several miles. Masonwork jetties for holding water were paired with deflecting walls arrayed at an angle at regular intervals in the riverbed, as in the Wadi Dura', for example.[16]

Another challenge is that of reconstructing the appearance of the Ma'rib oasis as it appeared in ancient times. One possible clue lies in the revival of crops such as alfalfa, cereals, and fruit trees that are now grown once again on the ancient fields. Set amidst these fields are hamlets and unfired-brick farmhouses, some fortified and

decorated with patterns in lime. The water now comes from mechanical pumps, however, and the communal management and distribution of floodwaters has long since disappeared. In antiquity,
the community decided jointly on equitable distribution of water.
The division of land into small parcels now requires each farmer
to manage and maintain his own irrigation system. Then there is
the task of planting and harvesting at least once annually. The job
requires many hands, no doubt mostly recruited from within the
family.

Crops and Forests

The plants under cultivation included sorghum, wheat, and barley,
but the principal crops were fruits and vines. Date palms thrived
in the irrigated zones. Pliny noted several species:

> The first type barely rises higher than a small shrub, and this type is
> generally sterile but nonetheless bears fruit in some areas. . . . There
> also exist forests of large date palms whose trunks are completely cov-
> ered in leaves with rows of pointy teeth. . . . Others are thin and tall,
> with bark that forms knots or closely spaced rings that allow the east-
> ern people to climb these trees easily by putting a willow hoop around
> the trunk and scooting up with surprising speed.[17]

Two ancient species of date palm have been identified, namely
Medemia and *Hyphaene,* the latter having since disappeared from
numerous regions of Hadramawt.[18]

Prominent among the many species of trees in the region is
Zyzyphus spina christi, a member of the jujube family, which was
used principally for construction but also had medical uses: "The
Arabian thorn even by itself by its thickening nature checks all
fluxes, spitting of blood and excessive menstruation, there is even
more potency in its root. The seed of the white thorn is a help
against the stings of scorpions."[19] Locust trees are also found in
the area bordering the desert, the most common species being *Tor-
tilis* and *Hamulosa,* with their characteristic flat-topped silhouette.
These species were used for the wooden frames commonly found
in the civil and religious architecture of Raybûn and Shabwa. The

forest cover during the period near the end of the occupation of these cities was probably similar to that of the current day; no natural vegetation succeeded it. A rare locust, myrrh tree, or tamarisk will be found here and there, but the mature standing forests praised by ancient writers have entirely vanished.

The deforestation is not limited to the areas around the cities of the lowlands; the same fate has befallen the mountains of Yemen, where the species mentioned above once thrived along with several species of ficus, juniper, *Dracaena, Olea africana,* and others (these species are also found at the same altitudes on the high plateaus of Ethiopia). There are several reasons for this clearing, mainly construction and domestic uses; the end result is that junipers now grow only in rare patches in Hujariyya, in the Taizz region, and in the mountains of the Asîr.[20]

The City of Ma'rib

With its impressive walls and numerous civic and religious monuments, Ma'rib was not only the capital of the Sabaean kingdom but the greatest city in all of South Arabia. "The city of the Sabaeans," as Agatharchides referred to it in apparent ignorance of its ancient name of Mariaba (Mryb, later Ma'rib), "is known as Saba, from the name of the entire Sabaean people; it is situated on a mountain which, though not among the highest, is by far the loveliest in all of Arabia."

The city grew up on the very edge of the Wadi Dhana, about eight kilometers east of the dike. It was defended by a high wall some 4.2 kilometers in length, the oldest sections of which are thought to date back as far as the beginning of the second millennium B.C. In the South Arabian era, the rampart was fortified with square towers and central gates with narrow entryways decorated with inscriptions. The most ancient known inscription is a dedication of construction dating back to the beginning of the eighth century B.C., under Yathî'amar Bayân, son of Sumhu'alî. Another inscription, dating to around 510 B.C., attests to the construction of towers and two gates by an unidentified sovereign. Other construc-

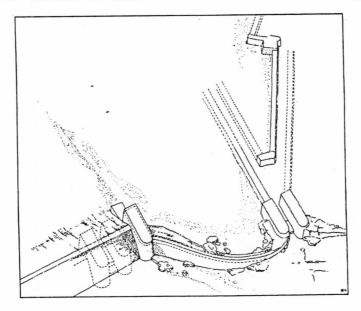

Waterworks at Maʾrib
(reconstructed by W. Herberg)

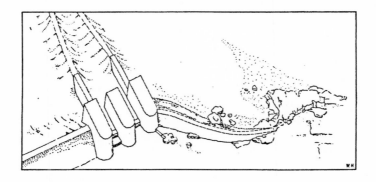

tion was undertaken in the middle of the second century B.C. and again toward the end of the first century B.C.[21] This vast fortification was partially dismantled some time in the 40s B.C. in order to build the governor's palace and other buildings. All that remains are two large gates, one on the western side and the other on the northern side; several towers; sections of curtain-wall; and the massive interior of unfired brick. The city's interior, which covers at least a hundred hectares, has yielded an accumulation of archaeological remains some fifteen to thirty-five meters deep, clearly attesting to the city's long history. The lower zone may have been used as a caravan stop, while today the city above is ringed by a village of houses made of unfired brick. Several stones with fragmentary inscriptions and decorations have been recycled as lintels or other building materials. At the foot of the hill lies the remains of the monumental portico of an ancient sanctuary, which currently serves as the entrance to the small mosque of Suleiman; inside, shafts from old columns and capitals have been reused to support the framework of the building on all sides.

The city's principal monument, the Salhîn (or Salhîm) Palace, has never been discovered. Built as the residence of the first Sabaean sovereigns, it was enlarged or heightened in the seventh century B.C. by the sovereign Karibʾîl Watar, who is named in an inscription: "[He] built the higher parts of his Salhîm Palace from the stonework and the walls." As symbol of the Sabaean dynasty, this palace's fame surpassed that of all other royal houses, notably the Shaqîr house in Shabwa and the Harîb house in Tamnaᶜ. The existence of other monuments—a Hirwam Temple to Almaqah, a church built after the Abyssinian conquest, and a synagague—can only be inferred from surviving inscriptions. The city was abandoned following the destruction of the dike, and was later occupied only partially during the Islamic era.

The Temples outside the City Walls

The principal known monuments of Maʾrib lie outside the city, 3.5 kilometers to its southeast, in the southern oasis. The first, locally

known as Mahram Bilqîs, or the Temple of Bilqîs, was partially excavated by an American expedition in the winter of 1951–52. This
expedition, which had the exceptional status of being authorized by
the imam, was devoted to the excavation of an entry court and
surrounding peristyle. The dig was undertaken in haste—perhaps
too much haste—and was cut short when members of the expedition were forced to flee to Bayhân under cover of night.[22] All the
excavated objects remained at the site, including the famous bronze
statue of Ma'dîkarib, now housed in the National Museum of Sana.

   This building is by far the most famous in South Arabia. It comprises the peristyle court, a vast enclosure surrounded by a high
oval-shaped wall, several related buildings, and an adjacent cemetery.[23] The principal entryway into the oval enclosure is through
the peristyle court, with the eight pillars of its propylon. The courtyard is 24 meters long by 19 meters wide and is bordered by a
32-pillar portico with a stone roof. The far wall is decorated with
"false windows" (or "recessed panels") distributed along the interior, with cursive inscriptions painted in red. Excavation revealed
hundreds of inscribed stones, some of which had been recycled as
paving stones, and twenty-four bronze statues. The oval wall, some
300 meters long and 13 meters high, remains unexcavated, and
therefore its character is unknown. The foundations are covered on
the outside with dedicatory inscriptions relating to their construction; the authors were apparently Sabaean sovereigns who reigned
between the seventh and mid-fifth centuries B.C. This sanctuary,
named Awwâm, is dedicated to the god Almaqah.

   The second temple, known as 'Arsh Bilqîs (the throne of Bilqîs)
and dedicated to "Almaqah, lord of Bar'ân," is among the best-
known ancient temples in Yemen.[24] This architectural ensemble
comprised a central structure with a low courtyard in front. The
building consisted of four integrated structures originally built between the ninth and fifth centuries B.C., of which only the so-called
Temple 4 is well known. On its western entrance was a monumental portico with six monolithic pillars with dentiled tops. Beyond
these pillars was a small porch opening onto a courtyard with porticoes on two sides; in the center of this courtyard was an adyton
sheltering a bronze lifesize idol of (doubtless) a bull, two stone al-

tars, and the statue of the donor. The large courtyard below, entered from the west, was bordered by porticoes on three sides. The temple was destroyed around the time of Christ and subsequently reconstructed with entrances aligned on an east-west axis in accordance with a change in rituals and a new name for Almaqah: "Lord of Maskat and He-Who-Resides-at-Barʾân." The sanctuary was reinforced with strong towers and remained in use until the fourth century A.D.

Like other cities in ancient Arabia, Maʾrib contained at least one sanctuary within the city as well as one or more temples on the outside. In the Sabaean regions and regions dominated by the Sabaeans, one or more of these temples were dedicated to Almaqah, their principal divinity. When the Sabaeans seized Jawf, they ordered the construction of a temple to Almaqah *intra muros*. Cities in Hadramawt had at least two sanctuaries, one within the walls, probably dedicated to Siyân, and the other on the outside, built against a nearby hillside.

Words Carved in Stone

In the oasis of Maʾrib, the vestiges of two sites in particular demand our attention. The first, found in the Jabal ʿAmûd 24 kilometers southwest of Maʾrib, is evidently one of the quarries of Maʾrib, similar to those found at Jabal Balaq al-Awsat. The quarry walls show low cuts clearly corresponding to the thickness of the limestone slabs. Several very ancient inscriptions in the rock have been found to commemorate the managers of the quarrymen who cut the stone slabs destined for breakwaters, ramparts, and sanctuaries. One of these quarrymen reported that he had cut the blocks for one or two bench seats and transported them to the site of a future banquet hall. Another prepared commemorative monuments intended for erection on ceremonial occasions.

The second site is located ten kilometers south of Maʾrib on the slopes of the Jabal Balaq (known locally as Janûbî, or "southern"), an arid spot with no vegetation. Here a vast array of funerary monuments were erected in drystone (i.e., without the use of mortar); many of these were arranged in circular formations known as "pillboxes" or "turret tombs." It is here that the numerous inscriptions referred to as "lists of eponyms" were found. Certain of these lists are thought to rank among the oldest known Sabaean inscriptions, though their exact age is in doubt. Here it is possible to see one of the birthplaces of Saba.[25]

The term *lists* is not totally precise here: they are more like short notices, of which only fragments remain, of lists of persons classified by generation. Specialists in epigraphy tend to interpret these lists as records of names of people entrusted with sacerdotal duties in the temple of the god ʿAthtar dhû-Dhibân; their names were probably added at the time when they left office. These people belonged to the dhû-Khalîl clan, apparently one of four original clans of the eponyms of later periods. Of particular interest is a series of notices known as Stone A, which includes lists whose most recent names were from the period immediately following that of sovereign Karibʾîl Watar, son of Dhamarʾalî, who reigned in the seventh century B.C. Despite the difficulty of interpretation of this stone, it is highly probable that it mentions at least a dozen successive generations of people who had all exercised the same function.

Saba is invariably linked to irrigation, and all these lists can be seen within the agricultural context of the Maʾrib oasis. Whether a priest was in service or had been discharged, the god ʿAthtar dhû-Dhibân would regularly water Saba during autumn or spring. One text reports that ʿAthtar watered the Dhana river, in autumn or spring, for an exceptional period of seven days, under the reign of sovereign Sumhuʾalî, when Dhamarhumû was priest. From this it seems clear that the priests of Saba prayed to a divinity who rewarded them with floods. Uncertainty as to absolute or relative chronology of the lists of eponyms highlights the challenges in studying Saba during the early centuries of its history.

2. THE CARAVAN KINGDOMS

The period spanning the last eight centuries B.C. was dominated by the caravan kingdoms that skirted the Sabʾatayn desert. The prosperity of these kingdoms was built on commerce in aromatic products. In these monarchies, organized around common cults, the sovereign played an important role.

In the eighth century B.C., South Arabia was politically fragmented. Each of the four major valleys that flow down to the desert was occupied by a state whose territory corresponded to the valley and its tributaries. From east to west, these were Hadramawt (in the wadis ʿIrma and Hadramawt), Awsân (in the Wadi Markha), Qatabân (in the Wadi Bayhân), and Saba (in the Wadi Dhana). The great valley of Jawf, which lies north of the Wadi Dhana, was divided up between Saba and several smaller kingdoms. In the early seventh century B.C., Saba extended its dominance to a large part of South Arabia and probably held this territory until the fourth century B.C., when Qatabân took it over until the first century A.D.

The Sources

South Arabia's most ancient inscriptions, known as "archaic" or "preclassical," date back at least as far as the eighth century B.C., but pottery fragments with painted and incised letters dating perhaps to the tenth century B.C. have been discovered at Yalâ and Raybûn. In southern Iraq, short texts in Arabic have been dated to the eighth century B.C. The Arabic language seems to have developed around the tenth century B.C., if not earlier; its alphabet shows similarities to Phoenician but with marked differences in order. The

29

alphabet of Epigraphic South Arabian belongs to a South Semitic branch which originated in Syria-Palestine in the second millennium B.C., whereas Phoenician belongs to a North Semitic branch. Its alphabet of twenty-nine consonants (with no vowels) was fixed around the eighth century B.C.; writing went either right-to-left or occasionally left-to-right, with the former becoming standard by the seventh century B.C. The distinctive letters conformed to clear aesthetic norms that rose to a virtually canonical standard during the era of Sabaean dominance of South Arabia. Whether etched in stone or carved in bronze, these inscriptions were destined to ensure the enduring fame of their writers for posterity. The inscriptions generally related to construction of public or private works, sacrificial offerings, royal decrees, decrees emanating from temples, demarcation of land boundaries, and religious practices. Although there are some 15,000 of these surviving texts, they presumably represent a mere fraction of the total output of this civilization. We have no surviving law codes, royal annals, official correspondence, or historical texts; nor is there any trace of literary texts such as epics, poetry, hymns, or stories. However, the number of surviving texts is still greater than those of the Phoenicians, Hebrews, Carthaginians, or Persians.

Twenty years ago, a secret archaeological dig brought to light sections of a tree branch carved with a cursive alphabet derived from the writing found on the monuments. Since this discovery, hundreds more texts, written on palm ribs, have been uncovered in Jawf and Hadramawt. These are leafstalks from ten to forty centimeters long and two to three centimeters wide, covered with ten or so lines of text written lengthwise from right to left. Among the texts that have so far been published are contracts, private letters, memoranda of debt, and lists of people or clans. All these documents, which relate in one way or another to the ancient rural economy, must have been catalogued in veritable libraries, and current research leaves room for hope that eventually an official archive will be found.[1]

At least four principal languages were in use in South Arabia, of which Sabaean is the best documented. Sabaean began as the

language of the tribe of Saba, which originally occupied only the
Maʾrib region and gradually extended its domain through conquest.
By the end of the fourth century B.C., the language had lost ground
and was spoken only in the area between Maʾrib and Sana.

Madhabian originated in Jawf, northeast of Sana, and was the
language of the Minaean traders (hence the alternate name Minaean). It spread throughout the Minaean colonies across South
Arabia and as far as Egypt. It disappeared with the kingdom of
Maʿīn around the first century B.C. In the kingdom of Qatabān,
which covered at least the entire southwestern part of Yemen,
people spoke Qatabanian, a language that has proven difficult to
decipher. As for Hadrami, it seems to have been spoken in the eastern part of the country, but survives only in three or four hundred
texts.

Given our total ignorance of ancient pronunciation, it is extremely difficult to differentiate between these four languages. And
in the absence of any knowledge of how vowels and consonant
pairs were treated, we must resort to speculative conventions of
transcription.

What Is Saba?

The kingdom of Saba was formed around a language, a common
cult, and centralized institutions. The Sabaean language is "closer
to Arabic than to Geʿze (ancient Ethiopic) or other South Arabian
languages, and is attested in the most ancient inscriptions of South
Arabia," dating back at least as far as the eighth century B.C.[2] Seemingly the oldest written language in the region, it is itself the product of a long evolution whose main outlines are unclear. Sabaean
appears to have endured at least into the fourth or fifth centuries A.D. In the course of its fourteen centuries of active use, it established itself as a model of durability among South Arabian languages, despite profound changes in morphology, vocabulary, and
syntax. It is also the best documented, with more than six thousand inscriptions extant. While the oldest inscriptions in Epi-

graphic South Arabian amount to little more than fragments count-
ing no more than ten or so words each, this body of evidence is of
great value to scholars.

The earliest Sabaean inscriptions are found in the Maʾrib oasis
and in the neighboring Highlands of Jabal Balaq and ʿAmûd.[3] Later
inscriptions have been discovered along the course of the Wadi
Dhana up to Sirwâh and its tributaries, including the Wadi Yalâ.
Plotting these points on a map clearly shows the extent of Sabaean
dominance in the region. The birthplace of Saba was clearly in the
region around Maʾrib, and Sabaean texts have been recovered in
the Jawf valley, especially on the south and north slopes, as well as
in Jabal al-Lawdh and on the high plateaus of the Sana region.

Saba was a community united around a single cult. Aside from
mentions in the lists of eponyms previously discussed, the name of
Saba first appears in three brief inscriptions referring to the sovereign as "mukarrib of Saba," in commemoration of construction or
dedication of monuments. The name of Saba was never limited to
a single tribe or kingdom and evidently referred only incidentally
to the territory originally identical with the region of Maʾrib.[4] Its
component groups formed a strongly integrated collectivity united
around the cult of Almaqah, who was viewed as their common
ancestor, and a well-defined pantheon of lesser divinities. Some
surviving inscriptions mention Saba and Alamaqah jointly to indicate the state whose sovereign is its leading representative. In the
lists of eponyms, the phrase "Saba and the union" referred to all
the inhabitants and lands watered by the god ʿAthtar, suggesting a
political unity extending farther still. The cohesiveness of this union was ratified and celebrated in formal ceremonies held under the
aegis of ʾAthtar dhû-Dhibân. These lists, along with certain inscriptions from the seventh century B.C., testify to a political awareness among the Sabaeans that apparently long preceded such thinking in neighboring populations.[5]

From its earliest origins, Saba seems to have imposed a notion
of centralized authority. A strong consciousness of unity was based
on shared cultural practices, an unchallenged occupation of the
Maʾrib oasis, and an awareness of the strong advantage of centralized power. The institution of monarchy was apparently very an-

cient here, though we don't know its origins. The early Sabaean sovereigns held the title of *mukarrib,* which originally meant "federator" or person in charge of rallying people together.[6] The title is evidence of an early quest for Sabaean dominance throughout the South Arabian peninsula. Rivalries arose as sovereigns from neighboring kingdoms vied for the title. Though not exclusively Sabaean, the term mukarrib was used by Sabaean sovereigns from the mid-eighth to perhaps the sixth century B.C., after which time it began to be used by the Qatabanites. The title was never invested with absolute authority or autonomy; instead, the sovereign made important decisions in consultation with several other important figures represented in "councils" or "assemblies" whose main concerns were typically related to irrigation. Each Sabaean city would be headed by one or more leaders chosen from among the local chiefs or personal representatives of the sovereign.

The capital city of the Sabaean confederation was Ma'rib, or Mariaba as it was most likely pronounced in ancient times. The city was located in the heart of a vast irrigated zone on the Wadi Dhana, less than ten kilometers from the gorges of Jabal Balaq. The residence of the mukarrib was located here, as was the seat of the "ministers of Mariaba," who were under his direct authority.

The First Mukarribs

The first mukarribs, in the eighth century B.C., had names like Karib'îl, Yathî'amar, Sumhu'alî, and Dhamar'alî, combined with epithets such as Bayân, Watar, and Yanûf. However, it is hard to identify any of these with any precision. The only one who is well known is Yathî'amar Bayân, son of Sumhu'alî. He reigned alone at first and was later joined by Karib'îl Watar, though he maintained seniority. His long reign—perhaps as many as thirty years—brought great prestige which probably went beyond the boundaries of the Sabaean lands. The annals of King Sargon II of Assyria (722–705 B.C.) mentions payments of tribute received from Sâmsi, queen of the Arabs, and from Ita'amra the Sabaean, at the time of a military campaign that took place around 716 B.C. Ita'amra has been

possibly identified as Yathî'amar Bayân, mainly on the evidence of
his precedence to Karib'îl, perhaps as a result of an earlier acces-
sion to the throne. Evidence for such a hierarchy is derived principally from the texts of al-ᶜAql, wherein Yathî'amar mentions great
ritual hunts with as many as a thousand victims.[7] But the possibility that Ita'amra was a predecessor to Yathî'amar can't be ruled out
entirely.

The first mukarribs presided over large construction projects
such as urban fortifications, temples, and irrigation works. The
houses in the ancient city of Hafarî (the modern Yalâ), located
about thirty-five kilometers southwest of Ma'rib, were built by one
of these early rulers. They were also responsible for officiating at
religious ceremonies, banquets, and ritual pacts. The evidence suggests that they solidified and maintained power over their domains
by building large-scale civil and military works.

The Reign of Mukarrib Karib'îl Watar

At the end of his reign, the mukarrib Karib'îl Watar left behind two
very long inscriptions on the faces of two monumental stones
erected within the fortified enclosure of the temple to Almaqah
at Sirwâh.[8] The first text describes eight successful military campaigns undertaken over the course of a very long reign, perhaps as
long as fifty years. He boasts of having extended Sabaean domination to all the edges of the desert.

Karib'îl Watar's goal was to control all the trade routes for incense and therefore all the so-called caravan kingdoms. Saba had
two major rivals, the first being Awsân, a kingdom set up in the
heart of the Markha valley to the southeast of Ma'rib. This ancient
kingdom may have come into being as early as the fourth millennium B.C. Its agricultural prosperity was evident in the growth of
numerous cities along the main course of the river; of these cities,
Hajar Yahir was probably the capital.[9] The sovereigns of Awsân
extended their territory toward the southeast, perhaps even as far
as the shores of the Indian Ocean. By finally laying hold of the title

of mukarrib, they were asserting a form of regional hegemony. Moreover, their lands were rich in aromatic spices, principally myrrh. But most important of all was their strategic location between Hadramawt to the east and Saba to the west. The Wadi Markha effectively formed a long, continuous line oriented along a northeast-southwest axis from the mountains all the way to the very outskirts of Shabwa. Every caravan that left Shabwa had to cross the Wadi Markha on the way to Ma³rib, either passing through a string of cities located on the border of the desert or through the villages situated at the foot of the Jabal an-Nisiyîn.

Saba's other rival was located to its northwest at Nashshân, the modern al-Baydâ³. This city's prosperity was derived from meticulous management of the wadis Madhâb and Kharîd, and spawned large-scale construction programs such as the temple of ⁶Athtar outside the city walls. Beginning in the eighth century B.C., if not even earlier, Nashshân slowly but steadily extended its influence, bringing the admittedly tiny neighbor states of the Jawf valley under its sway. This region formed an indispensable link in the relations with Saba to the south and with the region of Najrân to the north. Jawf was in effect an immense depression stretching along a northwest-southeast axis for more than a hundred kilometers and extending far into the Sab³atayn desert. Hegemony in the Jawf would eventually ensure control over the passage of the caravans. If Nashshân had been successful in its effort to dominate the small states of Kaminahû, Haram, and Inabba³, it would have constituted a real menace to the latter's own quest for hegemony. This reading of the ancient map suggests that Saba was hemmed in between powerful neighbors on either side of Ma³rib.

The first military campaign of Karib³îl brought him to the mountains of south Yemen, south of Taizz, in the Hujariyya.[10] This mountainous terrain is nonetheless fertile because it receives monsoon rains. Karib³îl claimed to have killed three thousand of his enemy and captured eight thousand more. He then proceeded to the southwestern part of the country into the kingdom of Awsân, where the Wadi Markha now runs. The ancient text describes terrible fighting in which sixteen thousand fell dead and another forty thousand were taken prisoner. Numerous cities were destroyed, agricultural areas were laid waste, and houses were burned. The palace of the sovereigns of Awsân, known as Miswâr, which probably stood in the city of Hajar Yahirr, was razed and all its inscriptions were carried off. Rarely has a military campaign exhibited such willful annihilation. The defeat was far from total, however; two subsequent expeditions were required before Awsân was reduced once and for all.

On the third campaign, Karibʾîl headed off to conquer all the low mountains that dominate the Gulf of Aden. This territory embraces the ancient Dahas (the region of modern-day Yâfî) in the northeast and the ancient Tubanî (Wadi Tubân) in the north, both possessions of Awsân. The Sabaean sovereign may have penetrated as far as the Tubân delta, near Aden. The site of Sabr was apparently destroyed with such fury that its residents were forced to flee without their belongings.[11] Archaeologists are still awaiting conclusive proof from analysis of very recent digs there. The final toll of this third campaign was five thousand people taken into captivity; the fourth campaign was waged in the same region and brought back another fifteen hundred captives.

The fifth and sixth campaigns took place in Jawf, about a hundred kilometers north of Maʾrib. The objective this time was the state of Nashshân. It seems that before entering the country, Karibʾîl took pains to secure the support or at least neutrality of certain cities, including Haram (modern-day Khirbat Hamdân) and Kaminahû (modern-day Kamna). He massed his troops near the entrance of the valley and proceeded to seize Yathill (modern-day Barâqish). He followed the route past Haram and on to Kaminahû, from which Nashshân is visible on the horizon barely five kilometers distant. On his arrival outside Nashshân, he inspected the powerful defensive walls built on a rectangular plan and surmounted by numerous towers. He then began to build a surrounding wall, presumably of earth, in order to starve the city into submission by the traditional method of the archaic Greeks. After a three-year siege, Karibʾîl was master of the city. He proceeded to raze the town and destroy its sanctuaries, and burn the Afraw palace. Curiously, he spared the sanctuary to ʿAthtar outside the city walls. The neighboring villages and their hydraulic installations suffered a worse fate. Line 16 of the inscription of Sirwâh reads as follows:

> [He] destroyed the fortified town of Nashshân to the point of saving it from any looting that it might have otherwise suffered had it been spared from the flames; he inflicted a similar destruction on the Afraw palace and the city of Nashshân; he imposed a tribute on the backs of their citizens, hitting the priests in particular; he ordered the massacre of all Nashshanites who hestitated to show devotion to the divinities; demanded of King Sumhuyafaʾ and Nashshân that Saba be established in the city of Nashshân and that Sumhuyafaʾ and Nashshân build the temple of Almaqah.[12]

Thus did King Sumhuyafaʾ of Nashshân suffer the harshest of defeats; but he was neither executed nor deported. Karibʾîl ensured a lasting victory by destroying the town and subsequently installing a garrison with Sabaean colonists. As for his allies, he rewarded Kaminahû and Haram by bestowing upon them the lands and breakwaters formerly controlled by Nashshân. Finally, he fortified the neighboring city of Nashq (modern-day al-Baydâ, "the White"), doubtless also settling farmers and soldiers and other colonists, and erecting a sanctuary to Almaqah.

The target of the seventh campaign is difficult to identify; but a likely region is Tihâma, on the coastal plain of the Red Sea, or perhaps even the other side along the Eritrean coast. The eighth and final campaign was apparently led against the territories and peoples to the north of Jawf. The tribes around Najrân (in modern-day Saudi Arabia) were decimated, with five thousand men killed and twelve thousand more taken prisoner along with some two hundred thousand head of livestock.

This considerable toll, while perhaps exaggerated, suggests the scale of the conquests of Karibʾîl. Vast agricultural areas were ravaged and entire populations were either massacred or reduced to slavery. The prisoners were assigned to work on construction or in the fields. The only part of South Arabia that was spared during these conquests was the high plateaus and western slopes of the Yemen. It is possible that these areas had already come under Sabaean domination, or even that their lands, located outside the main commercial routes, were not in contention. The kingdom of Qatabân also lay outside this conflict, despite its proximity to Maʾrib. Its sovereign Warawʾîl showed great prudence in seeking an alliance with Karibʾîl and was duly rewarded with the transfer of some of the spoils from the kingdom of Awsân.

Still farther to the east, the king of Hadramawt likewise chose to side with Karibʾîl. But this alliance seems strange when considered from the Sabaean perspective, since Hadramawt was the principal producer of frankincense, and Shabwa was the center of distribution. In the absence of relevant documents, it is impossible to tell whether Karibʾîl chose alliance over war with Hadramawt, or chose instead to delay his seizure of this vast region.

The Sabaean Peace

After completing these ambitious campaigns, Karibʾîl devoted his energies to consolidating his victories and making improvements in his territory. A long inscription listing the works he had so far accomplished was found on the back of two slabs of stone in the great temple of Sirwâh.[13] From this document it is clear that Karibʾîl had at his disposal a considerable workforce that he was able to move to various sites as needed.

This text first mentions the cities that Karibʾîl fortified: Barâqish (though it is difficult to identify with certainty which parts can be attributed to him) and al-Baydâ. These two establishments were situated to the west and east of Nashshân, respectively, and were therefore key to controlling access to Nashshân's former possessions. Two towns around Maʾrib, namely Wanab and Yaʾrat, were fortified. Karibʾîl subsequently turned his attention to the construction of hydraulic works, mainly in the irrigated lands he had acquired in the Maʾrib region, where he set up dikes and distributors, though none of remarkable size.

He sent colonists into his new territories and even beyond. Conquered cities like Nashshân received contingents of Sabaean settlers, as did newly created ones like Nashq. The expansion of Saba carried a wave of tradesmen and others even farther afield. Some put down roots in the former possessions of Awsân, in the region of the Wadi Markha, in the heart of the Wadi Dura², and in the Heights, above the plain of Dathîna; others ventured to the highlands south of Taizz, the region of Sana, and as far as the mountains of Nabî Shu²ayb. Still others settled in Hadramawt, at Shabwa (where a sanctuary is dedicated to Almaqah), and possibly even farther into the interior in Huraydha in the Wadi ʿAmd.

Sabaeans appeared in the region of al-Hurayda on the shores of the Red Sea, where they introduced their writing to the local population. The presence of Sabaeans across the sea in Ethiopia is attested as early as the reign of Karib²îl Watar. Sabaean inscriptions have been found in the region of Aksum at sites in Matara, Haoulti, and Yeha. Sabaean artisans and traders were probably drawn to the area's vegetation and climate, which are similar to that of Yemen. Most settlers probably came from Ma²rib and, in lesser numbers, from the plain of Sana. Masons and stonecutters brought with them building techniques acquired on the other side of the Red Sea, as is evident in the sanctuary of Yeha, located south of Aksum. Its architecture and construction techniques are strangely evocative of Sabaean temples of the same period, especially in their use of monolithic pillars and dentiled cornices. Throughout the region, monumental inscriptions, incense altars, ibex friezes, bell-shaped pitchers, and other objects bear testimony to the arrival of the Sabaeans and the regular contact that followed between the two coasts of the Red Sea.[14]

The Sabaean language spread through all these regions. By the end of the reign of Karib²îl, Sabaean was spoken in a large part of South Arabia, and certainly all around the edge of the desert. It also spread into Ethiopia, where several texts mention the names of Sabaean divinities (dhât-Himyam) and a sovereign of Saba, though carvings on vases made by the local population were in a dialect distinct from Sabaean. In any case, the Sabaean language exerted an important influence on local populations, who used certain terms and turns of phrase in a number of dedications from al-Huraydha in Hadramawt.

Reasons for the Success of the Sabaeans

How do we explain fifty years of Sabaean victories? The political environment of Arabia was certainly favorable to Karibʾil, allowing him to take advantage of the fragmented power of many small states. This was the case with Jawf, which was divided into autonomous cities; Karibʾil was thus ensured of gaining the alliance of the cities of Haram and Kaminahû against Nashshân. The northern regions near Najrân lacked the unity to resist the Sabaens, and the same was true for the tribes of the mountainous regions above the Gulf of Aden and the Indian Ocean. Nashshân was ultimately a single city which, though important, could muster far fewer resources than Saba. In the end, only the kingdom of Awsân was able to resist Saba, despite the latter's relentless and fierce efforts to reduce it.

The supremacy of Saba was due in large part to a superior level of agricultural prosperity. The sheer size of the Maʾrib oasis and its exploitation through intensive farming gave the region a clear advantage over its neighbors in terms of resources. This advantage was optimized by the highly organized collective known as Saba. Tribal cohesiveness was perhaps the single greatest reason for Sabaean dominance over their neighbors.

The prosperity of Saba was also due in part to the frankincense trade. As early as the eighth century B.C., the countries along the eastern Mediterranean (with the exception of Egypt) had begun to consume aromatic products, and consumption increased in the seventh century. Saba attempted to gain early control of this trade, and the campaigns of Karibʾil were undertaken at least in part with the intention of taking over the principal routes. An alliance with Hadramawt may have appeared more profitable to him than outright domination resulting from warfare. There is evidence to confirm that the reign of Karibʾil roughly coincided with a period of growth and development in the consumption of frankincense in the Near East, and commerce grew proportionately. After all, a certain Karibilu, king of Saba, offered precious stones and spices to Sennacherib, the sovereign of Assyria (705–681), during the commemoration of a temple at the festival of the New Year.[15]

But this economic power alone does not explain the success of the Sabaeans. Agricultural wealth brought with it strong demographic growth in the Maʾrib region. It is not known if the military superiority of the Sabaeans was due to superior numbers of men under arms—the surviving texts mention only enemy losses—but it seems likely that a high number of Sabaeans were settled in the conquered lands. Colonization was doubtless linked to Saba's demographic vigor, though it is unclear whether this growth came from a high birth rate within the country or through the arrival of groups from without. Demographic advantages seem to have been critical to Sabaean expansion even more so than tactical superiority in war, in the absence of any evidence suggesting outstanding military genius or superior weaponry on the part of Karibʾîl.

Saba: Kingdom without a Queen?

The Sabaean inscriptions from the era of Karibʾîl make no mention of a queen. So where does the mysterious Queen of Sheba come from? Her encounter with King Solomon in the Bible's First Book of Kings brought her lasting fame:

> Now when the queen of Sheba heard of the fame of Solomon concerning the name of the Lord, she came to test him with hard questions. She came to Jerusalem with a very great retinue, with camels bearing spices, and very much gold, and precious stones. . . .
>
> And when the queen of Sheba had seen all the wisdom of Solomon, the house that he had built, the food of his table, the seating of his officials, and the attendance of his servants, their clothing, his cupbearers, and his burnt offerings which he offered at the house of the Lord, there was no more spirit in her.
>
> And she said to the king, "The report was true which I heard in my

own land of your affairs and of your wisdom, but I did not believe the reports until I came and my own eyes had seen it; and, behold, the half was not told me; your wisdom and prosperity surpass the report which I heard." (1 Kings 10:1–7)

This passage directly precedes a description of a similar visit from Hiram of Tyre, with whom Solomon maintained extremely close relations; the effect of this juxtaposition is to invite comparison between the queen and Hiram and imply that foreign kings were coming from all directions to celebrate the magnificence of Solomon. The story's historicity is not necessarily undermined by its political apologetics. There is little doubt that an early version of this passage was assembled some time in the seventh century B.C., with a final version appearing in the next century, but traces of an ancient popular legend remain. It would be imprudent to dismiss a certain historical reality here, despite the fact that the Sabaeans were as yet unknown in the tenth century B.C. The Book of Ezekiel had already located them in South Arabia, with Genesis later placing them in North Arabia.

Could King Solomon, who reigned in the tenth century B.C., have received a Queen of Sheba? It is far from certain whether diplomatic ties could have existed between Jerusalem and Saba at that time, especially considering that, besides the First Book of Kings, only Jeremiah and Ezekiel make so much as a reference to the existence of Sheba (or Saba). The biblical evidence yields no sign of Sheba between the tenth and seventh centuries B.C. The earliest South Arabian inscriptions, recently discovered in Jerusalem, belong to a period no earlier than the seventh century B.C. That a queen could have undertaken such a mission is quite astonishing. Queens were only known to exist in North Arabia, examples being Zabibê, Queen of Qédar, who paid tribute to the Assyrian King Tiglathpileser III (744–727 B.C.), and Sâmsi, queen of the Arabs, a contemporary of Sargon II (722–705 B.C.).

The mention of the Queen of Saba is presumably attributable to the compiler and the reference was perhaps originally to North Arabia. The story was a panegyric celebrating the glory of Solomon;

if at first it was based on real facts, these facts must have been profoundly modified over time. Moroever, there is a certain vagueness underlying the whole story, particularly in the fact that the queen's name is never mentioned. It is not inconceivable that the name of Sheba was added simply as an embellishment to the story.

The Decline of the Sabaean Empire

Let us pause to examine the two monumental inscriptions from Sirwâh. Composed at the end of the reign of Karib'îl Watar, or perhaps after his death, these inscriptions celebrate the founding of the Sabaean empire, which by then had spread over a large part of modern-day Yemen. Though the exact dates of his reign are unknown, it was likely during the first half of the seventh century B.C. According to J. Pirenne, the written form of these painstakingly carved texts is significant as an early example of the so-called classical style of the seventh to sixth centuries B.C. According to Pirenne's analysis, which is based exclusively on the evolution of the script, this period follows the so-called premonumental or preclassical period.[16]

The empire of Karib'îl was apparently far too vast to have much of a chance of surviving very long, although it is difficult to say exactly when it began to disintegrate. It is known that one of his successors sent military expeditions into diverse regions, with the earliest interventions apparently in Jawf, only a hundred kilometers or so from Ma'rib. The kingdom of Ma'în attempted to regain its autonomy and take control of Barâqish, prompting the Sabaean king to lay waste the entire area. Later, Karib'îl led a campaign as far as Najrân, north of Jawf, where the local tribes were becoming restless. The situation was far graver in the southern region around Yafa' and in the Highlands overlooking the Gulf of Aden, where the kingdom of Qatabân was attempting to lure certain tribes away from Saba's sphere of influence. Qatabân, a former ally of Saba, had become its rival. The Sabaean mukarrib was thus forced to take action against a tribe of Dahas in the Wadi Tudan, where he massacred some four thousand people. The emergence of Qatabân at the end of the sixth century B.C. was a major development in the region.

The Rise of Qatabân

The heart of Qatabân was located in the Wadi Bayhân, whose sources were high in the mountainous regions of Rada at altitudes near 1,700 meters above sea level. The wadi's two principal branches meet just below the village of Bayhân al-Qasâb (commonly known as al-ʿUlya). Farther north, especially on the right bank, traces of canals, remains of locks, and carved decrees on the boundary stones bear witness to intensive agricultural exploitation of the area below. Ten kilometers downstream, the wadi erodes the slopes of the tell of Hajar Ibn Humayd, a modest settlement occupied as early as the eleventh century B.C. and which later became Qatabân's principal city.[17] Still farther north stand the tall buildings of Hajar Kuhlân, rising above the ruins of the ancient Tamnaʿ, capital city of Qatabân. With 1,850 meters of defensive walls and four gates enclosing an area of some twenty hectares, Tamnaʿ was by far the more prosperous city in the region. In 1951, American archaeologists excavating part of the city behind the southwest gate came upon a large monument that provided evidence of the ancient occupation of the site.

There is no doubt that the early Qatabanite sovereigns had their residence at Tamnaʿ. Though little is known about them, some were already attempting to gain the prestigious title of mukarrib, and eventually the title did pass from Saba to Qatabân, triggering several wars between these powerful neighbors. Qatabân appears to have been the eventual victor, judging from the Qatabanian texts found in several regions formerly held by Saba. The expansion of Qatabân was first directed toward the valleys to the west, in Harîb and Jûba, and later toward those which bordered the Jabal an-Nisiyîn to the east. The Qatabanites later extended their presence into the southwestern mountains of Yemen, in the regions of Radâ, Yafaʾ, and Yarîm, and into the mountains rising above the Gulf of Aden. This expansion was a symptom of Sabaean retreat, a reversal confirmed by Strabo, who cited sources from the second century B.C.: "The territory of the Cattabanians [Qatubanites] extends down to the straits [Strait of Bab al-Mandab] and the passage across the Arabian Gulf; their royal seat is called Tamnaᶜ."[18] Pliny reported that the Qatabanites also controlled a port on the Red Sea at Okélis, the modern-day Shaykh Saîd.[19] On the ancient map, these points described a vast empire both on land and at sea.

In certain respects, Qatabân and Saba owed their prosperity to the same sources. Agriculture was their main asset. Aerial photography has revealed that Qatabân's main riverbed was the site of remarkable development, from al-Haraja in the south all the way to Muqanna some forty-five kilometers to the north. The area under cultivation was at least as large as that of the Maʾrib oasis. Qatabân also derived significant wealth from the spice trade. We learn from Pliny that all frankincense was exported via the intermediary of the Gebbanitae (Qatabanites), and that the great route toward the Mediterranean began at Thomna (Tamnaᶜ).[20] In its break from Saba, Qatabân perhaps aspired to gain a greater share of the revenues from this trade. But it did have another sizable rival in Maᶜîn.

Maᶜîn and the Minaeans

The power of Maᶜîn was out of proportion with its territory, which was always minuscule. Established on the main course of the Jawf, it was hemmed in between the possessions of Haram, less than six kilometers to the west, and Saba. It contained just two neighboring cities, Maᶜîn (known in ancient times as Qarnawu) and Barâqish (the ancient Yathill), along with their irrigated fields and a few dry wadis to the north of the Jawf. The oasis of Barâqish measured about 1,350 hectares, and that of Maᶜîn less than 2,000 hectares; their combined area has less than half the size of the lands of Maʾrib.

The wealth of Maᶜîn stemmed from the Minaeans' capacity for organization and control of the frankincense trade, which gave them a special role in South Arabia. While other tribes were mainly concerned with agriculture and military exploits, the Minaeans made commerce their specialty. None of the surviving Minaean texts mention military campaigns, though there are mentions of commercial expeditions, some to very distant places. The Minaean sovereigns never attempted to claim the title of mukarrib, nor did they colonize their people or even coin their own money.

Trade remained the principal activity of the Minaean people. They were successful in establishing close relations with Hadramawt; Shabwa was less than 200 kilometers away, across desert trails, and therefore some Minaean traders must have lived at Shabwa. The Minaeans later forged close ties with other cities involved in the spice trade and settled initially in small numbers in towns such as Haram, Tamnaᶜ, and Aswân, and ultimately ventured north all the way to the eastern shores of the Mediterranean. Traces of their presence have been found in Najrân, Qaryat al-Faw (280 kilometers northwest of Maᶜîn), Dedan, Gaza, Egypt, and northwestern Arabia. They traded with Egypt, the Phoenician coast (Tyre and Sidon), Syria (or the Transeuphratene), Assyria, and Babylonia. They eventually made their way across the Mediterranean to settle on the island of Delos, joining numerous other traders from the east, and in Ionia.

The texts which mention commerce are often silent on the subject of the political evolution of Maᶜîn and the history of its relations with its neighbors. Even if Saba offered more or less informal protection over Maᶜîn, the latter left no evidence of having adopted the Sabaean pantheon, language, or political institutions. Hadramawt seemingly maintained an enduring alliance with Maᶜîn. One of the kings of Hadramawt even financed construction of one of the towers on Maᶜîn's eastern gate.

Hadramawt

In its narrowest sense, the name Hadramawt refers to the valley that runs parallel to the Indian Ocean between the arid high plateaus known as Jawl and the plateaus that continue east along the Wadi Masilah to the boundaries of a region known as the Mahra. In a wider sense, Hadramawt designates the entire expanse of land including the regions to the south and north of this valley, as well as a large number of tributaries oriented more or less north-south. On the western side, these plateaus terminate in an abrupt escarpment that rises on both sides of the opening of the Wadi Hadramawt, overhanging the sites of Barîra and Shabwa. This line of cliffs naturally forms a powerful barrier that allows easy control of access through the wadis. Hadramawt is exceptional for its large area and the fact that it faces both land and sea.

It is an established fact that some of these valleys were in use as early as the second millennium B.C., but the history of Hadramawt up to the early first millennium B.C. remains relatively obscure. The Sabaean sovereign Karib'îl made an alliance with Yad'îl of Hadramawt, doubtless to ensure peaceful conditions favorable to commerce. Both sovereigns later proclaimed themselves mukarrib.[21] Fierce competition may have ensued between Qatabân and Hadramawt to procure this prestigious title. Lastly, the inscription refers to several kings whose chronological order is not certain.

Shabwa gradually asserted its power to the detriment of neighboring cities. The city of Barîra, in the Wadi Jirdân, became an increasingly important center of activity for Sabaean soldiers waging war in the region. Barîra's location on the trade routes was most beneficial to Shabwa, whose fortunes depended on its role in commerce. (Paradoxically, the city is located twenty kilometers south of the Hadramawt valley.) The city was established at the mouth of the Wadi 'Irma, where floods were small and infrequent compared with those of the wadis Dhana, Bayhân, or Markha. Barîra developed a network of mountain trails connecting it to the interior valleys of Hadramawt, and also built the 'Aqaybat and Futra passes as well as gravel roads along the summit of the high plateaus.[22] Shabwa was strategically located at the crossroads of several important routes, some of which led through the desert directly to Ma'în or Najrân, others along the rims of the high plateaus; still others connected Shabwa with the port city of Bi'r 'Alî (the ancient Qana'). Shabwa also benefited from the presence of salt deposits that had accumulated in the hills to form a defensive triangle, naturally sheltering the city from floods and siltation. The area's first occupants arrived as early as the middle of the second millennium

B.C., and practiced intensive agriculture with irrigation from the floodwaters of the Wadi ʿIrma. These early settlers created a network of canals and earthen aqueducts on both sides of the riverbed.[23] Their houses were constructed of unfired brick on stone foundations. Their pottery somewhat resembled the Palestinian styles from the Late Bronze Age.[24] At Shabwa and Raybûn, archaeologists suspect they have found the earliest evidence of ancient culture in Hadramawt, predating even the South Arabian era.

There is a scarcity of texts relating to Shabwa in the archaic period. While several Sabaean inscriptions have been discovered at Shabwa, their contents are difficult to assess, since Shabwa was not a Sabaean city and its inhabitants wrote in the local Hadrami dialect. But Sabaeans, perhaps merchants or soldiers, settled here and brought with them their god Almaqah, to whom they probably erected a temple, though its location is unknown. In any event, evidence of the use of the Sabaean language in this area suggests a political as well as cultural influence and possibly an explicit relationship of protection by the Sabaean mukarrib Karibʾîl Watar. The city of Barîra, south of Shabwa, apparently had a similar relationship with Saba, remaining under Sabaean influence while not itself Sabaean.

The details of the earliest cultures in Hadramawt fell into obscurity as their ancient practices yielded to Sabaean influences. Over time, states began to forge closer ties, and evidence of the melding of different peoples and their gods is evident in Shabwa as in other ancient urban centers. Minaean traders settled in Shabwa and introduced the cult of ʿAthtar dhû-Qabd, and a number of Qatabanites passed through or settled there.

More Than One Arabia Felix?

As a geographical entity, South Arabia is so vast that it is difficult to grasp as a whole. It embraces starkly constrasting regions, from the coastal plains of Tihâma to the western mountains to the interior desert to the plateaus of Hadramawt. And along with great variety in topography and climate are diverse cultural practices and forms of social organization.

The coastal regions are oriented toward the sea: Hadramawt has Mahra and Oman to its east along the coasts of the Indian Ocean, and Tihâma looks across the Red Sea toward East Africa. The Sabʾatayn desert, which forms a sprawling depression between Hadramawt and Maˁîn, extends all way from the Persian Gulf to Assyria and the eastern Mediterranean. Crossing this desert has always been treacherous.

Between these geographical extremes, the mountains of western Yemen rise up to create an environment that is very difficult to penetrate, and the evidence suggests that people were dispersed from this region as if by centrifugal force. The fringes of the interior desert saw the settlement of the principal states and the development of their urban centers, but each of them was focused around one or more wadis, with arid desert land separating them. The region was politically fragmented, with the tiny territory of Jawf divided up into city-states. Distinct regional styles flourished despite a common language. The sanctuaries of Hadramawt, for instance, bore little resemblance to those constructed in Jawf during the eighth century B.C., and the style of decorative carvings of animals, plants, and people rarely traveled beyond the city limits.

Amidst this diversity, however, there was considerable unity. In general, the period from the Neolithic Age down through the Bronze Age and the South Arabian period was marked by continuity. The third millennium B.C., commonly accepted as the period during which the first irrigation networks were constructed, showed a continuity of techniques of operation, as with, most likely, cultivation (date palms, for example). In certain regions such as eastern Jawf, similarities between Bronze Age sites and those from the South Arabian period imply that these territories had been inhabited for a very long time. The duration of occupation was surely long, if intermittent, in other wadis such as the ˁIrma or Jûba. These establishments traded with the people of the upper valleys in exchanges of complementary products from different regions. There is also evidence of commercial relations with the Bronze Age people of the Levant. The cultural unity of South Arabian civilization appears to have been the result of long evolution.

Around the beginning of the first millennium B.C., each state used a different South Arabian language—Sabaean in the Maʾrib region, Madhabian around Maʿîn, etc.—but it is likely that the different states were able to communicate with each other to some degree. During this time, use of the Sabaean language was expanding along with Saba itself, and an ability to speak Sabaean brought ever-increasing prestige. By the seventh century B.C., Sabaean had established itself as the principal language of law, cults, and historical texts, and was probably spoken by local aristocracies outside of Saba. Surely there were pockets of resistance and a later resurgence of local dialects after the Sabaean empire's disintegration. Local dialects probably continued to be spoken in the home; evidence of these local dialects has been found in the names engraved on funeral stelae in the tombs.

Along with its language, Saba imposed its cultural models, institutions, and religion. The result was a discernible unity among different territories, at least in the period from the seventh to fifth centuries B.C. Various techniques in use among the Sabaeans, such as stonecutting (limestone, alabaster, etc.) and construction with diverse materials such as stone, wood, and metal, were adopted thoughout the region, as were designs for civil and religious buildings. Sabaean expansion brought with it numerous pottery designs, especially the high-quality, streamlined patterns in red paste, as well as steatite vases, obsidian utensils, seals, etc. There is a large body of evidence pertaining to funerary practices and ideas—a sphere marked by great stability over the centuries. Despite a great diversity of funeral rites, there is a underlying similarity of conceptions in the erection of funeral monuments, notably in the notion of the "eternal dwelling place." The tomb was seen as a place where the deceased enjoyed some form of continued survival (stripped of any sensation), and fitting honors were paid to the dead. (Burial practices will be discussed at length in chapter seven.)

In the end, all of the urban establishments were connected by a single activity, namely, the incense trade. Seen in their regional context, these cities on the borders of the Sabʾatayn desert were not isolated entities but rather were linked by commerce. Central to the question of regional unity is the debate over the domestication of the camel and when it began to be used for transportation rather than solely as a food source. Moreover, in ancient times the records used in the spice trade were probably somewhat standard throughout South Arabia and northward toward the Mediterranean.

3. FRAGRANCES OF ARABIA

> Furthest to the south of all the world is Arabia, and this is the one
> country on earth for growing myrrh and cassia and cinnamon and
> gum-labdanum. . . . There is a most marvelous sweet smell from all
> this land of Arabia.[1]

Thus did Herodotus of Halicarnassus imagine, in the fifth century B.C., this exotic land perched on the very edge of a flat world.
The details he describes, even the country's very existence, were
based solely on fragmentary reports from intermediary sources in
the region from the Nile to the Euphrates. The legends seemed to
grow more poetic with every mile they traveled. The geography was
hazy, and all that emerged was fragrances and myths, as the following passage from Herodotus vividly demonstrates:

> They collect frankincense by burning storax, which the Phoenicians
> export to Greece. This burning is a part of the harvesting of the frank-
> incense. For the bushes that grow frankincense are guarded by tiny
> winged snakes, of dappled color, and there are great numbers of them
> around each bush. . . . There is nothing that can drive them from the
> bushes except the smoke of the storax. . . .
>
> And this is how they get their cassia: they bind ox-hides and other
> kinds of leather over all their body and their faces, except their eyes,
> when they go out to get cassia. This grows in shallow ponds, and round
> the pond and in it there live winged creatures, very like bats, with a
> dreadful squeak and very ready to fight. You must ward these off your
> eyes if you are to harvest the cassia.
>
> Their method of collecting cinnamon is even more remarkable.
> Where it grows and what sort of land produces it they cannot say,
> except that they declare, with a show of reason, that it grows in the

places where Dionysus was reared. They say that great birds carry these dry sticks, which we have learned from the Phoenicians to call cinnamon, and that the birds carry the sticks to their nests, which are plastered with mud and are placed on sheer crags where no man can climb up. The Arabians have found the following trick to deal with this. They cut out the limbs of dead oxen and asses, taking as much of the limbs as possible, and carry them to the part of the country where the nests are, and there they put them near the nests and themselves withdraw to a distance. The birds swoop down and carry off the limbs of the beasts to their nests, and the nests, being unable to bear the weight, break and fall down, and the Arabians approach and collect what they want. Thus is cinnamon gathered in these parts, and so from there it comes to other countries.[2]

Theophrastus's Natural History

Theophrastus of Eresos (372–287 B.C.) was far more familiar than his predecessor with the principal tribes of Arabia and the riches they possessed:

> Now frankincense, myrrh, cassia, and also cinnamon are found in the Arabian peninsula about Saba, Hadramyta [Hadramawt], Kitibaina [Qatabân], and Mamali [Maʿîn]. The trees of frankincense and myrrh grow partly in the mountains, partly on private estates at the foot of the mountains; wherefore some are under cultivation, others not; the mountains, they say, are lofty, forest-covered, and subject to snow, and rivers from them flow down into the plain. . . .
>
> The whole [mountain] range, they said, belongs to the portion of the Sabaeans; for it is under their sway, and they are honest in their dealings with one another. Wherefore no one keeps watch; so that these sailors greedily took, they said, and put on board their ships some of the frankincense and myrrh, since there was no one about, and sailed away. They also reported another thing which they said they had been told, that the myrrh and frankincense are collected from all parts into the temple of the sun; and that this temple is the most sacred thing which the Sabaeans of that region possess, and it is guarded by certain Arabians in arms.[3]

Some time between 120 and 110 B.C., Agatharchides, a renowned grammarian, provided perhaps the most poetic picture of the plants and people of Arabia Felix:

> In the interior of the country there are dense forests of mature standing timber where the trees grow very tall. Myrrh, frankincense, and cinnamon are all found here, as well as fragrant palm and rockrose and other similar species, which grow in such a way that words cannot describe the impact on the senses. The sense of wonder transcends the sheer pleasure of the aromatic products, which are stored and aged, or even the creative force that nourishes them; most awesome of all is the flourishing of a fully divine and mature exhalation of wondrous perfume.[4]

Myrrh

The name derives from *murr,* a Semitic word meaning bitter. The Greeks distinguished between *myrrha,* or red myrrh, and *stakté,* the fragrant oil of myrrh. In the Gospels, the magi brought gifts of gold, frankincense, and myrrh (*smyrna*) (Matthew 2:1–11). The Latin generic term *Commiphora* has several modifications according to the species: *myrrha, erythrea, simplicifolia,* etc. Like frankincense, myrrh belongs to the family of *Burseraceae,* or balsam, characterized by the presence of resins under the bark. Pliny classified different species of myrrh by place of origin, distinguishing between types from Maʿīn, Qatabān, and Hadramawt. He provided a fairly precise description:

> Broadly speaking, however, the proof of goodness is given by its being in small pieces of irregular shape, forming in the solidifying of the juice as it turns white and dries up, and in its showing white marks like fingernails when it is broken, and having a slightly bitter taste. The second best kind is mottled inside, and the worst is the one that is black inside; and if it is black outside as well it is of a still inferior quality.[5]

According to the Greek geographers, "the frankincense-tree, it is said, is not tall, about five cubits high, and it is much branched. It has a leaf like that of the pear, but much smaller and very grassy in color, like rue;[6] the bark is altogether smooth like that of bay. The myrrh-tree is said to be still smaller in stature and more bushy; it is said to have a tough stem, which is contorted near the ground, and is stouter than a man's leg."[7] This is how myrrh appears to present-day travelers; it grows at the foot of the dunes north of Ma'rib or in the region of Markha. It is a vigorous shrub that grows to a height of two to three meters, with a knotty and spiny trunk, coarse bark, and small red flowers when in bloom.

The following observation is reproduced in a work by Strabo and attributed by him to Eratosthenes, the librarian to Ptolemy III at Alexandria in the third century B.C.: "Cattabania [Qatabān] produces frankincense and Chatramotitis [Hadramawt] produces myrrh; and both these and other aromatic plants are bartered to merchants."[8] This description corresponds closely to the geographical distribution of these plants today. Myrrh grows mainly south of the line stretching from Ma'rib to Shabwa, in the Bayhān and Markha valleys, in the Dathīna, and in Yafa'—regions brought under Qatabanite domination in the third and second centuries B.C. Botanists have also found the plant in Asīr, Jawf, the Highlands, and Tihāma. Conversely, several varieties of frankincense thrive alongside myrrh trees in Hadramawt.

The ancients found several uses for myrrh. In the time of Moses, according to Exodus, the Lord ordered that a sacred oil be prepared with liquid myrrh (môr), sweet-smelling cinnamon, aromatic cane, and olive oil, for the anointment of the great priest.[9] Later on, the Greeks dissolved red myrrh in olive oil and wine to create a "bitter and stimulating aperitif." They used the smoke of myrrh in perfumery, and medicinally in the form of a balm. The Cypriots were the great perfume makers, both in Crete and on the Peloponnese. After all, it was the island of Cyprus that gave the Greeks the myth of Aphrodite, the blonde goddess of Love who emanated a divinely alluring scent. Then there was Myrrha, the plant personified, who was struck with a violent passion for her father Cinyras, the king of Cyprus, whom she seduced under the cloak of darkness. When the king realized what his daughter's passion had caused, he recoiled in horror and tried to kill her. As she fled, she begged the gods to save her, and her prayers were answered: she was metamorphosed into a myrrh tree. Her tears emerged as the drops of resin from the tree. Myrrha's baby, trapped within the bark of the tree, could not be delivered without the help of the gods. His name was Adonis, god of perfumes and the future lover of Aphrodite.[10]

Frankincense

Frankincense was another tree of legend which brought lasting fame to Arabia Felix. Long before its first mention alongside myrrh in Greek and Roman sources, frankincense was known through the Sabaean term *libnay*, which spread early through all the languages of Syria, Mesopotamia, and Greece—proof of frankincense's origins in the southern part of the Arabian peninsula. Though the ancient Egyptians were apparently unfamiliar with this term, it was certainly current in Somalia or Sudan on the east African coast. Frankincense was known as *lubbunîtum* or *labanâtu* in Assyrian; the Greeks called it *libanos,* and in Latin it was known variously as *libanus, libanum,* or *olibanum.* It was later known as *lubân* in Arabic. Frankincense was mentioned in Assyria as early as the second half of the eighth century B.C., and in Palestine from the end of the seventh century, and it is possible that it was used even earlier in these areas.[11] The first square incense altars made a sudden appearance in the private residences of Palestine in the seventh century B.C., around the same time that the use of animal fats was definitively supplanted by incense in ceremonial sacrifices.[12] It was also in the (late) seventh century that the poet Sappho made the first recorded mention in Greek of frankincense, myrrh, saffron, and cassia from the Orient. The literary sources agree with the findings of archaeology, which date the arrival of frankincense in the Near East from South Arabia to the seventh century B.C., if not earlier.

Frankincense is a resin derived from any of several varieties of tree known to botanists under the generic name of *Boswellia*. As is the case with *Commiphora,* the genus of *Boswellia* embraces as many as twenty related species, mostly found in Somalia, Eritrea, and South Arabia. More than six different species have been identified on the island of Socotra alone, with ten more in the southern part of Yemen. The most common species, known as *Boswellia sacra,* has been the subject of numerous studies. Théodore Monod describes this species as typically growing from three to seven meters high, with vertical stems branching out from the base and then spreading outward (only in rare cases does this plant have a single trunk). The plant spreads out fairly wide at its peak, like several varieties of the African acacia. The trunk is generally composed of four or five strata, one of which is a thick, reddish-brown secretory layer several centimeters thick; gum-resin is exuded from the deepest layer of the bark.[13]

The various species of frankincense grow chiefly in the southern and eastern regions of the Arabian peninsula. Their western limit is generally around forty-seven degrees east latitude, which corresponds roughly with the descent of the plateaus of Hadramawt.[14] Small populations of Boswellia can be found near ʿAmaqîm and Habbân to the south, and in all the valleys that slope down from the high plateaus toward the Indian Ocean. Clumps of *Boswellia* are also fairly common in the hinterlands of Mukalla, Shihr, and Sayhût at altitudes below 1,000 meters. Even greater numbers of frankincense trees are reported farther east in Zufar, where natural conditions are especially favorable. The mountains in this region soar as high as 1,500 meters above sea level and receive the full force of monsoon rains from June to September; the plants also benefit from dense cloud cover throughout this period. Theodore Bent wrote in 1895 that "this peculiar district of Arabia, which supplied the ancient world with frankincense, is of very small size . . . perhaps, now not bigger than the Isle of Wight. . . . The valley is covered with this small shrub for miles around."[15] And Théodore Monod concurs that this same area, around the Qara and Samhan mountains, is the veritable "home of the frankincense tree."

The methods of harvesting frankincense have for the most part remained unchanged over the millennia. Pliny described the procedure in the first century A.D.:

> It used to be the custom, when there were fewer opportunities of selling frankincense, to gather it only once a year, but at the present day trade introduces a second harvesting. The early and natural gathering takes

place at about the rising of the Dog-Star [Sirius], when the summer heat is most intense. They make an incision where the bark appears fullest of juice and distended to its thinnest; and the bark is loosened with a blow, but not removed. From this incision a greasy foam spurts out, which coagulates and thickens, being received on a mat of palm-leaves where the nature of the ground requires this, but in other places on a space round the tree that has been rammed hard. The frankincense collected in the latter way is in a purer state, but the former method produced a heavier weight; while the residue adhering to the tree is scraped off with an iron tool, and consequently contains fragments of bark.[16]

Théodore Monod noted recently that this method requires only a small incision of roughly 10 centimeters by 5 centimeters in the secretory layer, without extending down into the central core of the tree. Very soon thereafter, viscous droplets of an opaque white liquid begin to well up like small pearls. Today, harvesters use a double-edged instrument resembling a raclette knife to score the bark with one edge and then scrape away the beads of frankincense with the other.

Two Harvests a Year

Pliny left a detailed decription of the harvest:

The forest is divided into definite portions, and owing to the mutual honesty of the owners is free from trespassing, and though nobody keeps guard over the trees after an incision has been made, nobody steals from his neighbor. . . . The frankincense from the summer crop is collected in autumn; this is the purest kind, bright white in color. The second crop is harvested in the spring, cuts having been made in the bark during the winter in preparation for it; the juice that comes out on this occasion is reddish, and not to be compared with the former taking; the name for which was *carfiathum.* the other being called *dathiathum.* Also the juice produced by a sapling is believed to be whiter, but that from an older tree has more scent.[17]

Pliny's account may be compared with that of Theodore Bent some twenty centuries later:

> The Bedouin choose the hot season, when the gum flows most freely, to do this puncturing. During the rains of July and August, and during the cold season, the trees are left alone. The first step is to make an incision in the trunk, then they strip off a narrow bit of the bark below the hole, so as to make a receptacle in which the milky juice, the *spuma pinguis* of Pliny, can lodge and harden. Then the incision is deepened, and after seven days they return to collect what are, by that time, quite big tears of frankincense, larger than an egg. . . . It is collected only in the hot weather, before the rains begin and when the gum flows freely, in the months of March, April, and May, for during the rains the tracks of the mountains of Gara are impassable. The trees belong to the various families of the Gara tribe; each tree is marked and known to its owner, and the product is sold to Banyan merchants, who come to Dhofar [Zufar] just before monsoons to take it away.[18]

Reports have come from other travelers crossing Zufar, such as the following account from 1932:

> The harvest of *lubān* is mainly done in the summer months. The crop is stored in caves until winter and only then shipped to the coast, since boats can't take to the sea during the monsoon storms in the southwest. The product is allowed to dry during this interval, although it is ready for export as soon as ten to twelve days after harvest.[19]

The double-cutting method was evidently familiar to Pliny, who noted that the frankincense known as *carfiathum* was the product of the harvest collected in autumn (*kharîf* in South Arabian) and *dathiathum* was from the spring (*datha*ʾ) harvest.

The ancient inhabitants of Zufar probably made first their incisions in April or May and then returned ten days later to collect the resin and make new incisions, which they would leave for ten more days before gathering the incense and storing it in a dry place. Work would cease upon the arrival of the monsoons sometime in July or August. In September, the bundles of frankincense would be packed and shipped to Shabwa, a journey of twenty to thirty days.

Beginning around the first century A.D., part of the shipment may have traveled by boat as far as Qanaʾ (modern-day Biʾr ʿAlī) and from there joined the caravans overland to Shabwa. The Zufaris would repeat their incisions in November, with a lower yield of frankincense. By February, preparations would have been completed for a new expedition to Shabwa either overland or by sea. This well-established cycle of production remained in effect for more than a millennium.

Other Spices

Besides myrrh and frankincense, several other aromatic plants graced the land of South Arabia. *Lâdan,* or gum-labdanum, which the Romans called *ladanum,* is a sticky oleoresin derived from various species of rockrose (genus *Cistus*), a scrubby bush that can grow in stony ground.[20] According to several authors, the undertaking of its harvest involved great risks. Goats—notoriously harmful to all leafy plants but particularly keen to nibble this plant's scented stalks—love to graze on the stalks just when the buds are at their swollen peak, as if they appreciated their commercial value to humans. In their tireless pursuit of the sweet liquor, the goats mop it up until their pointy beards are dripping with sap, which gathers dust as it hardens in the sun. This explains why goat hairs are often found mixed in with gum-labdanum. We learn from Pliny that in some countries gum-labdanum was harvested by tying off the stem of the plant with cord. Pure gum-labdanum has a harsh smell and a withered appearance. When burned, it gives off a bright flame and a strong but agreeable odor.[21] It is in high demand for its uses in perfumery and medicine.

There are at least four species of cassia, of which the only one definitely native to Arabia is so-called false cinnamon (true cinnamon comes from Ceylon). Cinnamon was harvested on the coasts of India and shipped through Arabia, and thus the confusion in the minds of Herodotus and Theophrastus.[22] Cassia is known as *salīkhat* among the inhabitants of Arabia, who use its leaves and hulls medicinally. Pliny commented on several legends which described cassia as growing on the edges of swamps, guarded by fearsome bats and winged serpents:

> Stories like these are purely fictional and are created only to raise prices. . . . The actual shrub of the cinnamon is only about three feet high at the most, the smallest being only a span high, and four inches thick, and it throws out shoots as low as six inches from the ground; it has a dried up apearance, and while it is green has no scent; the leaf is like that of the wild marjoram; it likes a dry soil and is less fertile in wet weather. . . . The finest quality with cinnamon belongs to the thinnest parts of the boughs, for about a span's length; the second best is to the next pieces for a shorter length, and so on in order; the worst in quality is the part nearest to the roots, because it has least amount of bark. . . . Some writers mention two kinds of cinnamon, one lighter and the other darker in color; and in former days the light kind was preferred, but now on the other hand the dark is praised, and even a mottled kind is preferred to the pure white. . . . The lowest value is attached to it when it is soft or when the bark is falling off.[23]

Numerous species of aloe grow on the island of Socotra (or Dioskoridês to the Greeks) about 300 miles off the coast of Hadramawt. The most celebrated of these is Socotra aloe, whose sap is highly praised; this variety is not to be confused with aloe wood, an aromatic used for perfume and incense, which is in reality agalwood.[24] This isolated island was well known for this latter substance; after all, it was Aristotle who advised his pupil Alexander the Great to lay claim to the island and settle Greek colonists there so that they could send aloe back to Greece and Syria. Pliny also emphasized the exceptional quality of this product. The aloe is harvested in September, right after the rainy season, when its fronds are swollen with juice, and stored in a ditch covered with rocks or goatskins. The sap is later extruded onto the goatskins and dried in the wind for about six weeks, until the sap has become a very dark brownish-green. This sap is used in traditional medicine as a digestive aid and for burns and other flesh wounds.

Socotra also grows a reddish resin known as dragon's blood.[25] Pliny recounts the fanciful tale that this resin originally came from the blood of a dragon that was felled and trampled by an elephant. The tree, identified in the nineteenth century as *Dracaena cinabri Balfour*, grows only on Socotra. Beads of its reddish-purple resin ooze naturally from the bark and are collected in small goatskins; a knife blade is sometimes used to detach the beads of resin. Dragon's blood is used medicinally to stop hemorrhages and to treat diseases of the eye; it is also used as a red stain for precious woods.

The inhabitants of Arabia imported perfumes, notably *costus,* a root harvested in the Indus delta for its properties as a stimulant and calorifacient root. Arabians also favored storax, a fragrant balsam derived from the *Liquidamabar orientalis* tree (an Asian tree of the witch hazel family), which they imported at great expense from Cyprus and Anatolia. True storax was used medicinally for treating catarrh, colds, aphonia, buzzing in the ears, digestive disorders, etc.; these applications seem more likely than the fumigation of winged serpents and insects in the harvest of frankincense as reported in Herodotus.[26]

Unknown Quantities

The absence of textual sources prevents us from accurately estimating the volume of incense production in ancient South Arabia; while it is possible to glean some details from Greek and Roman authors, they too were often poorly informed. Calculations based on figures supplied by Pliny allow us to estimate that between 1,300 and 1,700 tons of frankincense and between 450 and 600 tons of myrrh were delivered annually to the Roman Empire—but these figures should be regarded with some skepticism.[27] In any case, it is clear that the Romans were aggressive consumers of aromatic products and created a demand that vastly exceeded supply. Livy made an annual offering at the temple of the Palatine that consisted of a large root on a golden platter onto which droplets of sap would ooze out. The Emperor Vespasian later dedicated gold crowns encrusted with cinnamon as offerings to the sanctuaries of the Capitol and Peace. Finally, Pliny confirms that the quantity of frankincense Nero burned in the funeral rites of his consort Poppaea exceeded an entire year's production:

> Then reckon up the vast number of funerals celebrated yearly throughout the entire world, and the perfumes such as are given to the gods a grain at a time, that are piled up in heaps to the honor of dead bodies! Yet the gods used not to regard with less favor the worshippers who petitioned them with salted spelt, but rather, as the facts show, they were more benevolent in those days.[28]

Information about ancient incense production can also be inferred from more recent statistics: in 1875, for example, 300 tons of frankincense and 70 tons of myrrh were reportedly shipped to Aden for export. During a six-month period in 1977, the production of frankincense in Hadramawt was estimated at 4,200 kilograms. But even modern statistics such as these tend to be incomplete or even contradictory, and therefore must be taken with a grain of salt.

Frankincense Routes through South Arabia

Some imagination is required in attempting to retrace the original frankincense trade routes from the regions where it was produced up to the eastern Mediterranean. There is little doubt that the caravans tended to follow trails according to the features of the landscape, such as river valleys and high mountain passes, while staying as close as possible to sources of resupply for both man and beast. Very few traces remain of encampments used by these ancient travelers, besides a few tombs and graffiti; the sand has covered their tracks.

Archaeologists are just now beginning to retrace the trail from Zufar to Shabwa, a stretch of nearly 700 kilometers, but in the meantime this route can only be sketched hypothetically. Travelers had a choice between an interior route to the north of the plateaus of Hadramawt and the route to the south via Mahra. From Mahra travelers could rejoin the Wadi Masilah, which flows year round, and go up the Wadi Hadramawt as far as the Wadi Dhuhūr, which led to Shabwa via a system of rocky passes. Beginning around the time of Christ, a portion of the frankincense cargo from Zufar went by sea as far as Qanaʾ, whence the shipments would continue either north along the wadis Bīna and Hajar or west along the wadis Mayfʾa and ʿAmaqīm, finally reaching Shabwa via the Wadi ʿIrma. These two routes may have been used at the same time or successively; their respective advantages for ancient travelers remain unclear. In any case, it seems certain that Shabwa represented a point of convergence for all the trails and was a principal trading center.

Shabwa's central importance as a caravan stop was due to several factors. Its oasis provided pasturage for animals, and its water supply was regularly replenished by the Wadi ʿIrma. Its vast open space was protected by fortifications that ringed the surrounding hills.[29] Years of archaeological excavations have still not brought to light the warehouses and market buildings that must have existed there to handle transactions for the large cargoes that passed through the city. Since none of the inscriptions that survive from the site expressly mentions the incense trade, we must rely once again on Pliny's relatively late description, from the first century A.D.:

> Frankincense after being collected is conveyed to Sabota [Shabwa] on camels, one of the gates of the city being opened for its admission; the kings have made it a capital offence for camels so laden to turn aside from the high road. At Sobata a tithe estimated by measure and not by weight is taken by the priests for the god they call Sabis [Siyân], and the incense is not allowed to be put on the market until this has been done; this tithe is drawn on to defray what is a public expenditure, for actually on a fixed number of days the god graciously entertains guests at a banquet.[30]

Elsewhere Pliny explains:

> When the men bring [their harvest to Shabwa], each one sets aside a pile of his [frankincense] and myrrh and entrusts it to the keeping of the guards. Each pile is labeled with a tag describing the contents, weight, and sale price. When the merchants come to examine the writing, they choose the merchandise that looks right for them and leave

the payment in its place. The priest then comes along and deducts a
third of the price for the god, and the balance is held in security until
the owner comes to claim it.[31]

Though Pliny's description is more vivid than any South Arabian
inscription likely ever to come to light, there is no guarantee of its
accuracy.

Two possible routes were available to caravans departing Shabwa,
one leading directly to Tamna[c] and the other leading northwest
across the Sab'atayn desert toward Jawf or even farther north to
Asîr. The former led west from Shabwa past the foot of the black
dome of al-cUqla, alongside the great dunes to the west, and followed a strip of land about three to four kilometers wide which
eventually rejoins the lower course of the Wadi Markha. Caravans
then climbed south until reaching Hajar Yahirr, the old capital of
Awsân, where they would make a stop. On the next leg of the journey, they would continue west up the course of the Wadi Dumays
along the edges of the shiny black heights of the Jabal an-Nisiyîn,
to Tamna[c]. This route was no more than 150 kilometers long and
had the advantage of passing through an inhabited region with reliable sources of drinking water from the wadis Markha, Jifa', and
Jiba. Use of this route would have involved the active participation
of the Qatabanites, since the caravans would need to head north for
Ma'rib and Macîn, a 200-kilometer voyage that took about a week.[32]
According to Pliny, camels had to follow "a single, narrow trail"
across the kingdom of Macîn; this trail was surely well defined and
tightly controlled, though it has not been identified by modern
scholars.

The alternate route from Shabwa leads north over the rocky
spur of Nasr, then threads its way through the narrow gulley of
Shuqayqat, amidst the dunes, and up through the rocky peaks of
al-Arayn and Thaniya which loom high over small plains that grow
green after the rains. The hills of Ruwayk and al-Alam are recognizable from afar by their rows of turrets and tombs where the caravans buried their dead.[33] Twenty kilometers farther on, the caravans entered the Wadi Jawf, with fifty kilometers still remaining to
Macîn. The distance between Shabwa and Macîn was about 250

kilometers, or eight to ten days of difficult traveling, the main challenge being lack of water. The route from Ruwayk to Najrân is more
direct.

From Arabia to the Mediterranean

At Najrân, principal city of ʿAsir, the caravans left behind the South
Arabian world. The caravan trade had a unifying effect on South
Arabia—an effect mainly absent in the varied landscape of central
and northern Arabia, except for limited ties beween the caravans
and certain pastoral communities. Najrân lies about 2,200 kilometers south of the Mediterranean port of Gaza, and the distance from
Tamnaʿ to Gaza was measured at 2,437,500 paces, a journey of
sixty to eighty days and sixty-five camel stops, according to Pliny
and other ancient sources.

This trip was punishing even in winter, when the absence of
summer's burning winds eased travel. The villages were far apart,
water sources were few, the nights were cold, and the trails were not
always clearly marked. Caravans had to be tightly organized and
amply financed. Pliny's commentary is instructive even though
based on unverifiable sources: "Fixed portions of the frankincense
are also given to the priests and the king's secretaries, but besides these the guards and their attendants and the gate-keepers
and servants also have their pickings: indeed all along the route
they keep on paying, at one place for water, at another for fodder,
or the charges for lodging at the halts, and the various toll-houses;
so that expenses mount up to 688 denarii per camel before the
Mediterranean coast is reached."[34]

The essential stages of the journey from Najrân to Gaza were as
follows. From Najrân, the caravans headed north toward Yathrîb
(modern-day Medîna), first passing alongside the mountains of
Yemen and then up through the fertile region of Thumals-Tabâla
(known today as the plain of Bishah), avoiding the great lava fields
of central Arabia. They stopped at Dédan, capital of the Lihyanite
kingdom (al-ʿUla), and again at Hijrâ (modern-day Madaïn Salah,
known to the Nabataeans as Egra), where the Minaeans met up

with their compatriots. The final leg of the journey took them
through the oases of Taymâ, Tabûk, and al-Qurayya, then on to
Petra and Gaza.

Other caravans went east from Najrân to Qaryat al-Faw near the
region of Riyadh, reaching Qatif on the Persian Gulf, or toward
lower Mesopotamia or Babylonia via Yathrîb. On reaching Gaza or
Alexandria, the spices would be shipped on by boat to Greece and
Rome.

Some Prices

The length and difficulty of the voyage explain the high prices
charged for Arabian spices in the markets of the West. Few actual
figures remain, and once again we must rely on Pliny for the clearest surviving account. The most expensive item was *Cassia Daphnis*
at 300 denarii per pound; ordinary cassia brought 50 denarii per
pound (or 520 grams of coined silver per kilo).[35] Frankincense cost
only three to six denarii per pound (or from 31 to 62 grams of
coined silved per kilo), depending on quality; gum-labdanum was
4 denarii (40 assis, or 26 grams of coined silver per kilo), etc.
Curiously, the best quality myrrh, known as *stakté,* cost 50 denarii
per pound, whereas cultivated myrrh was only 11 denarii per
pound, or twice the price of frankincense. These prices were high
but not prohibitive, assuming that average annual income in Syria-
Palestine was approximately 120 denarii. A soldier in Caesar's
army earned around 72 denarii per year, the equivalent of six kilos
of frankincense. Pliny recorded that a kilo of frankincense was
equal in value to thirty to forty kilos of flour in the first century A.D.

Pliny indicated that the cost of bringing one camel-load to market at Gaza was 688 denarii. Assuming that a camel can carry a
payload of up to 150 kilos, then 1.5 denarii per pound, or a quarter of the sale price, would be sufficient to defray shipping costs.[36]
This seems like a reasonable enough mark-up, but still the Romans
complained about being gouged by middlemen. Pliny himself made
such a lament:

And by the lowest reckoning India, China, and the Arabian peninsula take from our empire 100 million sesterces every year—that is the sum our luxuries and our women cost us; for what fraction of these imports, I ask you, now goes to the gods or to the powers of the lower world?[37]

One hundred sesterces was roughly equivalent to nearly eight tons of gold, or eighty-five tons of silver coin. If Pliny estimated that India's share of this trade cost the Empire no less that fifty million sesterces, then the balance of twelve million sesterces must have gone to Arabia.

Not all modern historians are persuaded by Pliny's observations and calculations. Without the ability to calculate exchange rates in the modern sense, it is likely that the Roman Empire was effectively required to pay in gold, particularly in its dealings with Arabia. Archaeological discoveries in India have confirmed the prevalent use of Roman coinage in exchanges between the East and the West, although discoveries of Roman gold pieces in South Arabia have been so far very rare. For example, so far only one gold aureus, dating to the time of Hadrian, has been found in Shabwa.

Organization of the Caravans

None of the surviving South Arabian texts or the writings of ancient Latin authors provide any detailed information about how the caravans were organized. Strabo likened them to veritable armies shuttling back and forth between Arabia and Petra, but his comments lacked any precise details. It is only from the works of Arab writers describing caravans to Mecca in the early days of Islam that any details can be gleaned.

There were no horses or mules yet, but caravans consisted of up to a thousand camels in the company of anywhere from a hundred to three hundred merchants and escorts; convoys with as many as 2,500 camels were not exceptional. These expeditions were led by guides who managed the itineraries and were responsible for choosing rest stops, finding regular watering points (while avoiding flash floods), steering clear of labyrinthine detours, and identifying trails

in the aftermath of rains or sandstorms. Competent and reliable
guides did not come cheap, and even the best were capable of be-
traying their clients. Arab chronicles abound in stories of guides
who disappear just before a raid, after being tipped off to the presence of bandits or perhaps even conspiring with them. For this
reason many convoys resorted to bringing along an armed escort.

Nomads normally derived a great part of their livelihood from
protecting these enormous convoys, and local tribes often reaped
windfalls from the lease of safe pasturage to convoys camped
nearby. In the era of the Prophet Mohammed, fees for guides
and payments to local tribes for the use of wells and pastures could
add up to a quarter of travel costs, a proportion similar to the figure previously mentioned for ancient taxes.[38] The nomads were
known for devising ingenious pretexts for a multitude of fees and
charges, and for generating ever-new demands. For this reason it
was essential to negotiate with the nomads in advance, or, better
still, enter into long-term alliances. (The details left by early Islamic
chroniclers are sketchy and far removed in time from Sabaean
times.)

No amount of preparation could eliminate the possibility of raids
in a region that was continually ravaged by tribal wars. This is clear
from a long inscription carved on one of the walls of Barâqish describing the adventures of two Minaean traders named ʿAmmîsadaq
and Saʾd. First they escaped a raid by a group of Sabaeans from
Maʾrib who were joined by inhabitants of Sirwâh. The attack came
just as their caravan was leaving Maʿîn for Najrân; they emerged
victorious in the confrontation and credited the gods for averting a
tragedy. They later arrived in Egypt just as the so-called Medes were
launching an attack. (The attackers were actually Persians in a campaign waged during the reign of Ataxerxes III in 340 B.C.) Once
again, the gods protected the caravan, which managed to return
home safe and sound.

The following text is exceptionally informative and deserves to
be quoted at length:

> ʿAmmisadaq . . . and Saʾd, . . . leaders of the Minaean caravan, a group
> [?] who had left with them on a trading expedition to Egypt, Assyria-

Babylonia, and the Transeuphratene [modern-day Syria] . . . when ꜥAthtar dhû Qabd, Wadd, and Nakrah saved their lives and their possessions and turned away the attacks of Saba and Khawlân against their persons, their goods, and their beasts of burden on the trail between Maꜥîn and Ragmat [Najrân], and from the war which was raging between the south and the north; and when ꜥAthtar dhû-Qabd, Wadd, and Nakrah let them escape with their lives and their goods from the heart of Egypt during the conflict that was taking place between Egypt and the Medes. . . . [39]

Maritime Routes

In the fourth and third centuries B.C., the land route was not the only way from Arabia to Persia or the shores of the Mediterranean. The Egyptians had in fact opened up a sea route as early as the third millennium B.C. when they launched expeditions to Punt (probably the coast of Sudan or even Eritrea) seeking aromatic products. Around 1500 B.C., Queen Hatshepsut attempted to naturalize trees from that area in the gardens of Thebes. An image of thirty frankincense trees, each carried by a team of six men, decorates the walls of the queen's burial temple at Deir al-Bahari.

Darius the Great sent Scylax to study the possibility of navigating the Indus River and the Indian Ocean. He made it to the opening of the Persian Gulf and then to the Indus delta; then he followed the southern coast of Arabia and crossed the strait of Bab al-Mandab, making his way into the Red Sea as far as the Kamarân Islands.[40] At the same time, the first exploration was underway to reach the Red Sea from the Mediterranean side via a reopening of the Nile canal. This two-pronged effort, from both east and west, suggests that Arabia had been entirely circumnavigated by Achemenid ships. Otherwise it is difficult to explain the omission of any mention of the journey between Muscat and the Gulf of Aden in Scylax's account. The texts argue against the notion that there was a pressing need to open up a commercial route between Persia and Ethiopia for the purpose of delivering a few rare payments of tribute. The project was quickly abandoned, and none of Darius's successors pursued his dream of creating a maritime route from the Suez to Persia.

One hundred and seventy years later, Alexander the Great dispatched his fleet, under the command of Nearchus, along the coast of the Persian Gulf as far as the mouth of the Indus in a grand reconnaissance expedition; Alexander was preparing to conquer Arabia on the fleet's return.[41] In the account left by Arrian, our only credible source, there is little doubt as to Alexander's motives: to establish domination over the entire region and control the incense trade as well as its sources of production. "Some historians have even asserted that Alexander intended to have his fleet circle most of Arabia, Ethiopia, and Libya." In fact, the fleet led by Nearchus never got past the cape of the sea of Oman. Nearchus's refusal to venture past this point "was the reason that Alexander's force came through safely; for they would have been lost if they sailed past the desert parts of Arabia."[42] In 324 B.C., the year before Alexander's death, Nearchus rejoined Alexander at Susa and the project was abandoned. Thus Pliny was wrong in his description of Alexander's conquest of Arabia:

> Alexander in his boyhood was heaping frankincense on the altars in lavish fashion, when his tutor Leonides told him that he might worship the gods in that manner when he had conquered the frankincense-producing races; but when Alexander had won Arabia he sent Leonides a ship with a cargo of frankincense, with a message charging him to worship the gods without any stint.[43]

Travelers, merchants, scholars, and botanists returned to the Mediterranean from a great Asian expedition with seeds of medicinal plants and other crops, but mainly they brought back an immoderate desire for aromatics and a sense of smell that was more exacting than ever before. The aristocracies of the Hellenized cities gave themselves over to the consumption of new perfumes, luxurious oils, and aromatic resins. King Seleucus sent a large quantity of silver items to the great sanctuary to Apollo of Didyma, and with it came 360 kilograms of frankincense, thirty-six grams of myrrh, and 1,200 kilograms each of cassia, cinnamon, and Indian frankincense (*kostos*).[44]

The captains Alexander sent into the Persian Gulf and the Red Sea never even came within 1,000 kilometers of each other, and most of the stretch between them was left undiscovered. Nevertheless, there were numerous sailors in the Red Sea, if the texts can be believed, especially in the era of the Ptolemies (330 B.C.–30 B.C.). It was Agatharchides who, on his journey to the far end of the Persian Gulf, gave us the descriptions of the Sabaean port on the southeast coast and made mention of crossing the straits of Bab al-Mandab. The goal of his trip was primarily to find not only aromatic spices but also precious stones and tortoise shells. Commerce in these items was a monopoly controlled by the sovereigns, and states bought and resold merchandise at fixed prices. But the sovereigns also engaged in relationships with merchants wherein they would advance money and share the profits on their return, as was the case between Ptolemy VII Evergetes and a certain Eudoxus in the middle of the second century B.C.[45] The result of these voyages was a steady accretion of geographical information that prepared the way for future expeditions in the Indian Ocean.

There is no doubt that merchants of cassia and cinnamon used the Indian Ocean to bring their cargoes from India and Ceylon. The following is recounted by Pliny:

> The Cave-dwellers buy it from their neighbors and convey it over the wide seas in ships that are neither steered by rudders nor assisted by any device of art: in those regions only man and man's boldness stands in place of all these things. Moreover they choose the winter sea about the time of the shortest day, as an east wind [the winter monsoons] is then chiefly blowing. This carries them on a straight course through the bays, and after rounding a cape a west-northwest winds brings them to the harbor of the Gebbanitae [Qatabanites] called Ocilia. On this account that is the port most resorted to by these people, and they say that it is almost five years before the traders return home and that many perish on the voyage. In return for their wares they bring back articles of glass and copper, clothing, and buckles, bracelets, and necklaces; consequently that traffic depends principally on having the confidence of women.[46]

4. CITIES AND VILLAGES

A Sparsely Populated Land

According to the ancient view, South Arabia's climate was so agree-able and its natural resources so abundant that it could support a large population. Roman authors listed a great number of tribes, suggesting a dense network of cities and large villages. Though the reports of these Latin authors were based mainly on guesswork, they nonetheless suggest a relatively advanced state of urban devel-opment in the region.

In Yemen's Highlands, climatic conditions were favorable to agri-culture, but arable terrain was limited to the small basins nes-tled among the mountains. In the area surrounding the Sab'atayn desert, conditions were very different: agriculture required irriga-tion and was confined to the areas around the mouths of the sea-sonal wadis. The area's dense population depended on a very lim-ited area of productive land, a situation similar to that of the Nile valley. The oases were separated by vast expanses of sandy or rocky land that are barely habitable even today, although there is evidence that it supported a very sparse population in ancient times.[1] On the edges of the desert, urban settlement was neither dense nor regu-lar, with barely thirty cities of any importance. In Jawf the major cities were, from east to west, Inabba', Ma'īn, Barâqish, Khirbat Hamdân, Kamna, as-Sawdâ', and al-Baydâ. The cities of al-Asâhil and Khirbat Sa'ûd were located farther south in the Wadi Ragwân. The Wadi Dhana and its tributaries supported the major city of Ma'rib as well as Sirwâh and Yala. Hajar ar-Rayhani lay still farther south, in the Wadi Jubâ. Hinû az-Zurayr and Kuhayla were in the Wadi Harîb; Tamna' was in the Wadi Bayhân; and Talib, am-Barka,

Lajiyya, and Yahirr were in the Wadi Markha. Finally, on the margins of the Hadramawt plateau were Barîra, Shabwa, and Naqab al-Hajar, with Hurayda, Raybûn, Sûna, Shibâm, and Tarîm in Hadramawt's great interior valleys.

The area of these cities was typically between six and ten hectares. Barâqish occupied about 7.25 hectares, Ma'în five, and Kamna barely ten. Their defensive walls were generally less than one kilometer around; the relatively large cities of Kamna and al-Baydâ had walls measuring 1,350 meters and 1,500 meters respectively.[2]

The capital cities of Qatabân, Hadramawt, and Saba were the largest. The walls of Tamna', capital of Qatabân, measured some 1,850 meters in circumference—a modest size considering that Tamna' was at one time capital of a vast empire.

Shabwa, capital of Hadramawt, was located in a large area within a triangle of three hills; the city proper was built on the southern slope of the al-'Aqab ridge and girded by powerful walls measuring some 1,500 meters in circumference. Beyond, a ring of lower walls ran along the hilltops for four kilometers, enclosing a total area of approximately fifty-seven hectares. Saba's capital at Ma'rib was the most impressive of all, with 4.5 kilometers of walls and an area of some ninety hectares, making it the largest city in Arabia and the only one whose prestige was acknowledged outside South Arabia. The exact populaton of Ma'rib remains a great riddle; it was probably much lower than ten thousand.

Fortified Cities

There were several reasons for the fact that every city in ancient South Arabia was surrounded by defensive walls. The cities were built on flat areas along the edges of the desert, and therefore natural defenses were for the most part lacking. Benefiting from its fertile oasis, a city harbored all sorts of riches within its houses and sanctuaries. Moreover, the city was the seat of power for local chiefs and sovereigns. Their walls were designed to protect them from their neighbors as much as from the eventual menace of nomads.

The origin of these defensive systems is uncertain, but they were already in place by the eighth century B.C. The expansion of

Sabaean power was marked by its destruction of the fortified cities, as exemplified in the razing of the ancient walls of Nashshân after that city's conquest. Sabaean mukarribs built or rebuilt large-scale defensive structures; they created fortified cities like Nashq (al-Baydâ) in order to control Jawf and specifically Nashshân. The earliest inscriptions left by the Sabaean mukarribs make frequent mention of the construction of towers and curtain walls.

The fortifications of al-Baydâ were apparently typical for a Sabaean city, surrounded by shrubs and acacia trees, around the bend of one of the branches of the Wadi Madhâb. An ancient traveler approaching the city would first encounter a low but still quite impressive oval wall reinforced at regular intervals by prominent towers, with two entry gates.[3] The following dedicatory inscription from this site is typical of those found on the walls and curtains at the time of construction: "Ilisam Nabat, son of Nabatʾalî, king of Kaminahû [Kamna] . . . built these two towers for Almaqah and the kings of Maryab [Maʾrib]." Ninety-one such inscriptions run in large characters along several slabs of stone. The western gate, which is well preserved, contains two towers crowned by a crenellated battlement, with a deep passageway into the city. The quality of the masonry is surprising: blocks of stone two to three meters in length are squared off and joined with mortar; the workmanship is so impeccable that a knife blade won't fit between the slabs.[4] These stonecutters had developed remarkable abilities as early as the seventh century B.C.

At the edge of Jawf, the high walls of Barâqish (the ancient Yathill) offer an even more impressive spectacle. These walls, which run for several kilometers above rolling hills and gray fields, are in an exceptionally good condition and rank among the best examples today in Yemen. The city is built along a sandstone ridge in an irregularly shaped semicircle approximately 276 meters in diameter. Its fifty-six towers rose to a height of fourteen meters; only one remains, on the southern side. The remains of the ancient walls are easily recognizable by their perfectly aligned foundations, the blocks decorated with a meticulously carved stippling and joined without mortar right up to the coping of the walls. The city was inhabited until the seventeenth century A.D., and various irregularities in several places provide evidence of later efforts to repair the walls. The interior surface of the walls is made up of a thick layer of unfired bricks that have been protected from erosion by the outer walls. Originally these bricks probably supported wooden structures with several stories connected by stairways, but the latter have long since disappeared. Entry into Barâqish was through a gate situated within a recess on the southwest side and defended by a tower; farther to the east, a postern provided access to the sanctuary of Nakrah.

It was Karib'îl Watar who built the fortified city of Barâqish. The original walls were probably stone, but the remains that are visible today were probably built sometime between the fourth and second centuries B.C.[5] The great southwest gate was built first, then work progressed east and north. On the tower of the eastern wall, there is an inscription left by two caravan chiefs named 'Ammîsdaq and Sa'd.[6] The northern and western parts of the enclosure seem to date to the era of Saladin, an imam who is known to have resided in Barâqish and undertaken important restoration work there.

There were other motivations besides defense for building walls of such great height and fine quality. Nomads could hardly have caused such concern, for they were not known for expertise in the art of capturing cities. It would have taken the full army of an enemy state to take Barâqish, and even Karib'îl had to wait three full years in his siege of Nashshân before its residents finally surrendered. In fact these fortifications were above all a measure of the wealth of the cities they defended. It is hardly surprising that the cities that benefited most from the spice trade, especially Ma'în, Barâqish, and Shabwa, built defensive walls of prodigious dimensions, and that caravan chiefs bragged about having financed these projects.

A Distinctive Urbanism

The ancient cities of South Arabia differed from their counterparts in the Near East. There is even less of a parallel with the cities of the Mediterranean world, for the very idea of a city organized on a more or less regular plan simply did not exist in South Arabia.

There is little evidence of streets in the sense of predetermined lines drawn for the purpose of siting houses. In South Arabia's ancient cities, it is difficult to tell public buildings from private homes, or public squares from market areas, and even more difficult, in certain cases, to distinguish between civilian dwellings and temples.

Much ink has been spilled in addressing the question of the nature of ancient city life; the debate began amongst the ancient writers themselves. Pliny counted sixty-five temples in Tamna^c and sixty in Shabwa.[7] When Major Hamilton completed his excavation of what he thought to be Shabwa in 1938, he concluded that the site had been a mausoleum—the city as vast necropolis.[8] Historians were unable to locate any house sites in certain cities such as Ma^{c}în, Mayfa$^{\circ}$at, or Tamna^c, and were led to reconsider the very nature of these cities.[9] Their problem was due to the difficulty in identifying all the buildings, a situation that is unlikely to change, since ancient builders seem to have used the same plans and building techniques for temples and private homes. One approach is to estimate the original elevation (number of stories) of each building, but centuries of erosion, plunder, and fires have erased almost all useful evidence in this regard.

Archaeologists have learned to compare ancient sites with the traditional architecture that still pervades the landscape. Back in 1942, Leonard Woolley surmised that ancient houses resembled their traditional counterparts in Hadramawt, and suggested that the buildings in Shabwa were neither temples nor mausoleums. But a lack of ancient remains made it difficult to prove his theory. The evidence that he sought didn't surface until the 1980s, when excavation revealed socle stones that had apparently served as foundations for very tall buildings. The contributions of the dig at Shabwa proved decisive in this regard.

A Visit to Shabwa

Set among gray pebbled hills overlooking irrigated fields that stretched for a distance of about fifty meters, Shabwa would have been visible to ancient travelers approaching from the west. Beyond the fields, about hundred meters from the city, ran the canalized Wadi ʿAft and the southern slope of Qarat al-Hadîda, which was crowned with fortifications joined to the city's inner wall. Moving past the corner tower of Dar al-Kafîr, travelers would come upon a vast, triangular depression formed by three hills: al-ʾAqab to the south, al-Hadîda to the west, and al-Firân to the east. This expanse is known today as as-Sabkha (the saltworks) after the numerous salt mines found there.[10] The ancients were well aware of this natural resource, and its exploitation was probably the main factor in the success of this city. This terrain has always been unstable, spongy, and covered with a whitish crust in the aftermath of the first rains.

Continuing alongside the wall with its mighty towers, our ancient traveler would reach the great north gate, where a main road opened up before him. (This "main road" was not quite a highway—its path was meandering and its width irregular until much later.) More than a hundred buildings of similar construction rose up on both sides of this road.[11]

Let us attempt to imagine what these buildings must have looked like around the time of the birth of Christ. Built on a rectangular plan and generally rising several stories, they were hulking structures with a base of socle stones one to two meters thick, an ungainly stairway entrance, windows on the ground floor, and a monotonous succession of stories and upper terrace. These houses resembled towers more than normal residences, as is apparent from Strabo's commentary:

> And, farthest toward the east [is the land inhabited by] the Chatramotitae [Hadrami people], whose city is Sabata [Shabwa]. All cities [in Arabia] are ruled by monarchs and are prosperous, being beautifully adorned with both temples and royal palaces. And the houses are like those of the Egyptians in the manner in which the timbers are joined together.[12]

The most remarkable of these houses straddled the northern gate more than five meters above the large road. This huge edifice, excavated by French archaeologists between 1975 to 1985, comprised two structures. The central building (A) consisted of magnificent socle stones originally surmounted by several floors built out of wood. It loomed above a second building (B), which probably began as a single-story building with a vast, paved courtyard. The eastern and western wings of building B partially enframed building A, leaving only a narrow entry into the courtyard, which was divided into two parts by a surrounding wall. The inner part contained a large stone stairway to the entrance of building A, whose ground floor was raised about four meters above street level. This monumental complex has been identified as the Shaqîr Palace, residence of the kings of Hadramawt.[13] The palace was burned by the Sabaeans in the beginning of the third century A.D. and rebuilt several decades later; it was completely ransacked around the fifth century A.D. All that remains today are the socle stones and a few vestiges of brick wall on the ground floor.

The main road (such as it was) led south to the monumental Temple of Siyân.[14] It is virtually impossible to imagine this temple's former magnificence. Its halls were filled to bursting with sculptures and other objects, all of which have disappeared. A monumental stairway was framed by four statues and four bronze-covered pillars. At the eastern side there stood a colossal bronze statue mounted on a massive monolith, flanked by terraces with statues of animals, probably oversize horses, among others. All this was most likely just the entryway to a temple in which absolutely nothing remains. The above describes the temple in the first few centuries A.D.; in earlier times there had probably been just a few steps leading up to a platform.

It is still possible to follow the trail that leads to the temple from the eastern part of the city, now buried under the remains of the earthen buildings of al-Mathna. In ancient times, the houses in this area were built close together, sometimes even touching (though not sharing a common wall); they formed a fairly regular row with narrow passageways between them. The streets were nothing more than open spaces between the tall buildings; no doubt the visual effect was similar to that evoked in the modern city of Shibâm in Hadramawt.[15] No doubt the city was plagued by acute overcrowding, a problem compounded by inadequate ventilation, though no surviving texts shed light on measures that ancient city-dwellers may have taken to deal with these conditions. There were apparently no sanitation systems or canals, just individual sisterns within each house or perhaps just outside. Nor is there any trace of a central marketplace along the lines of a Greco-Roman agora with shops in sheltered porticoes.

Another mystery is how land was divided, sold, and parceled out in lots. Individual tribes may have controlled specific areas with the exclusive right to settle their members, which would suggest relatively homogeneous neighborhoods. Comparison with more recent models tends to support such a hypothesis. But there may have been an open market for land, and thus a certain amount of tribal diversity within the city. In any case, construction costs would have prevented all but the most prosperous families from settling within the city walls.

Wooden Houses

All the buildings were built on stone basements which were raised about two to four meters above grade. Each socle stone supported a frame for the interior walls, which were joined at right angles to form a storage cellar. The elevated foundation was designed to support a heavy load from the floors above. Buildings could be torn down and rebuilt on the same base, which was extremely solid and resistant to erosion. Thus they were a staple amid such sites in ancient landscapes. The walls were (curiously) made of wood. A stairway ran along an exterior wall to a ground-floor entrance a few meters above street level. The framework of wooden beams was filled with unfired bricks or earth. This frame formed the main part of the wall, and the pattern was repeated on each floor. This method of construction may seem a bit strange for a country that is now almost entirely deforested. It is definitely tempting to infer the existence of ancient forests from the use of wood in buildings over the millennia.

Tower-Houses

The original height of these ancient buildings is unknown. The few surviving wall fragments rise no higher than two meters. In an ef-

fort to resolve this question, archaeologists have examined the dedicatory inscriptions created at the time of construction of some of
these buildings. Some mention the "four stories" or "six levels and
six stories [palace], whose upper part comprises two stories."[16] Bas-
reliefs provide the additional evidence of miniature depictions of
houses with distinct floors, decorative posts enframing the openings, and terraces with merlons. The tall dwellings of contemporary Yemen appear to be direct descendants of these ancient structures, preserving an age-old tradition. Even if we may overestimate
the number of stories, it seems certain that the prevalent type of
ancient house was the so called tower-house.

The prevalence of the high-rise building testifies to the importance of defense in ancient domestic architecture. The elevated base
prevented easy access; there were only a few narrow openings on
the ground floor—just enough for shooting arrows through—and
the upper terraces enabled residents to guard the entrances by hurl-
ing projectiles at invaders. The buildings served as refuge and fortress for their inhabitants in Yemen down through their history,
even in relatively recent times. The only major vulnerability of
these houses was their exposed wooden frames, which could easily
be set afire.

This type of tall building was not limited to South Arabia. The
Aksumite palaces of Ethiopia, which began to show up around the
end of the first century B.C., consisted of several stories of wood
over a stone base, and the obelisks of Aksum were visually similar in exterior decor. Multistory brick and wood buildings with
small openings and pigeonholes were found in the Nile delta. Models as well as Pompeiian paintings and mosaics have provided a
glimpse of these massive yet graceful houses. In southern Syria,
tower-houses ensured adequate surveillance of orchards and vine-
yards. Tall buildings of this kind appeared in Cilicia during the
Hellenistic period. This type of housing was generally favored in
agricultural areas or in areas that were menaced by nomads.

The phenomenon of tower-houses survived well beyond antiquity. Multistory houses were built in the Middle Ages and even
later, from Italy to the Caucasus and from Dadès to Draa. But vertical orientation was the norm in Yemen. Homes built in the wadis
Hadramawt and Daw'an also served as citadels, and those built in

the oases were essentially fortified farms. They testify to the memory of combat, pillage, and destruction. Over the years their fortifications were improved with the addition of loopholes in the walls, machicolations above the entrances, merlons on the battlements, interior gates, etc.[17] Subsequent addition of ramparts did not alter their appearance. Defense was the main reason for tall buildings both in the city and the countryside. Some scholars have cited high land prices as a cause for the height of buildings in modern-day Sana, or Shibâm in Hadramawt, but there is no persuasive evidence that this observation should apply to ancient times. The prestige of tall buildings as an indicator of the owner's wealth, however, was certainly as relevant in ancient times as it is today.

A Wealthy Man's Home

The grandest houses were built out of a variety of materials including stone, wood, and fired brick, requiring the specialized services of stonecutters, masons, and carpenters, all of whom had to be paid and fed during the construction process. Such an undertaking required significant financial resources on the part of the proprietors or sponsors.[18]

Only the most influential members of a tribe could afford to build large houses. We know their names and origins from inscriptions they left behind to commemorate their achievements. One building in Shabwa, for example, was built in a joint effort by Rafʔan, Yaʔîl, Nimram, Ilisharah, and Marthadum.[19] All of the several hundred ancient buildings identified in Shabwa seem to have belonged to members of a privileged social class. Some parts of the city were so densely settled that there was barely room to add another building, even one of modest proportions. The peasants lived amidst the irrigated fields outside the city. These separate living conditions reinforced a distinct social hierarchy in antiquity.

Let us try to imagine a visit to one of these tower-houses. After climbing a steep stairway one would pass through a heavy wooden portal secured by brass bolts. A hallway on the ground floor would lead through the length of the building past narrow, dark rooms with high thresholds; these rooms were reserved for grains and forage, or perhaps used as stables. In one of the houses in Yalâ, there were two small rooms on the ground floor with stone cisterns; a corner room on the ground floor of a royal chateau in Shabwa had four stone troughs. In the houses of Sana, the rooms on the ground floor also held grain, woodpiles, or fuel. Animals were stalled there overnight, and water was stored in jars or basins.[20] In Shibâm in Hadramawt, goats even climbed up to the second floor, where several rooms were reserved for them.

A stairway along the far wall at the end of the hallway led to the upper floors, which were used as both entrance hall and living area. Among the numerous inscriptions attesting to the existence of multistory houses, one late text mentions that the owner had restored, refurbished, and repaired damage and destruction to all floors of his palace of Shabʾân, including all the entrances, the reception hall, the porticoes, and all outbuildings.[21] The *maswad*, or room of honor, is mentioned in numerous texts, but its exact location remains unclear.

Today the better homes of Sana have a *diwân*, or a salon where the men can receive guests in a serene setting; a *manzâr*, a room from which to contemplate the landscape; and a *mafraj*, always situated on the top floor and often quite spacious, reserved exclusively for men.[22] In the tallest buildings, the fourth or fifth floors contain living rooms used either year-round or seasonally; the upper floors are generally used for a variety of functions.

Comparing traditional Yemeni architecture with its ancient models can lead to forced and even misleading conclusions if one fails to consider how much has changed in the daily life of the area's residents over the course of two millennia. But it is clear nonetheless that Yemen's traditional architecture has its roots in the pre-Islamic era and has changed little due to long periods of isolation from outside influences.

Austere Dwellings

Ancient homes offered little variety in terms of decoration. Their foundations were most often made of bare stone. Only the finest houses featured fastidiously carved patterns or elaborate masonry work. The frames of the upper stories were always visible as repeating squares, though usually covered with a thin coating of mud applied by hand. The exterior wooden beams of the magnificent palace of Shabwa were faced with a cladding of limestone slabs and decorated with a regular stippling pattern, but this level of workmanship is exceptional.

Exterior decorations were generally limited to alabaster doorways and window frames whitewashed in lime or perhaps studded with variously colored stones. In the palace of Shabwa, one or more layer of angled slate protected the façade from runoff, in a style also found in certain houses in the mountains of ʿAsir.[23] Rooftops were apparently unadorned, and no decorations such as merlons, sculpture, or ibex horns have been discovered at their base. In the Greco-Roman era, several palaces were decorated with metallic ornaments of human or animal figures. Among the most remarkable of these are two bronze plaques from the façade of the Yafash house at Tamnaʿ. Measuring about 52 by 61 centimeters and mounted on inscribed bases, the ornaments depict nude cherubs riding lions.[24] The royal palace of Shabwa was also decorated with bronze figures including a horse, an archer, a ram, and a roaring lion. These items were most likely cast and installed by itinerant artisans from the provinces of the Roman Empire. In the absence of late additions the exterior of ancient houses was for the most part austere-looking. This was also the case with the incense altars and recessed panels imitating the woodwork on the façades. Their appearance was a far cry from the somewhat exaggerated image favored by authors such as Agatharchides:

> It is said that they [the Sabaeans] constructed many gilded or silver columns, and that the ceilings and doors were highlighted with precious gems; the areas between the columns were equally magnificent.[25]

Functions of the House

Construction dedications have been helpful in providing insight into the type of work performed and materials used in ancient houses. Ahram and Dharʾam, the two sons of Saʾadum, and one of their sons, Banû Thaʾaym, announced they had laid the foundation and built their house from the ground up, floor by floor; they posted a notice of construction asserting their incontestible claim to the site.

Building a house affirmed the owner's power and prosperity derived from exploitation of his farmlands or perhaps success in war or commerce. Thus the possession of a large home was a way for tribal chiefs, noblemen, and members of the royal lineage to proclaim their high social status. A palace served as base of operations from which their master managed his lands, collected taxes, ruled over members of his tribe, assembled his chiefs, etc. The house affirmed not only his power but the legitimacy of his successors, who would also live there: the kings of Saba lived in the Salhîn palace, the kings of Nashshân in the ʿAfraw palace, the kings of Awsân in Miswâr, those of Qatabân in Harîb, and those of Hadramawt in Shaqîr.

Several texts mention other works underway during the construction of a given house by the same owner. One owner acquired the lot adjacent to his building site; another had irrigated fields; a third oversaw a palm grove and a water well; a fourth built a stable. Several members of the Shaybân tribe in the Wadi Jawf recorded in an inscription that they had put their entire fiefdom under cultivation and built the Shabʾan palace.[26] In the Wadi Bayhân, Ahdab and Saʾdum, along with their sons and companions, built the houses that served mainly as warehouses for the piles of booty they had acquired, including slaves and prisoners as well as the products of the neighboring lands and taxes (which were no doubt collected in kind).[27] All this evidence suggests that houses played both a political and economic role in ancient life.

Houses were also used for religious functions, though their exact nature is difficult to reconstruct. The largest houses probably had one or more rooms reserved for cult practices, with private shrines that may have been outfitted with incense altars, images of the gods, places made ready for sacrifices, and even votive objects. The Hadath house in Tamnaʿ contained a curious hand-held lamp mounted on a bronze plate, inscribed with the following dedication:

[He] has offered to his god and lord . . . a hand that sheds the light of
an oil lamp and a dedication, just as he had promised in his oath. He
has committed to the master of Yaghûl his faculties, powers, and his
offering against whosoever should try to move it from its place.[28]

But the uses of these objects are not clear, and the evidence discovered in certain houses is not sufficient to determine their function.
The fact that the word *bayt* was used to denote both house and
temple is proof that the South Arabians tended to conflate the two.
Archaeologists have also been interested in determining the precise nature of certain large buildings with central courtyards. This
particular architectural formula seems to have been common to
both temples and palaces and is found, with subtle variations, in
the temple of Barʾan in Maʾrib, in the royal mansion of Shabwa, and
in the main building of Tamnaᶜ.[29] Knowing the structure of the
central building (whether a multistory building or a single low area
with a roof resting on a row of hypostyle columns) would allow us
to make certain distinctions, but the disappearance of the super-
structures makes this type of identification extremely difficult. We
can only try to determine whether the same buildings served si-
multaneously as sanctuary and home, or if their uses changed over
the course of their long occupation.

The Villages

The textual evidence at our disposal is uneven, and surviving
sources only describe houses belonging to the most privileged vil-
lagers. Besides several names, the villages and the farms around
them have yielded very few texts. One reason for this is that researchers have become interested in South Arabian villages only
recently, since most of these villages lie buried under the silt of two
millennia. The temptation, not entirely unreasonable, is to imagine
them as similar to the villages we see on the South Arabian landscape today: a collection of smallish houses of unfired brick, adobe,
or stone, rising one or more stories.
    One type of settlement that seems to have in common in the

regions of Jawf, Maʾrib, and Bayhân, consisted of an unbroken ring of houses.[30] This array is useful for light defensive purposes, as the adjoined houses created an unbroken exterior wall; if the houses are several stories high, the result is a veritable fortress. This outer ring protects an interior space for other houses or sanctuaries. Access is gained through one or more passages between the houses of the outer ring. One notable village of this type is al-Janâdila, located not far from the Wadi Markha. This settlement, built in an irregular oval shape of up to 210 meters in diameter, contains a ring of rectangular buildings either pressed up close against each other or sharing a single or double wall. Also visible in the western part are the remains of stone foundations of the wealthier residents' houses; the upper floors—built of stone or unfired brick?—have since disappeared. The city of Hajar am-Dhaybiyya, in the Wadi Duraʾ, was also defended in the first centuries A.D. by strong buildings arrayed in a circular formation. Excavation of deeper layers indicates that older buildings were designed in a similar fashion.[31]

The arrangement of buildings juxtaposed in a protective ring seems to have been characteristic of numerous smaller villages but was also found in larger urban centers such as Najrân. This city, the modern-day Ukhdûd, consisted of a ring of buildings with stone foundations and several stories, originally of wood. Numerous other cities in South Arabia used this original system, which may date back to the Bronze Age. Villages of this type are known to have existed in the Negev Desert as early as the eleventh century B.C. and in Sabaean regions from the eleventh to the tenth century B.C. In the time of the early Sabaean mukarribs, towns sprang up suddenly with continuous rings of defensive ramparts. This is the case with Yalâ, not far from Maʾrib, where a ring of houses was enclosed within an outer wall.[32] Other towns such as Hinû az-Zurayr and Najrân conserved their original ring of contiguous houses for a long time.

This architectural model presupposes a relatively cohesive form of social organization. Considerations of defense precluded any gaps in the ring of buildings, and thus the original plan must have been conceived in advance of building. Such a community could not tolerate discord among its members; around the beginning of the first millennium B.C., these were relatively small and close-knit groups. It is curious that the Arab populations who began to settle in the wadis around the desert a thousand years later built their settlements on a similar model. In the Wadi Markha, certain villages built with juxtaposed houses, such as Hajar an-Nâb, Hajar Tâlib, and Hajar Hizma, probably originated during this later era.[33]

Farmhouses

There were few farmhouses in the proper sense of the term, and very few have been excavated. The most ancient is Farmhouse A in al-Huraydha.[34] Like most buildings of its type, it was built of unfired brick. The walls were about 0.4 meter thick, suggesting that it may have originally risen more than two stories, if not three. Tall buildings were therefore not an exclusive privilege of the wealthy. On the ground floor, some rooms opened onto an open-air courtyard, and others were furnished with benches; the former had a large quantity of animal waste, and the latter contained ceramic objects dating back to a time from the mid-fifth to fourth century B.C. Other farmhouses have been excavated in the countryside around Shabwa, in an area known as al-ʿOqm. Sadly, only foundations remain, but they reveal a juxtaposition of small cisterns strongly indicative of a ground-floor plan.[35] A roofless interior cooking area provided women with privacy and shelter from the wind; among the objects found there are flour mills, stone vases, and a fragment of wooden beam in the shape of a boar's head.

Earth was not the only construction material; numerous villages from Bayhân and Markha were built entirely of stone. Seminomadic settlers have taken up residence in some of the farmhouses that have survived nearly intact, and they continue to live in the structures to this day, adding only new roofs, as is the case in the villages of Surban.[36] These structures vary in size from six meters on a side to fifteen or twenty meters in more complex buildings, with the most elaborate measuring as large as three to five hundred square meters. The varying functions of these buildings attests to the diversity of this ancient society. The largest houses presumably belonged to peasants who had enriched themselves through acquisition of land. The Bedouins of today routinely dig around in these sites and have recently uncovered beautiful ceramic artifacts dating from the eighth to sixth centuries B.C.[37]

Current research has provided only tantalizing glimpses of the evolution of ancient living quarters, but it is already clear that a great variety of building materials were in use. In the areas around the great mountain ranges, granite and schist were dominant, whereas elsewhere the prevalence of limestone resulted in an abundance of fired-brick housing. All ancient buildings seem to have been of rectangular design and high elevation; tower-houses offered the critical advantage of allowing residents to survey and guard their territory.

5. ECONOMY AND SOCIETY

A Unique Society

The oasis environment surrounding the deserts of South Arabia provided a limited but livable habitat for the populations organized around irrigation of the seasonal floods. The success of these societies depended initially on a cooperative arrangement wherein water was distributed equitably to the fields regardless of distance from the source, and the regular maintenance of the canals was shared among the population. This collective of small groups of agricultural workers probably came into being as early as the third millennium B.C., albeit in a primitive form. In the Maʾrib region, agriculture based on collective exploitation of the oasis led to the birth of Saba around the eighth century B.C. In the lists of eponyms inscribed on stones, the term Saba was consistently used as the direct object of the verb signifying irrigation. In this sense, Saba was conceived as a sedentary society defined by the land and its productive cycles.

The areas on the edges of the desert were occupied by a fairly dense network of towns of varying size such as those in the large valleys of Jawf and Hadramawt. Even in ancient times people tended to live in distinctly urban settings—passing through gates on which official edicts were carved, frequenting sanctuaries and marketplaces, and living in houses whose design and functions were in widespread use. The architectural setting of the town suggested its own form of communal practices, which are worth considering in relation to the practices of the rural peasantry. In between the towns and villages were sacred territories with temples on the hillsides facing the towns, or in the oases, or in even more remote areas. A few, like that of Jabal al-Lawdh, were apparently open to all visitors, which suggests a general awareness of the rules governing these structures. This was also true for the sacred and inviolable enclaves that later came to be known as *haram,* where sanctuaries were often built and where people were subject to tribal laws.[1]

A comparison of these settings suggests that social life did not vary considerably from one community to the next. While they didn't worship the same gods, with the exception of ʿAthtar, and there was no single language common to all the communities, the South Arabians still had much in common besides agricultural organization. They shared a common writing system and techniques for using monumental inscriptions in architecture; their buildings were similar in design and decoration; and the fact that they traded with distant regions suggests a certain level of organization both for ensuring the security of the goods while in transit and for the distribution of the revenues. Whether or not they considered themselves to be part of the same community, their ways of life certainly had a lot in common.[2]

Tribal Organization

Greek and Roman authors were well aware that the South Arabians were a group of sedentary tribes, not nomads. This form of social organization characterizes modern Yemen just as it did in ancient times. However, the details of tribal organization in ancient times are not easy to reconstruct. Current research is only beginning to unearth the physical culture of the region's ancient population, and their society is still largely mysterious. The historical tradition informs us that Semitic tribes from the north gradually settled in the southern end of the peninsula, mixing with local populations as they went and adopting their practical knowledge, religious beliefs, and, most likely, social organization.

In ancient South Arabia the tribe was a vast unity comprising anywhere from dozens to hundreds or even thousands of members. Each group occupied a territory of corresponding size and collectively managed the irrigation of the fertile valleys skirting the desert. Such agricultural endeavors required a collective approach to management. The tribes were formed out of a loose alliance of small clans whose reliance on kinship ensured tight cohesion. There were six principal tribes: Haram and Maꜥīn, in Jawf; Saba, in the Wadi Dhana; Qatabân, in Bayhân; Awsân, in Markha, and Hadramawt, in the valley of the same name. While kinship was their primary basis, these tribes also defined themselves as citizens of such and such a town.

The Maꜥīn tribe was settled in a territory of barely a hundred square kilometers, bordering the independent towns of Haram about five kilometers to the east and Kamna only ten kilometers to the east; mountains provided a natural barrier to the north and south, and the towns of the Wadi Ragwân lay to the southwest. The territory of Maꜥīn had only two cities, Maꜥīn and Barâqish, along with several villages and the irrigated lands surrounding them. The two cities were very small in area, covering between five and eight hectares. The population of the Maꜥīn tribe was no more than a few thousand.[3] The tribe was composed of clans (ahl), and subclans (also known as ahl) organized by kinship; the smallest unit of the clan was the individual family household. Clans are attested in several different Minaean sites. These groups probably lacked territory of their own; membership was reckoned by tracing kinship back to an imagined ancestor.

Among Minaean tribal members whose identity is known today, the Saꜥad family stands out as a relatively rich family of caravan outfitters. Like many other Minaeans, they belonged to the Abꜣamar lineage, which linked them to the subclan of the ꜥAmân, one of thirty or forty subclans in the region. The ꜥAman in turn belonged to the royal Gabaꜣan clan, who were responsible for building the towers and curtain walls at Barâqish. The Maꜥīn tribe was made up of about twenty of these clans, whose principal city was Maꜥīn (modern-day Qarnaw). A Minaean took his identity from his clan and tribe, but the city was not named for any one clan.

This pyramid of tribe, clan, and subclan was also the basic social structure in the Highlands, although kingdom, tribal confederation, federation, and tribe were all defined by territorial associations rather than strictly through kinship. Each tribe (*sha²ab*) took its name from the territory in which it was located; it belonged to a larger tribe (also called *sha²ab*) which in turn belonged to a larger *sha²ab*. Thus the most solid and durable level of the pyramid was that of the tribe, rather than clan affiliation as was the case for the Minaeans. A certain Za²d was said to come from Yafa², a property situated north of Sana, where he paid rent to the "lords of Yafa²"; a certain Ma²dîkarib was said to be from the tribe of the Khawlân (southeast of Sana), where he dug a well to irrigate his lands; Ilîsa²ad and his four brothers described themselves as Bakîlites (i.e., from Bakîl) who lived in the city of ʿAmrân. This form of tribal organization is very ancient and has been remarkably stable through the ages; indeed, some of the most ancient of these tribes, including the Bakîl, the Hashîd, and the Sinhân, still exist today. The Bakîl and Hashîd have migrated over the centuries (the former having moved eastward from their original location west of the modern Sana-Saada route, the latter moving westward). Today the Hadramawt and Radmân tribes take their names from the territories they inhabit.

A Hierarchical Society

If the shape of South Arabian society was an immense pyramid, each level helped ensure the stability and cohesion of the whole. At the top of the pyramid were the great noble families, city-dwellers who derived their wealth from the exploitation of vast domains on the edges of the desert. They did not carry any particular title. The sovereigns, who were descended from these grand families, did not enjoy absolute power but were assisted by a city "council" (which numbered twelve people in Barâqish and eight in Haram) or a tribal assembly, that worked with the sovereign to publish decrees and enact various laws.

The social structure of the Highland tribes was also hierarchical, with the city at the top of the pyramid. The tribal assembly and the nobles possessed real power and political autonomy within the tribe. At each level of the pyramid, there were institutions in charge of military and commericial expeditions, maintenance of hydraulic works, perhaps certain cult functions, and other activites affecting the group.[4] Whether their political power was real or imagined, these groups enjoyed autonomy due simply to the difficulty of communication and limited terrain of their mountainous lands. By the end of the first century B.C., the second highest power was that of the tribal confederation, which was directed by a king and his barons (qayls), a council, and confederate assembly. Below the barons in the social hierarchy were the notables, who headed up the various clans and tribal subgroups and were "clients" of the "lords" of the great noble families. The slaves (ʿadam) were, of course, at the bottom of the hierarchy, below the members of the clans and subgroups—or more accurately outside it altogether. Slaves belonged to families or clans rather than to individuals; they were allowed to own property and worked in the fields or stone quarries but were not allowed to travel freely or to carry arms.[5] Around the end of the first century B.C., their lot does not seem to have been particularly tragic.

People's occupations were generally determined by this hierarchy: the nobles engaged in warfare and agriculture while tribal members were left to work in trade or the handicrafts (the aristocracies of the great tribes such as Saba and Qatabân were disdainful of commerce). The Minaeans specialized in commerce and thus may have been regarded as socially inferior. Agricultural self-sufficiency was a prized value for the Yemeni people, and this antimercantile bias has persisted in Yemen's predominantly agricultural society over the centuries. Even in modern times, the term qalîbî, or "tribal man," retains the meaning of farmer. Traders were looked down upon as dependent on the men of the tribe for their subsistence.

The Place of Women

Though it is difficult to understand the role of women in South Arabian antiquity, they seem to have had more autonomy than in traditional Yemeni society, even if they did not achieve full equality with their male counterparts. Of the few relevant texts that survive, some mention women enjoying a certain amount of financial autonomy. One example is that of Abîrathad, who had a tower and a tomb built with the aid of her husband and sons, though largely through her own finances; another is that of Khâlhamad, who had a house built entirely on her own.[6] At Qaryat al-Faw, north of Najrân, a women made on offering of an incense altar inscribed with a dedication, implying a certain level of affluence and social prestige.[7] Women are known to have made offerings in sanctuaries without the intervention of a man and to have constructed funerary monuments or even had their names inscribed in stone, as at Tamna[c]. Magnificent tombs were erected to perpetuate their memory. Women made dedications to the divinities requesting favors outside the family circle, and certain women played a public role, though only in exceptional cases. There is no evidence of any historical parallels to the queens of North Arabia who led their troops into battle, nor was the so-called Queen of Sheba properly in that category. In fact, ancient South Arabian society seems to have been dominated by men.

Descent was patrilineal for the most part, though there are some instances of descent traced through female family members, a phenomenon that was common among the Nabataeans to the east. Of three surviving inscriptions referring to matrilineal descent in South Arabia, two involve a Sabaean king who ordered the members of one family to be integrated into a larger tribal group; the text names the men "with their brothers, sons, and [male] relations," and also the women "with their sisters, daughters and [female] relations." In the third text, three women and their daughters, who are from the same family and are referred to collectively as "[the women] of Gurhum," consecrated four statues, one male and three female, for their children (a boy and three girls). Despite the presence of the boy, all four children are referred to as "the daughters of [the women of] Gurhum," a phrase which very probably designated daughters born into the clan and still unmarried.[8]

These three texts also inform us that the man could live in his spouse's household. Moreover, a curious passage from Strabo (who, as an outside observer, is less than totally reliable) hints at matriarchal practices in South Arabia:

> One woman is the wife for all; and he who first enters the house before any other has intercourse with her, having first placed his staff before the door, for by custom each man must carry a staff; but she spends the night with the eldest. And therefore all children are brothers. They also have intercourse with their mothers; and the penalty for an adulterer is death; but only the person from another family is an adulterer.[9]

Anthropologists have studied the customs of the Bedouin tribes of South Arabia in an attempt to see if traces of matrilineal descent have survived into modern times. Among the Humum, a sedentary and seminomadic tribe who inhabit the plateaus south of Tarîm, women are permitted to bear children out of wedlock; children are given their mother's name, or the name of their maternal uncle.[10] Adulterers are not necessarily punished for being unfaithful, although a woman is judged severely if she is unfaithful to her husband while he is present in the home. Whatever the case, the Humum women seem to enjoy a fair measure of sexual freedom both before and after marriage. Another practice, observed in Yemen by medieval travelers, allowed women of the Sarû tribe to take a lover while her husband was away. It was customary for travelers to be offered the woman of the house for the night, and certain villages practiced "sexual hospitality." Women of Yemen may not have been constrained by a severe moral code but instead may have been allowed to control their own destiny in some ways. A woman's brother may have assumed responsibility for raising her children. These customs were in stark contrast with those of Islamic times, of course, and may have applied only to a small minority of the population.

The texts also mention polyandry, polygamy, and even temporary marriage, but these instances surely reflect isolated occurrences rather than prevailing social mores. Khâlhamad, who was married to two men (perhaps brothers?), had a house built for her, and she helped her two husbands by repaying a debt of a thousand pieces of coin on their behalf. In another instance, two women, both childless and married into the same family, agreed to have sex with the same man and gave thanks to the gods when one of them became pregnant.[11] It was presumably the women who took the initiative, not the husband, though it is unlikely that this was a temporary marriage arranged by one of the women. On the contrary, the mother of the child may well have been married to the man, or perhaps neither woman was married to him. The evidence about ancient South Arabian sexual mores is contradictory, and it is difficult to come to any firm conclusions; the instances described above were probably peculiar to nomadic tribes. It is hard to imagine such disparate social practices coexisting within a settled kingdom such as Saba.[12] For the overwhelming majority of this ancient society, descent was patrilineal, and the general practice was for a woman to move into her husband's home and take his name at the time of marriage.

The Peasants

South Arabian society was predominantly agricultural, as is plainly seen through the many inscriptions referring to the construction of farmhouses, the working of the fields, the planting of palm groves, etc. Conflicts among different states did little to change the basic conditions of life for the peasant population, a hard life cast in the mold of long tradition.

Life on the edges of the desert was largely determined by the annual flood cycle. Peasants prepared their fields in advance for these seasonal inundations, by shoring up dikes and irrigation canals. It was the peasants who formed the labor pool for constructing the large breakwaters and deflecting walls that steered the water into the network of canals and toward the fields that lay beyond. The entire peasant population would gather in the fields for several hours at the height of flooding, and the official in charge of irrigation would oversee the distribution of the floodwaters to ensure that each parcel of land received its share. The quantity of water would be measured the following evening by the movement of the stars, and the next day according to the length of the shadows. An in-

scription on wood records that two clans turned over one day's al-
location of water, taken from their own quota and reserved for the
next winter season, to an individual who was probably an irrigation
official.[13] This official apparently had the power to collect water
from some people and turn it over to others. In Nashq (al-Baydâ)
in the third century B.C., we have learned that one of these "water
masters" was named Wahabʾawâm, son of Awsim.[14] During the dry
season, peasants were kept busy with ongoing maintenance of the
waterworks. Various inscriptions mention digging a quarter of a
well, an entire well, several wells, and (earthen) aqueducts above
the fields. Small-scale jobs such as maintenance of existing channel
inlets, cisterns, or sections of canals were also undertaken during
the dry season to improve dispersal of floodwaters. Several dedicatory inscriptions mark the start of projects to repair a large hydraulic station, improve a palm grove, or level a field to grade. The most
common type of inscriptions are invocations asking the gods for
rain or protection from natural disasters.

The peasants mainly cultivated cereal crops such as wheat, barley, and sorghum, from which they would make flour for cakes.
Sesame was also harvested and pressed for oil. Two varieties of
wheat, *aethiopicum* and *dicoccum,* apparently predominated in ancient times.[15] Lentils and fava beans were prized for their high nu-
trient value and formed a significant part of the ancient diet. In the
irrigated zones, peasants apparently raised fruits more than cereals
or legumes. One surviving text, in which a person asked his cor-
respondent to supply two measures (of unknown quantity) of sesame (*gilgilân* or *gulgulân*), a sack of flour (*daqîq*), and five measures each of salt (*milh*) and lentils (*bilsin*), provides a rough idea
of the quantities of food reserved for personal use.[16] Indeed, the
same words are still in use two thousand years later.

The most prized crops of all were vines and date palms. Grapes
were used for wine (though the exact process is unknown) and
other daily uses. One text describes three hundred camel-loads of
wine of two types destined for workers undertaking the repair of
the dike at Maʾrib—clear evidence of the central importance of this
project. However, no traces of a wine press have surfaced yet. There
are a number of palm groves in and around the oasis, and the irri-

gated fields of Maʾrib and Raybûn still retain a large number of
traces of stumps and roots. The date palm is a tree with many uses,
including construction; though not particularly strong, it was used
regularly in the roofing of farmhouses and other modest structures.
The dates themselves were a highly prized commodity; Pliny tells
us the fruit was used for wine, a type of bread, and, among certain
populations, animal feed. Growing date palms requires great care
and attention; the plants were started in nurseries and then trans-
planted after a year or two. Pliny gave a description of how the
plants were thought to pollinate:

> It is stated that in a palm-grove of natural growth the female trees do
> not produce if there are no males, and that each male tree is surrounded
> by several females with more attractive foliage that bend and bow to-
> wards him; while the male, bristling leaves erect, impregnates the rest
> of them by his exhalation and by the mere sight of him, and also by his
> pollen; and that when the male tree is felled the females afterwards in
> their widowhood become barren. And so fully is their sexual union
> understood that mankind has actually devised a method of impregnat-
> ing them by means of the flower and down collected from the males,
> and indeed sometimes by merely sprinkling their pollen on the fe-
> males.[17]

Some peasants were beekeepers. Honey was a prized commodity
in ancient times and remains so today. Hives were built of wood
and a mud mortar and lodged in small stone cavities in several valleys of Hadramawt. In Yathûf, in the Wadi Jirdân south of Shabwa,
hives were nestled in the crevices of the rock, and nearby paintings
of the hives showed a miniature crenellated tower in white with a
dark red lower border, surrounded by a cloud of black dots representing bees. All around the tower, the artist inserted the names of
people, the word for honey (dhaʾbas), and images of antelopes, camels, and hunters.[18] Other hives in the region were built with planks
and mortar and outfitted with two openings; some had red lines,
others a red-and-white checkered pattern. The modern-day descendants of these ancient beekeepers in the valleys of Hadramawt
continue to use these stone cavities for hives. They distinguish between the easily accessible crevices, which they use primarily for

stocking and capturing larvae, and the higher, more remote hives. They also set up new hives in hollow tree trunks or build them out of wood in the shape of long boxes. Beekeeping was considered a benign activity in ancient times, as is evident from the observations of Strabo ("a fertile land abounding in beehives") and Pliny ("The Sabaeans . . . produced honey and wax").

The evolution of ancient agricultural practices is difficult to assess. The earliest societies apparently used a communal approach in which the land was collectively owned among rural and urban communities. Land for palm plantations and cereal crops seems to have been combined in the same areas. A number of edicts promulgated between the fourth and second centuries B.C. suggest that the fund of communally owned property gradually diminished while that of individual landowners increased. These decrees opened the way for individual members of the community to secure grazing rights on these lands, even as the community retained control over the property. By the end of the first century B.C., private property rights seems to have become predominant along with a legal distinction between grazing lands and crop lands. This juridical evolution bears witness to profound social transformations.[19] It is basically impossible to make any reliable estimates on crop yields during this period, and it is uncertain whether any new species of plants were introduced—the olive seems never to have been in regular cultivation in Yemen—or whether the region benefited from technical innovations in agriculture.[20] The system of irrigation based on *qanats*, or underground drainage tunnels, was introduced perhaps as early as the fifth century B.C., but the dating of this advance remains far from certain.[21]

Animal Husbandry

The raising of animals played a large part in the village economies of South Arabia, and animals were often involved in sacrificial rites in which their owners would ask the divinities for prosperity. Various types of domesticated animals are mentioned in the accounts of the military campaigns of Karibʾīl Watar in the seventh century

B.C., which make reference to the capture of some 150,000 camels from the tribes north of Jawf, and 200,000 more animals, including cattle, donkeys, and various small livestock, from the tribes of the Najrân region. The importance of these small livestock is evident from their frequent mention in accounts of war and pillage. Archaeological explorations of Raybûn, in Hadramawt, show that the raising of small livestock played a central role in the economy of that region. References to animal husbandry are frequently found in lease agreements carved in palm leaves; one of these agreements shows that a woman named Barâ' rented three adult ewes from three members of the Gan'ân clan, from the Nashshân tribe, for a one-year period. Barâ' was responsible for feeding the animals, but their wool and any offspring were to be shared among the contracting parties. The agreement specified that the Gan'ân family would bear any unforeseen risks such as illness, drought, or sterility. In return, Barâ' was responsible for protecting the animals from being eaten (presumably by wild animals), and she would be liable in any claims if the animals were to cause damage to other people's property. At the end of the year, the lessors had the right to reclaim full ownership of the three ewes along with their share of the offspring.[22] The text referred to here reflects a slow diffusion of such agreements involving the sharing of farm animals and is far from an isolated case.

Two types of animal deserve particular mention. First and foremost was the camel, whose unique ability to travel across extended tracts of desert land—as far as a hundred kilometers or more in a single day—proved indispensable to the caravan trade. Not surprisingly, the camel is the most commonly found image in surviving terra-cotta, stone, and bronze statuettes, and the only animal explicitly mentioned in dedicatory inscriptions. It was used for more purposes than any other animal in the region. (Horses remained unknown in South Arabia until a much later date—certainly no earlier than the second half of the first century A.D. The diffusion of the horse throughout South Arabia is attested by inscriptions that describe the presence first of four, then five, then perhaps ten horses in combat. By the third century A.D., a few dozen horses were reported in battles; hundred of horses were in use during the wars of the fourth century.)

The Rural Economy

The agricultural lands of Qatabān are the most clearly documented, thanks to the survival of a number of regulations carved into the southwest gate of Tamnaᶜ as well as on large stones in the fields.

Landowners in the Wadi Bayhân had wrongfully extended their areas under cultivation and seized parcels of communal land from the kings and their subjects. In the third century B.C., Yadaʾab Dhubyân published a decree to halt development of agricultural lands and any planting in certain fields; the decree also banned the sinking of wells and other work in the area. Another edict restricted the use of water and grazing rights on certain lands belonging jointly to the king and the community. Stone inscriptions showing the text of these laws served as boundaries in these lands, which were located on the edges of the wadi.[23] Yet another decree, concerning a poorly irrigated palm grove, called for the creation of new canals that would cross the territory of another tribe. In all these cases it is apparent that agricultural activity was regulated by sovereigns and tribal assemblies.

Other Qatabanites possessed lands in Dathîna, about a day's march from Tamnaᶜ. One farmer named Kahad was given the right to farm fields in this area in exchange for rent paid both in kind and in cash through various taxes.[24] Two later inscriptions detail the types of regulations in effect and describe an effort by these Qatabanite landowners to form a legal association of unkown duration. A so-called employee (ᶜamîn) was chosen from among these landowners and designated to collect taxes. This agreement was placed under the authority of the patron divinity of both tenant farmers and the property owners. One of these texts authorizes the king to place copies of the contract in certain towns like Tamnaᶜ; a formal appendix limits the role of the king to the recording of agreements entered into by members of the private sector.

A long Qatabanian inscription in the Wadi Dura, about a hundred kilometers east of Tamnaᶜ, records that a man from the Qasamum tribe was developing eight thousand units of land (the exact area is unknown) for his family: through the use of wells, canals, plowing, terraces, and control of plantations, this portion of the valley was turned into a productive oasis from the fourth century B.C. onward.[25]

None of the surviving documents provide a clear picture of the effect of taxation on the peasantry, but it does not seem as if they were crushed under burdensome taxes. Scholars are inclined to think of the peasantry as having been treated with a fair level of sensitivity by their royal or private landowners, inasmuch as there is no surviving evidence of peasant uprisings or massacres of tax collectors. Inscriptions on wood show short-term contracts among different groups, suggesting an orderly preservation of fair terms between parties. The agricultural world of the third and second centuries B.C. seems to have been characterized by a proliferation of agricultural decrees and the practice of publishing various copies of these documents for public view.

A barter system of agricultural products prevailed in the archaic period, but this yielded gradually to a system of monetary exchange. The first coinage appeared no earlier than the last decades of the fourth century B.C. Following the model of the old-style Athenian silver tetradrachma, these coins also incorporated a letter (or letters), a monogram (or monograms), the symbol of Almaqah, or even a six-character legend. These coins were struck exclusively from silver, but no more than a few thousand pieces were likely to have been in circulation; the rarity of gold coins was due to a lack of mines. Bronze coinage spread slowly through the towns and countryside. Two farms in the area around Shabwa have yielded more than a hundred bronze pieces, including one Hellenistic piece from around the first century B.C., dating the occupation of one of the farms. One possible conclusion is that bronze coinage was in use among the town's residents during that time, and that the coin mentioned earlier was an exception. In addition, numerous contracts signed in Jawf made reference to payment in a currency known as *balat*. One text mentions two sterling *balat* pieces received as payment for grains; another contract stipulated that one of the parties turn over a specified sum in coins to a temple.[26]

Finally, two inscriptions furnish a fairly detailed view of rural exchanges in the final centuries b.c.[27] The first details how two rural landowners named Urayn'at and Taw'um put a farmer in charge of sacrificing a small animal to the divine Patron. The landowners thanked the farmer for his shipment of musk (a luxury item probably imported into South Arabia), asked him the price, and then sent back a shipment of goods of equivalent value. Another text documents that a woman named Amwathan sent her sister four baskets and two sacks of spices along with flour, lentils, and baskets of flax seeds.[28] Agricultural products were therefore convertible into cash, as were the spices and musk that circulated in the countryside

The Urban Economy

It is difficult to characterize the relationship between agricultural and artisanal activities in ancient times. The only concrete evidence of a notion of a marketplace comes from a decree published at Tamna' that aimed to centralize commercial activities in the market known as Samar, and to control the exchanges between the villages of the Qatabanite territory. The decree's first clause, proclaiming Samar a single market under the authority of a chief, apparently addresses fiscal concerns. The text goes on to distinguish between Qatabanites and foreigners, the latter being subject to special taxes on entry into the city as well as being forced to do business in association with a Qatabanite partner. Within the villages, only authorized Qatabanite merchants were permitted to hawk their wares. In the cities, owners of buildings rented to foreign (especially Minaean) tenants were subject to special taxes. Nighttime commerce was prohibited, mainly to ensure enforcement of these restrictions. This decree sought to protect Qatabanite merchants by defending the interests of small shopkeepers from their richer competitors and prohibiting transactions between nonresidents. Such legislation was presumably spurred on by the collective business interests of Tamna^c merchants.

The merchants and landowners of Tamna^c constituted an independent urban community with enough autonomy to resist even the sovereign, who was prohibited from conducting business within the confines of the town and could exert his power over the citizens of Tamna^c only through the agency of the group of merchants and landowners. A similar type of relationship between town and king is attested in the Hellenistic monarchies of Asia Minor, but the South Arabian institutions were earlier and therefore not borrowed from the Greeks.

The Fragility of the Urban Economies

In a mainly agricultural economy, the city's original function was that of trading center. Agricultural products were bought and sold according to fairly strict rules, as in Tamna^c, and members of the landed aristocracy were not necessarily enriched by these exchanges. The great landowners, who financed the development of farmlands and collected rent and taxes on the land they owned (often far from their city), probably relinquished the business of trading in these goods, focusing instead on large-scale business. Moreover, it is reasonable to assume that commerce in valuable agricultural products was left to foreigners, especially the Minaeans. Indeed, irrigated farming gave only a small group access to a limited zone of arable land. The existence of pastoral nomads or seminomadic peoples resulted in the importation of complementary goods from distant lands, but the oasis was the principal source of wealth. Moreover, agricultural productivity depended not only on the volume of seasonal flooding, which varied significantly from year to year, but also on the principle of collective organization. Areas under active cultivation gradually declined as a result of the inability of the local workforce to cope with the steady siltation of the fields by seasonal flooding over the long term. The fields demanded such meticulous care that any outbreak of epidemic disease or military conflict was enough to sap the landed aristocracy of its ability to make necessary investments in the maintenance of their agricultural lands.

In the precarious context of urban dependence upon a concentration of local resources, external factors also played an important role. The prosperity of the cities was closely tied to the caravan trade, whose development depended in turn upon security and political stability along the entire route through various kingdoms. Wars between neighboring states were apparently frequent, and commercial relations would cease for the duration of these conflicts. The economic prosperity of the towns along the caravan routes was, therefore, at the mercy of an uncertain political climate.

The relationship between the rural economy and large-scale commerce has been very difficult for modern researchers to grasp in the absence of any relevant statistics. For instance, there is no proof that profits from commerce ever resulted in large-scale investments in agriculture. On the contrary, it seems more likely that such profits were invested in civil or religious construction projects. Financial reversals seem to have forced sponsors to abandon certain of these projects before their completion.

The cities along the main frankincense routes seem to have primarily served the movement of the caravans, and secondarily served as transshipment points for products traveling long distances. These cities did not produce any exports of their own, and artisans seem to have played a fairly minor role. Archaeologists have so far uncovered no evidence of luxury goods, and the iconography of items found so far suggests only the weaving of linens. The only information we have on the trades is limited to builders and scribes.

The Builders

Construction workers probably constituted an important part of the overall labor force of skilled workers in ancient South Arabia. At the bottom of the scale were the quarrymen who worked in the limestone deposits above the city of Shabwa. These workers performed the initial extraction and rough-cutting of the stone in the actual mines while other work teams moved the slabs downward toward the city. In Jawf, workers in white-marble quarries extracted large monoliths that were then used in construction of local sanctuaries. The rough-hewn slabs were marked to identify ownership and then warehoused at the quarry site. Some of these blocks, such as those found at the Temple of ʿAthtar in as-Sawdâ', weighed as much as six or seven tons, and some mystery remains as to how ancient workers were able to transport these massive monoliths and lay them in place.

Once the rough-hewn rectangular slabs arrived at the building site, they were laid as the foundations of the structure.[29] Workers would then use heavy hammer blows to square off the stones; on the upper floors the blocks were cut more carefully, since these would be visible above ground. The stonecutters demonstrated an astonishing ability to shape the blocks in such a way as to ensure a snug fit between layers, despite irregularities in the stone. Their prowess is especially striking in the stonework at Maʿîn and al-Baydâ, where the blocks are virtually seamless. With meticulous care, the workers used a malleable device that took the imprint of the block below, and they were then able to transfer the slightest contours and irregularities to the next layer, ensuring a perfect fit. In many cases the stones are so elegantly joined that a knife blade would not fit between them. Even modern stonemasons are impressed at the level of technical ingenuity brought to bear in these ancient structures.

Blocks averaging half a ton each were hoisted atop walls as high as eight meters in Maʿîn and fourteen meters in Barâqish. Carpenters were brought in to build scaffolding and bridgework along the exterior sections of the walls to provide temporary flooring for teams of stonecutters who would then dress the stone and add the finely chiseled stippling motifs which are a typical feature of South Arabian architecture. As a finishing touch, these specialists would then carve monumental inscriptions on the walls.

Bustling amongst the stonecutters were other artisans working on the wooden parts of the structure. The discovery of several hundred wooden beams among the ruins of the royal palace of Shabwa confirms that a form of wooden framework was erected along the base of the building. The framework consisted of prefabricated post-and-beam units of identical dimensions that could be assembled as needed with mortise-and-tenon joints. Carpenters made use of shorter beams by cutting them to half-length and staggering the joints or by incorporating them into dentiled ornaments, often painted red. The work of these specialized teams was coordinated by a foreman who had authority over the entire site. There were artisans who made the unfired bricks which were built into the wood frames, and smoothed out the earthen panels as they went up; in the finer homes, a separate team would install stone slabs on top of these panels and then finish the surface with decorative stippling.

For large construction projects like defensive walls and royal palaces, a skilled workforce would be mobilized for a long period of time, requiring significant financial backing. Construction must have ground to a halt during the occasional periods when financing was interrupted, and the ongoing demands of agriculture must have diverted a large portion of the labor pool. Factors such as these may explain the unfinished state of the fortifications of Maʿîn and as-Sawdâʾ, where entire sections of wall were apparently abandoned before they were finished.[30] Not surprisingly, large-scale projects such as these often spanned the reigns of several sovereigns, as was the case at Barâqish, where work seems to have continued through the sixth and fifth centuries B.C.

A large number of specialized craftsmen were associated with these ancient construction projects. There were artisans who made the alabaster plates mounted in wooden frames as windows or skylights. Sculptors created friezes with ibex heads and pseudo-bondstone motifs to surmount the walls, as well as decorative paneling that ran along the stairways and was typically painted red. Other workers dressed the surfaces of the stone blocks and incised the bands of epigraphy. Some of the great ornamental alabaster plates in the temple of Barʾân and Maʾrib, with borders depicting crouching or standing ibex, are veritable masterpieces. Some works, such as the limestone statuettes that were common in sanctuaries and tombs, were created in the artists' own workshops. One of the

characteristic types of artwork designed for use in architectural settings in South Arabia was the alabaster bust encrusted with semiprecious stones for eyes and hair of white mortar. Finally, there
were the bronze-casters who executed small and medium-sized
statues such as those found in the temple of Awwâm at Maʾrib, and
large quantities of compartmentalized boxes, lamps, statuettes of
bulls and camels, plates, and small vases.

Scribes and Clerks

It was long supposed that ancient scribes drew up texts for engrav-
ers who would later recopy them in large characters onto stone. But
this assumption has been undermined by the discovery of a single
text that shows that a king of Qatabân once ordered publication of
a text on both wood and stone; the king signed the original, probably on wood. The recent discovery of hundreds of palm stalks
sheds new light on the occupation of the scribe in ancient times. It
is now clear that professional scribes engraved texts directly onto
wood and that these were then stored in archives.

Scribes selected the best palm stalks, stripped their bark, and
then wrote on them while holding onto one corner. They scored the
margins and wrote lengthwise from right to left, scrolling down
according to the length of the text. At the end of the text they would
draw a line at an angle and would sometimes sign their name. The
minuscule lettering on these documents testifies to a remarkable
fluidity and consistency that could only be the work of trained pro-
fessionals. Their writing implement was a stylet of iron or bronze;
ivory stylets have also been discovered and were evidently used to
write on wooden tablets that were covered with a layer of wax.
Scribes used gridlines for training; on one surviving tablet, some-
one attempted to inscribe the alphabet, made a mistake, and then
began again farther on, this time making it all the way to the
twenty-third letter.[31] Mistakes and false starts were not uncommon
in exercises of this type.

In the predominantly illiterate society of ancient South Arabia,
scribes fulfilled the indispensable role of intermediary for those

who could not read or write. Some scribes were entrusted with the drafting of contracts. The author of one surviving letter addresses the reader(s) in the second person but refers to himself in the third person, implying the intervention of a scribe. In another letter, a woman writes to her sister through a scribe. The resulting indirect epistolary style was well known in ancient Egypt, Akkad, and the Orient. Nonetheless, modern scholars are uncertain as to whether the prestige of writing earned scribes a corresponding level of social recognition.

Once a text was engraved it was then filed away. A large hole was first punched in the palm stalks, no doubt so that it could be hung by a string or bound up with others. One text refers to a document that has been sealed with wax. The filing was performed either by the scribe or by an archivist. One of the sticks contained a contract prepared in duplicate and signed by the sender, with instructions for the recipient to return one fully executed copy of the agreement, under seal, and retain the other.[32] It seems reasonable to infer that private or public archives were created to house documents of this type, even though the survival of specimens in wood is indeed exceptional.

Other specialized artisans inscribed texts in bronze, using a technique that allowed them to create large letters in relief by hollowing out the surfaces around the letters. The artisans shaped the letters by applying lengths of wax braid (known as "fowls'-dung" or "pigeon-dung") formed in the shapes of the letters and then levelling them off with a spatula. The result was a rectangular bronze plaque with raised lettering, such as the votive offerings which commonly hung on sanctuary walls. Vases and basins were also adorned with letters in relief, spelling out a dedication to a divinity.

The Steppes and the Deserts

Though the oases and the towns built around them played an important role in the economy of the country, the area they represented was extremely small compared to the entire territory of South Arabia. Most of the region consisted of arid and infertile lands that provided a crucial buffer between the towns of the region, as well as between the towns and their counterparts in central and northern Arabia and the eastern Mediterranean. The economy of these vast zones apparently complemented that of the oases.

Classical authors referred to these arid expanses as the lands of the Skenitae, or tent-dwellers. This was the name Strabo gave to the Arabs of Mesopotamia as well as to those who inhabited the area between the Euphrates and Syria, and also the land around Apamea in Syria. The tent was the primary characteristic of these nomadic and seminomadic populations. Though mobile, they were still vulnerable to having their tents destroyed, a prime means of fighting against them. "I inflicted a bloody defeat upon her," recounted Ashurbanipal in his struggle against Queen Adia.[33]

Ancient authors consistently referred to the Arabs as mainly shepherds with small livestock, goats, and sheep. Herodotus recorded that "there are two varieties of sheep that are worthy of wonder and occur nowhere else [outside of Arabia]. The one of these has a long tail, not less than four and one-half feet. If this were suffered to trail after the sheep, it would be injured because of the rubbing of the tail on the ground. As it is, every shepherd knows enough of carpentry to make a small cart on which to fasten the tail, one for each sheep. The other variety of sheep has a thick tail that is one and one-half feet broad."[34] So much for legend; in reality, the sheep of ancient South Arabia probably bore a strong resemblance to their modern descendants. This type of animal husbandry is only possible on the borders of the desert, where annual rainfall averages between 100 and 150 millimeters and the distance between watering holes is not too great. Shepherds tended to stay near the agricultural zones and engage in trade with the inhabitants of those areas, and thus regular contact was maintained between nomadic and sedentary peoples.

The camel was the most important of all animals in the economic life of the nomads, a fact clearly attested in all the surviving texts from the Assyrian inscriptions of the ninth century B.C. down to Strabo. The camel made its first appearance in warfare at the battle of Qarqar in Syria in 853 B.C., when Gindibu the Arabāya led a force of a thousand camels into combat. In that same era, mounted camels with one or two humps were depicted in bas-reliefs at Carchemish and Tell Halaf and in the bronze leaves of the gates of Balawât. The usefulness of camels in war had been known and exploited as early as the ninth century b.c. in the Fertile Crescent, where the animal was also used for transport and as food. The so-called Aribi (Arab) tribes used camels in military campaigns during the reigns of Tiglathpileser III, Sargon II, Sennacherib and Esarhaddon. The Assyrians seized camels as war booty or received them as tribute. Though figures are rarely supplied in ancient documents, the number of camels was surely significant. We know, for instance, that Queen Sâmsi lost thirty thousand camels in a single battle. The practice of breeding camels in the Syrian desert must have begun at least as early as the seventh century b.c. and progressed steadily thereafter.

The diffusion of the camel in combat and transport was probably related to the rise of the caravan trade which increasingly connected northern and South Arabia. One can even suppose that the original push was from north to south rather than the other way around.[35] It is unclear exactly when the caravan trade really picked up, but frankincense probably first reached the eastern Mediterranean in the ninth century b.c. Commerce was probably sporadic until around the eighth or seventh centuries, when it became more frequent and regular; around this time, frankincense arriving in Assyria was referred to by its South Arabian name of *libnay*. A trading post was set up at Hindanu in the central Euphrates around the ninth to eighth century b.c. The breeding of camels probably began to move southward at around this time, from Syria to South Arabia, which became the point of departure for the great caravans heading north. The impact of this commercial development on the areas bordering the deserts of South Arabia must have been considerable. Strabo mentions the Debae, who lived to the north of Yemen, as "nomads who get their livelihood from camels; for they carry on war from the backs of camels, travel upon them, and subsist upon their milk and flesh."[36]

The development of large-scale caravan commerce created an ongoing demand for camels and thus provided an ongoing stimulus for those who raised camels. The annual caravan runs probably included several thousand camels, all of which needed to be fed and outfitted, and here again the commerce between nomadic herdsmen and their sedentary counterparts was essentially complementary. Nomads and Arabs regularly entered into contracts with the South Arabians from the towns and countryside to serve as guides and soldiers. Although the South Arabians used both the terms "no-mad" and "Arab," it is not clear that they saw any sharp distinction between the two; the latter word seems to have meant essentially shepherd.

6. THE GODS AND THEIR TEMPLES

The gods of South Arabia were inextricably linked to the oases; many of their attributes were directly related to agriculture and irrigation, and one of the primary functions of the cults that surrounded them was to encourage rainfall. The various divinities worshiped among the great valleys had similar roles, though their influence was often limited to a specific territory, town, or even small village. The only god worshiped in all regions in ancient South Arabian was known as ʿAthtar. He was known by the same name throughout the various states and was always named first in the enumeration of the gods. As the influence of Saba spread throughout South Arabia, the cult of Almaqah was imposed upon tribal groups who already had pantheons of their own. The result was a hodge-podge of religious conceptions. Of the dozens of divinities mentioned in Sabaean inscriptions, most were native to Saba but some were worshiped in other kingdoms.[1]

Fragmentary Sources

Our knowledge of South Arabian paganism is severely constrained by our reliance on scant epigraphical and archaeological sources. Though some eight thousand religious inscriptions have survived, either carved in stone or cast in bronze in large characters, texts preserved in these media are less informative than other literary and religious texts that are noticeably absent but presumably did exist; details on rituals, lists of gods, magical texts, and oracles remain totally unknown to this day. We have only a single religious hymn, composed in a rhythmic style, dating to the first century A.D.

Even in the best cases, the surviving epigraphic evidence provides only the names or epithets of certain divinities at certain temples, and it remains virtually impossible to do more than infer the attributes of a given god from the dedications or entreaties addressed to him or her.

While it is true that archaeological exploration over the past twenty years has brought several sanctuaries to light, we are not yet able to give a precise description of all the rituals that were once performed in them. There are only a few examples of anthropomorphic statues that might represent divinities, and no bronzes have emerged from the great temples of Sayîn at Shabwa and Barʾân at Maʾrib. There are bas-reliefs depicting ibexes (sitting or standing), bulls, and gazelles, but it is unclear which gods these figures were meant to represent. Some inscriptions naming a particular divinity have been identified with fairly abstract images that accompany them, but these are neither numerous nor particularly rich. The religious iconography of the high periods was not particularly varied. It was only later, during the early centuries A.D., that the iconography of Greco-Roman religious artwork began to make its way to South Arabia. These imported gods were not referred to by name in the inscriptions, and we are therefore unable to identify the local divinities with which they came to be associated.[2]

These uncertainties are compounded by the vagueness of much of the epigraphical evidence. We can deduce the hierarchy of the gods from the order in which their names appear in the so-called final invocations in which dedications always ended; this formula places the subject of the dedication under the protection of several divinities. It is also possible to isolate pairs of gods, but in certain cases it is impossible to tell whether a divinity is male or female, since the latter are not always called by feminine names. Another ambiguity arises from the incorporation of the South Arabian pantheon into a triad of Bedouin gods known as Father-Moon, Mother-Sun, and Son-Venus.[3] Divinities with astral significance, such as ʿAthtar (closely related to the Mesopotamian Ishtar) and Shams (a female Sun goddess, rather than a male) were the minority among gods in the South Arabian pantheon. In contrast with the Assyro-Babylonian religions, astronomical preoccupations were somewhat foreign to the South Arabians, who do not seem to have had a specific cult devoted to the stars.

The classical sources express the views and conjectures of outsiders and are therefore of limited help in providing a view of religion in South Arabia. Writers such as Herodotus, Diodorus Siculus, Pliny the Elder, and Pliny the Younger all attempted to compare the gods of South Arabia to the Greek and Roman gods, and their efforts are not particularly enlightening. Later Arab sources are even less helpful, especially since their main purpose in preserving the memory of the religions that preceded the arrival of Islam was to denigrate them as symptoms of a shameful "period of ignorance."

The God ʿAthtar

The cult of ʿAthtar was commonly known throughout the tribes of South Arabia as the chief divinity in their pantheon. He was the god of thunderstorms and rain (as opposed to the artificial irrigation of the arid zones). ʿAthtar was the "God of Thunder" and was often known by the epithet Sharîqan, or "the Eastern god" after the morning position of the planet Venus; he was a vengeful god who was invoked against the desecrators of graves. He was primarily associated with the ritual hunt, along with another divinity known as Kirwam. Sabaean sovereigns conducted these ritual hunts mainly for the purpose of obtaining rain, which may explain why the gazelle is ʿAthtar's animal attribute. He also presided over the federation ceremonies which integrated diverse tribal groups into the Sabaean state.

The God Almaqah

Almaqah was the principal god among the Sabaeans, but the preeminence of ʿAthtar and Hawbas in earier periods prevented Almaqah from occupying first rank in the formal order of the gods. Almaqah was the god of agriculture and irrigation, probably for the most part the artifical irrigation which was the basis of successful farming in the oases of Maᵓrib. The god's animal attributes were the bull and, in later times, the vine. Almaqah was a masculine sun god; the divinity Shams (Sun), who was invoked as protector of the Sabaean dynasty, was his feminine counterpart.

Almaqah's central role in the development of the Sabaean state is clear from two large inscriptions of the sovereign Karibᵓîl Watar in Sirwâh, in which the Sabaean nation is "descended from Almaqah," the mythic ancestor of all Sabaeans. As the Sabaean state expanded, the cult of Almaqah spread to the conquered and even the allied territories. A king of Kamna who built the towers of the high-wall of Nashq dedicated these structures to Almaqah, the kings of Maryab (Maᵓrib), and Saba. When the Sabaeans seized the city of Nashshân, they forced its inhabitants to build a temple to Almaqah within the city walls as a sign of their subjection to Sabaean power. When the Highland tribes became allied with Saba, they either built their own sanctuary to Almaqah or made a pilgrimage to the shrine of this divinity. A number of such sanctuaries were built throughout the lands of the Bakîl tribe near Amrân and Raydâ, northwest of Sana.[4]

Numerous sanctuaries to Almaqah were also built on the fringes of the desert. The most majestic of these, referred to as Awwâm in inscriptions (modern-day Mahram Bilqîs), was dedicated to "Almaqah Thahwân, master of Awwâm." This was most likely the site where the faithful gathered at the start of their great annual pilgrimages, which probably took place around the month of July. A second temple situated in the nearby locality of al-ᶜAmâyid ("the pillars") is referred to as Barᵓân and also by the place name Arsh Bilqîs. In this temple the god was worshipped as "Lord of Maskat Who Resides at Baᵓrân."[5] There must have been a third temple within the walls of the city, but it has not been located. The immense sanctuary of al-Masâjid, known as Maᵓribum, was located about thirty miles south of Maᵓrib.[6] This sanctuary consisted of a sacred precinct measuring 110 by 46 meters, which was entered through a large pillared portal that has since been destroyed. In the center was the temple and a courtyard bordered by porticoes and a wing of cellae.

Hawbas

A little-known divinity, Hawbas was a male god according to some texts and a goddess according to others. References in the most ancient inscriptions prove that Hawbas was worshiped earlier than Almaqah. The name of Hawbas adorns some stone basins carved into one of the summits of Jabal Balaq overlooking Maʾrib, but the name disappeared during the time of the mukarribs and did not reappear until the sixth century A.D. The introduction of Hawbas into the official pantheon doubtless corresponds with the incorporation of new tribes within Saba. Hawbas is known to have enjoyed great favor among the Sabaean settlers in Ethiopia, where several dedications to the god are known.[7]

Principal South Arabian Divinities

In the kingdom of Maʿîn, the national god was known as Wadd, or "love"; this god probably originated in central or northern Arabia and has been attested in several kingdoms of South Arabia. He is a lunar god whose name is sometimes accompanied by the epithet Moon. As a patron god and mythical ancestor, he was sometimes invoked as Wadd-ʾAbb ("Wadd is father") a magical formula which was engraved alongside a crescent moon and the circular symbol of Venus on numerous amulets. The animal attribute of Wadd was the serpent, symbol of the fertility of soil as well as animal and human fecundity.

In Qatabân, the national god was called ʿAmm or "paternal uncle" in reference to his role in the pantheon; but this designation fails to reveal his full identity. The Qatabanites also called themselves the "children of ʿAmm" (or the "descendants of ʿAmm"). The idea of the Qatabanite state itself was expressed through the double name of ʿAmm and Anbî, the latter occupying third place after ʿAthtar and ʿAmm in invocations. The designation of ʿAmm as patron and the postulation of a mythic line of descent from him suggests that the sovereigns may have accepted the diversity of the tribes that constituted the Qatabanite state. ʿAmm was seen as the protector of the Qatabanite dynasty, and it was under his author- ity that the sovereign carried out agricultural projects, divided up lands, and guaranteed rights of ownership. The etymology of the name ʿAmm equates it with *anbî*, "he who declares," and thus this divinity can be compared with the Babylonian god Nabû, who was associated with the planet Mercury.[8]

The national god of Hadramawt was known as Sayîn, a Sun god. As in Qatabân, the inhabitants of Hadramawt referred to them- selves as the "children of Sayîn"; the state itself was described through a formula using two divine names which also referred to a double tribe: "Sayîn and Hawl and [king] Yadaʾil and Hadramawt." We have only meager information from classical authors about Sayîn and his cult. Theophrastus reported that frankincense was collected in the temple of the Sun, which he erroneously placed in Saba.[9] Pliny recorded that priests imposed a tax on frankincense that went to the god "Sabis," and in turn the god provided generous hospitality for his guests during a certain number of days.

There were a great number of sanctuaries to Sayîn in Hadra- mawt. The principal temple was built into the spur of al-ʿAqab at Shabwa, at the end of the great road. Another santuary outside the fortifications, on a hill facing the temple, was also probably dedi- cated to Sayîn. In Hadramawt the name Sayîn was frequently found alongside epithets, as with "Sayîn dhû-Halsum" ("Sayîn of [the place] Halsum") in the temple of Bâwtfa east of Tarîm; or "Sayîn dhû-Alîm ("Sayîn of the ritual feasts") in a temple near Shibâm. These divinities were generally worshiped in two sanctuaries, one in town and another just outside of town. But Sayîn may have also been worshiped alongside other divinities, as seems to be the case in one of the *extra-muros* temples of Raybûn, where he was associ- ated with ʿAthtar and dhât-Himyâm.

Other Divinities

Not all of the gods of these kingdoms belonged to the official pan- theon, even those whose following was widespread. Worship of some gods may have been limited to a single tribe, town, or region. The influence of Samî, for example, is known to have extended throughout Jawf and the Yemen Highlands in the region of Raydâ, north of Sana. The cult of Kuhâl is attested in this region over the course of a long period, before yielding to the cult of Almaqah in the course of Sabaean expansion. Among other were the domestic gods, often designated by the vague term *shams* (a common noun, not to be confused with the proper name Shams, the Sun goddess), meaning "protector" or "master of the house." A space inside the house was commonly reserved for cult rituals such as sacrifices to the gods, as is evident from the incense altars or libation tables discovered in homes.[10] Other divinities have been identified only in relation to other gods in the pantheon; among these are a "mother of ʿAthtar," a "son of Hawbas," the "daughters of [the god] ʾIl," and the "servants of Almaqah."[11]

The sovereigns were not themselves considered divine, unlike their Hellenistic counterparts; they did not have their own cults but rather were considered mere "servants of the gods." Nor did they have the authority to institute the worship of new divinities among their subjects.

Gods without Human Forms?

While a great deal of uncertainty continues to surround the question of whether the gods of ancient South Arabia were worshiped in human form, it seems there was no specific prohibition against human representations of divinities, as was later the case with Islam. Architectural digs have uncovered many statues and story panels in the sanctuaries, though none of these images can be identified by accompanying texts. Several sanctuaries in Jawf have yielded objects bearing human images, probably women, but no names appear in the inscriptions engraved on the pillars. These temples have also yielded bronze statuettes and alabaster busts, most likely votive offerings rather than divine images.

It is possible to detect variations among the traditions of different regions. The most ancient temples in Jawf, which date back to the eighth century B.C., contain elaborate decorative schemes with entry porticoes and interior pillars covered with decorative panels depicting animal, plant, and human subjects. The proliferation of decorative motifs is particularly impressive in the temple to ʿAthtar at as-Sawdâʾ and the temple to Matabnatiyân at Haram. The architectural styles of the Sabaean regions were far more austere than their counterparts in Jawf, and none of the great sanctuaries of Maʾrib or Sirwâh were as luxuriantly decorated. The presence of ibex plaques and friezes with pseudo-bondstones did little to lessen the overall severity of the architecture. These temples were filled with bronze statues and inscribed stelae, but their effect was not nearly the same as in the temples of Jawf. The Sabaean decorative tradition grew out of a fundamentally different conception of sacred space, one which had more in common with that of North Arabia.[12] As for Qatabanite sanctuaries, what little we know of them suggests that they were decorated even more sparsely than those of Saba.

The surviving artworks and temple decorations display a wide variety of animal forms including horned animals, cows, bulls, antelopes, and ibex. Some of the figures are easily identifiable—sitting bulls, oryx (with their long, gently curving horns), ostriches—while other species are less easily identified, especially when represented only by a head. The ibex, recognizable by its long curled horns, was certainly a very common sight in the mountains of Yemen in ancient times, though it survives today only in Hadramawt, where it is still occasionally hunted. The ibex, which was most commonly depicted in a sitting position, shows up frequently as a decorative motif repeated along the periphery of alabaster plaques in the Sabaean temples at Maʾrib and Jabal al-Lawdh. Its image is also found, either in the sitting or standing position, on the pillars and architraves of the sanctuaries in Jawf. It was also portrayed full-face in the repeating friezes like the one crowning the wall of the temple of Sirwâh. The ibex was often associated with the god Almaqah but was also found in the temple to ʿAthtar at as-Sawdâ and the temple to Matabnatiyân at Haram.

The bull seems to have been primarily the symbol of Almaqah, but other gods, such as Samiʾ, were represented by the same ani-

Defensive walls of Barâqish (photo by the author)

The city of Sirwâh, with the great temple of Almaqah in the center (photo by the author)

The village of Ma'rib, with the waters of the Wadi Dhana in the foreground (photo by the author)

Altar dedicated by Adbal son of Wahab'il, Shabwa, circa third century B.C. (photo copyright © The British Museum, London)

Perfume burner, Ma'rib, third century B.C. (photo copyright © The British Museum, London)

Processional plaque, Saba, fifth century B.C. Commemorates a ceremony in honor of the god worshiped in the temple of Niʾmān, probably located somewhere between Maʾrib and Sirwâh. (National Museum of Sana; photo copyright © Philippe Maillard)

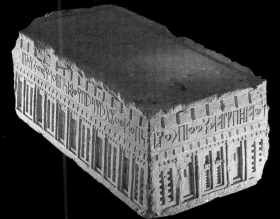

Miniature temple, Kamna, eighth century B.C. Decorations include (from bottom) a series of sunken panels, a long dedication mentioning a sacrifice, and a dentil frieze. (Sana Military Museum; photo copyright © Philippe Maillard)

Libation table, as-Sawdâʾ (Jawf), eighth century B.C. Monograms are those of Labʾûan, king of Nashshân (modern-day as-Sawdâʾ). (Photo copyright © Philippe Maillard)

Temple of ʿAthtar, west of as-Sawdāʾ

Decorative figures engraved on pillars in the temple of ʿAthtar, as-Sawdāʾ

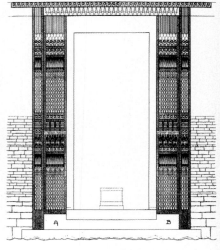

Western entry portico, temple of ʿAthtar: elevation of pillars A and B (reconstruction by G. Robine)

Statue of Maʾdīkarib, temple of Awwām, Maʾrib, sixth century B.C. One of ancient Arabia's most beautiful bronze statues. According to the inscription on his chest, ʿAmmīanas, father of five sons including Maʾdīkarib, offered this statue to the god Almaqah. (National Museum of Sana; photo copyright © Philippe Maillard)

Mural plaque, Maʾrib, Barʾân temple, fifth to fourth century B.C. Decorated with antelope and ibex heads and dedicated by an influential figure to the god Almaqah, this alabaster plaque was placed above the benches in the forecourt of the temple. (National Museum of Sana; photo copyright © Philippe Maillard)

Entry portico, Barʾân temple, Maʾrib (photo by the author)

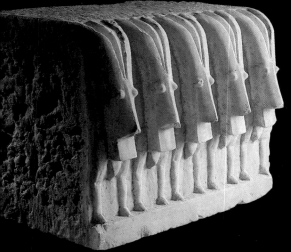

Ibex frieze, Barʾân ten Maʾrib, fifth century B (Museum of Maʾrib; photo copyright © Philippe Maillard)

Male head and female bust, Qatabān, third to second century B.C. *(private collection, Paris; photo copyright © Philippe Maillard)*

Seated figures, Jawf, seventh to fifth century B.C. *(National Museum of Sana; photo copyright © Philippe Maillard)*

Plaque depicting a woman in prayer, al-Jūba, south of Maʾrib. This alabaster plaque, offered by a woman named Barîlat, may represent the goddess dhât-Himyam or more likely the dedicant herself. (National Museum of Sana; photo copyright © Philippe Maillard)

mal. Images of the bull depicted full-face have also been found in the temple of ᶜAthtar. The image of the bull was used to evoke physical prowess or the notion of survival after death, qualities associated with the worship of several different gods. The bull's head appeared frequently as a decorative motif in Qatabanite and Sabaean regions. Splendid bull busts adorn alabaster funerary plaques from the first century B.C. to the first century A.D.; the most famous of these were discovered in Tamnaᶜ. The gutters of a great many civilian and religious buildings were also adorned with bull's-head motifs. The royal castle of Shabwa has yielded dozens of gargoyles with waterspouts more than a meter long, with the drain opening right above the head.

The eagle is the only animal whose image seems to have been identified with a single divinity. It was the attribute of Sayîn, who adorned the large coins of Hadramawt. The smaller bronze coins showed the god in the form of a bull.

Inscriptions consecrated to the gods are often accompanied by symbols. The best known is the crescent moon, often surmounted by a small circle which is generally interpreted as an image of the planet Venus. These two symbols show up together in a variety of contexts such as engraved plaques, incense altars, and buildings. The image seems to have been essentially a form of talisman to bring good luck and ward off evil, rather than being exclusively related to a specific divinity. Scholars have been so far unable to establish a link between each symbol and a particular divinity.

The Economy of Temples

The beginning of the South Arabian era was marked by significant building activity along the edges of the desert. The eighth to fifth centuries B.C. was an especially active period for architecture, and many of the temples whose traces remain visible today date back to this period. Magnificent sanctuaries were built in and around the large towns, and other, more modest structures were built in the countryside or on rocky sites. The large-scale buildings were characterized by great subtlety of architecture and careful execution, whereas buildings in outlying areas were more modest and displayed cruder workmanship in the masonry.

The temples bear witness to the wealth of their builders. While the small kingdoms of Jawf, Nashshân, and Haram were capable of designing and building sanctuaries of a very high level of quality, the Sabaean state produced the most majestic sanctuaries in all of South Arabia in the period between the seventh and fifth centuries B.C. These great buildings were clearly financed by wealthy sponsors, and the sanctuaries incorporated land as well, mainly irrigated fields, pasturage, and palm groves. Their properties were generally concentrated near the temples, as with the temple to Barʾân at Maʾrib and the temple to dhât-Himyam at Raybûn; some temples had lands dispersed throughout the oasis. The cost of irrigating these properties was generally covered by various taxes: thus did ʿAthtar ensure the proper maintenance of his fields. The exploitation of these lands was normally entrusted to third parties, while the property rights of the sanctuary remained with the temple administrators, who always retained control over the imposition and collection of taxes. The temple possessed herds of small livestock including goats and sheep. The god received tithes to support the priests and the upkeep of the temple, and other taxes were levied on certain artisanal and commercial activities. The sanctuaries to Barʾân at Maʾrib and to Sayîn at Shabwa, for example, collected tithes on aromatic products. A significant income was also derived from the offerings of pilgrims and other worshipers who came to ask favors of the gods. Inscriptions refer to offerings of bulls, small livestock, horses, etc.

Religious functions were performed by temple priests (*rashaw*) and administrators (*qiyân*). The priests were drawn exclusively from the noble families, though they never formed an autonomous class or constituted a powerful force in themselves. They were civilians with additional responsibilities in politics; moreover, temple inscriptions attest to a very small number of priests. In the earliest sanctuaries of Saba, priests were chosen from among a very small number of families; the priests of ʿAthtar dhu-Dhibân, who are mentioned in the lists of eponyms of Maʾrib, were descended exclusively from the lineages of Hazfar and the first-born of Khalîl, their chief. From the earliest times, years were named after the priest in office; presumably these were the names on the list of eponyms of Saba. In later times, a system evolved whereby the year was named after a group of four eponymous priests who changed annually. The priests were surrounded by a group of cult practitioners who seem to have been regarded as "protégés" rather than "slaves" of the divinity; this association was devoted to cult duties. The best known association was dedicated to the cult of ʿAthtar dhû-Yaharîq in one of the temples of Barâqish.[13]

Peculiar Rites

Divinities were honored with dedications of objects, people, and personal goods. The objects were primarily architectural elements such as the pillars or walls of a sanctuary, but other objects included stone furniture such as altars, libation tables, and incense-burners, or metal objects such as bronze plaques. The faithful also made offerings of animal and human figurines. In the temple to ʿAthtar at as-Sawdâʾ, thin bronze statuettes (three to four millimeters thick) with outstretched arms were inserted between the stones of the walls; a series of similar offerings originated in other sanctuaries in Jawf. In the great Sabaean temples, the faithful offered bronze or silver images of increasing magnificence over time. Two officers made an offering of a silver statue in thanks to Almaqah for saving a servant, and to ask him to protect them from their enemy's malevolence, spite, calumny, and the evil eye. Other statues were consecrated to Almaqah in thanks for a safe return from combat after the enemy was destroyed. Animal statues of bulls or camels were made out of bronze, stone, or (in rare cases) silver. Images of bulls were offered mainly to Almaqah, and camels mainly to dhû-Samawi; camel figures have also been found in the temple to Sayîn at Shabwa and the temple to dhât-Himyam at Raybûn. Dedications mention a male camel figurine made of gold, offered for the health of the dedicant and his camels; a female camel in gold for the well-being of a dedicant's female camel; he-mules, male horses, and so on.

In archaic times, believers principally made offerings of human figures, beginning with themselves. In one such case the worshiper offered his own person, his wife, and all of his children to ʿAthtar. This practice was evidently nothing more than a simple formula to express piety and certainly did not involve actual sacrifice. In one case, a subject of the king of Hadramawt pledged to Sayîn and to the gods of Shabwa "his own person, his faculties, his children, his worldly goods, the light of his eyes, and the understanding of his heart as a guard and protection in the hope that they might gratify him."[14] Another offered "his daughter and some gold": the offering of a human being may in some instances have been related to adherence to a cult association such as the example at Barâqish.

The faithful frequently consulted the gods for oracles. The divinity would make his will known through the priest as intermediary. If the oracle turned out to be favorable, the faithful would erect a stela in the god's honor, as happened in the case of a certain ʿAmmîkarib, who, on the basis of an oracular pronouncement, erected a statue to Taʾlab thanking the god for averting a vendetta. Others sought to learn the divine will through drawing lots, casting dice, and the interpretation of dreams. Religious practice was closely related to magic, though unfortunately no magical text has survived. All that remains are graffiti carved in stone, some of which are accompanied by magical signs and images of outspread palms which were thought to repel bad luck. Other texts mention a desire for protection against the evil eye or the hope that a child will be born under a favorable constellation.

The sanctuaries in the region of Maʿîn have yielded a certain number of inscriptions known as "ritual confessions" in which the dedicants express repentance for a range of infractions, most frequently related to purity. These texts almost always begin with a standard formula in which a person "confesses and repents" before the god; the confessor then admits his faults and closes with an expression of penitence and a request for forgiveness. The confession may concern either an individual or a collective offence. In an example of the latter, eight magistrates from Haram and officials from the surrounding rural area confessed to blasphemy, though it seems the offence was actually committed by only one of them. The group demonstrated their solidarity by assuming collective responsibility. A similar case was that of a certain ʿAmmyatha and the people of Maʿīn, who confessed as a group to having stolen the text of a dedication in a sanctuary at Barâqish. The king of Maʿīn himself was among the confessors, even though he could not have been the one to commit the offence; he demonstrated his solidarity with those who were actually guilty by lacerating his own face in repentance. In another instance, a man who had stolen a herd belonging to the god Halfân made amends by restoring the animals to the members of his clan just as they were departing on a pilgrimage.

Women were often responsible for individual offences such as the one committed by a certain Uhayyat in her house and in a temple; she was sent to the public square of her town without being purified and was judged guilty of a minor offence. Some women confessed to having kissed a man, having sinned (perhaps with a man?) in the temple, having entered the temple in an impure state, or having sinned "at night." A female servant named Hawliyat apologized for having "worn a soiled and threadbare mantle which she had mended in such a way as to hide its flaws from her lords [the gods] dhû-ʿAnyat and dhû-Samâwi." A woman of high social standing confessed to having had clients who acquired a stain— probably a moral stain—which had caused the god to turn away from them.[15] Public confessions were always recorded, either on a bronze tablet displayed in the sanctuary, or on a stone stela erected in or near the temple. In the case of the eight magistrates of Haram, the confession ended with an expression of their desire to regain the favor of the god Halfân, for apparently he had punished the entire town and tribe by depriving their lands of rain. However, their confession of blasphemy (which was no doubt a relatively minor offense) made no reference to any propitiatory rites or financial compensation. It must have taken considerable courage for the accused to make a public admission of guilt and have their offences published on a tablet in the temple for all to see, even if punishments tended to come only after the events had acquired public notoriety.

Sexual offenses seem to have been judged as matters of legal rather than moral propriety. Ancient South Arabians seem to have made a clear distinction between the sacred and the profane, and between pure and impure. The temple was known as the *mahram,* from the concept of *hrm,* denoting that which was forbidden. A woman was not allowed into the temple if she was in a state of impurity, nor was she to have contact with men. The legalistic administration of temples was such that an offender would receive a sort of certificate of remission of sin once the required services or payments of reparation had been rendered.

Inscriptions found mainly in Jabal al-Lawdh mention so-called ritual banquets. The typical formula was, "When he celebrated a ritual banquet for ʿAthrat dhū-Dhibān and offered him a sacrifice by fire at Tarah . . . " There is no evidence of banquets held in the honor of any other divinities besides ʿAthtar. The small sanctuary of Dish al-Aswad in the Maʾrib region appears to have had a central room with fourteen benches in parallel formation, with a forecourt also equipped with benches, though it is unknown which god this building was dedicated to.[16] Another banquet hall is known to have existed at Bab al-Falaj in this same region, but the most remarkable religious complex that has been found is the one at Jabal al-Lawdh, a mountain on the northern extremity of the Jawf valley.[17] Located beneath a rocky peak in the shape of a sugarloaf, its two large buildings contain open-air halls with benches. One of the buildings is 98 meters long by 41 meters at its widest point with two rooms preceded on the east by a series of masonry pylons. In each room there is a series of large, low benches with narrower benches interspersed. Such a plan is likely to have been devised to allow a large number of congregants to dine together, though probably not in great comfort. A narrow path leads east from the buildings up to a small stone sanctuary not far from the summit, in a place now called Mushjī, probably the ancient Tarah. Some sixty-five inscribed stelae, dating back to very ancient times, were discovered here. During the high South Arabian period it seems as if the sovereigns were the only ones allowed to visit this sanctuary. Karibʾîl Watar made offerings to a variety of divinities, including ʿAthtar dhû-Dhibân, Hawbas, and Almaqah, and organized ritual banquets and sacrifices by fire at Tarah. Later sovereigns including the kings of Saba and dhû-Raydân presided over similar ceremonies here.

Ritual banquets were not frequent; in fact, they only took place around ceremonies marking the pacts of union as part of the formula of federation between the various related tribes in Saba during its high period. On these occasions the Sabaean mukarribs would convene the representatives of all the conquered or allied tribes and join them together in a union implying the recognition of the gods ʿAthtar and Almaqah. ʿAthtar was always recognized as supreme, and his name was always recited first in the invocations, even though his role may have been somewhat limited. The integration of various tribes into a single political body was underpinned by their common recognition of Almaqah as the patron god. The Sabaean mukarribs concluded pacts of federation on three occasions: under Karibʾîl Watar son of Dhamarʾalî, under Yadʾil Dharih, and under Yathîʾamar Bayân in the seventh century B.C. The first pact may have corresponded to the foundation of the Sabaean state under Karibʾîl Watar, with subsequent unions simply reaffirming the original alliance on the occasions of the change of a sovereign. To celebrate such a pact, the sovereign would offer a ritual feast to the entire tribal assembly, most likely in the great halls of Jabal al-Lawdh. These ceremonies provided an opportunity for the sovereign to forge a personal connection with the tribes as well as to pronounce measures of collective security and other decrees whose details have not survived. The sovereign would presumably decree the inviolability of certains sites or even certain people, and reaffirm rules protecting the security of commercial exchanges.[18] Several inscriptions provide evidence that other federation ceremonies were held after the seventh century B.C. under the aegis of Saba, continuing as late as the third century B.C. The main function of these ceremonies seems to have been to place a certain number of sanctuaries under the common protection of all the tribes who were adherents to the pact. In the first century A.D., Dhamar Alî Watar, the first king of Saba and dhû-Raydân, organized a new union, though it is unclear whether this pact continued a regular practice or was an attempt to revive a ceremony that had fallen into disuse.

The Sabaean sovereigns also presided over ritual hunts. In the times of the early sovereigns, the hunt had explicit religious connotations and was held in honor of a divinity: in Saba, the gods were ᶜAthtar and Kirwam, and in Qatabân it was the Sun-goddess Shams. The hunt was led by the sovereign, who was personally involved in the meticulous performance of various rites. While no animal is explicitly mentioned in descriptions of these ritual hunts, the number of victims is recorded in the texts of the Yalâ region: ten, twenty, fifty, sixty, 150, 200, 460, and one thousand.[19] The ibex seems to have been the most abundant animal and thus the most frequently captured or killed. One late inscription mentions 4,000 ibex killed in a single hunt on the high plateaus. Other animals such as cattle, young camels, cheetahs (or panthers), and lions also figured in the hunt.

Large-scale pilgrimages were organized to honor the divinities; the most important of these was doubtless the pilgrimage of Almaqah at Maᵓrib. If this ceremony took place in the temple of Awwâm, that fact would help account for the large size of the building as well as its layout and the presence of a large oval space there.[20] It was probably held sometime in July, during the rainy season. Pilgrims would be required to perform certain rites asking for rain, in a ceremony know to the Arabs as *istisqâ*. A pilgrimage in honor of Almaqah is attested at Amrân, north of Sana, and another, in honor of the god dhû-Samâwî, is attested at Barâqish. In Hadramawt, the great pilgrimage in honor of Sayîn was held at Shabwa.

Some Ceremonial Costumes

The iconography of the temples included human representation, though it is unclear whether these images depicted divinities or their mortal worshipers. The most common figures are dressed in long tunics, probably linen, which fall to the feet or to about mid-calf and are sometimes held by a simple belt. The earliest statuettes of seated men portray a full-length garment that extends all the way to their bare feet, while the women are depicted with a garment that loosely conforms to their breasts. The faces were oval in form with prominent noses and eyebrows framing diamond-shaped eyes with hollow pupils. Numerous examples of this type of statuette exist, and though their origins are uncertain, they most likely date back to the beginning of the first millennium B.C. Another type of statuette depicts a standing subject with a similar close-fitting tunic falling to about mid-calf and held by a cloth belt with one end hanging between the legs; some figures are shown wearing a simple, low collar.

Besides these statuettes, the greatest number of human representations has been discovered in the archaic sanctuaries of Jawf, notably on the pillars of the sanctuaries at as-Sawdâ', Haram, and Maʿîn. These figures are twenty centimeters high and a maximum of about twelve centimeters wide, and they are always shown on a a pedestal and enframed in a chevron pattern.[21] The male is represented frontally but with his feet in profile; he wears a long garment decorated with chevrons and fitted to his form by a belt and rings at the feet. Another type of garment falls in a double fold behind the forearms and appears to be fastened by two crossed straps. The hair is turned up in symmetrical tufts, and parts of the head are entirely shaven. The right hand holds a bent instrument which in some pictures is split in two at the end; the left hand holds a long, bent cane. Beyond the presence of breasts, which are barely indicated as faint circles, there is no outward sign the figures are feminine. These figures show a few variations; some wear garments that are flared at the bottom with contours highlighted by netting in the background; others have shorter, tighter-fitting robes with a dentilled trim. Some of the pillars in the sanctuary at as-Sawdâ' show stocky figures (clearly masculine) wearing a short skirt under a tunic and with tousled hair; in their right hand they hold a musical instrument that forms an acute angle. This instrument, which is always curved and is split in two in some cases and not in others, could have represented a scepter—or a farmer's hoe. These figures all play a central role in the decorative schemes of sanctuaries of the eighth century B.C., and certain clues suggest they may have existed quite a bit earlier. The exceptional quality of execution implies an ancient and evolved artistic tradition that was probably related to proficiency in the textile arts.

Outstanding depictions of human figures can be seen in stone blocks from the sanctuaries of Maʿīn. One such stone shows a procession of (presumably) dancers or perhaps musicians divided between two panels. The figures are drawn in profile and wear either a tunic or animal skin over the shoulders. Their heads are shaven and their eyes are round and disproportionately large; their chins are very prominent (some have false beards) and curiously turned up. Two of the musicians are playing a short-stringed harp held horizontally, while six other musicians are holding a type of strange curved instrument similar to the example found at the temple of as-Sawdâʾ. The figures in another stone carving from Maʿīn are dressed even more strangely. One is much taller than the other six, who are split among two panels; the tall one is bare-chested, wears a fairly short, pleated skirt, and carries a fluted staff.[22] Each of the others is dressed in animal skins with a tail that curls behind him. Four of these figures are holding this instrument with the curved end in their right hand and seem to be resting their left hand on the handle of a dagger. A fifth figure is leaning on a straight cane, and a sixth is holding a vase with a branch coming out. These two panels may depict processions in the honor of one of the local divinities of Maʿīn.

The use of animal skins seems to have had more honorific than symbolic meaning in these images. The bronze statue of Maʾdīkarib that was found in the temple of Awwâm at Maʾrib depicts a figure dressed in a short tunic with a lion skin draped over it; the lion's paws are crossed, with two over the shoulders and the others around the figure's legs. The entire area of the tunic is covered with a long text. The tunic is secured by a large belt that also holds a decorated dagger. This style of carrying a knife is also found in other images, and some also include a straight sword.

Women and men appear in equal numbers. Representations known as "goddess plaques" are busts of a woman holding a sheaf of wheat in her left hand and raising her right hand in a sign of benediction. She is shown dressed in a tunic, open to mid-shoulder or the base of the neck, which accentuates her figure. In some cases the tunic covers only her forearms and in others it covers the entire arm, and it is decorated with stripes or large ornamental designs. The female figure wears a collar consisting of one or more rings stacked together or, in some cases, small ornamental bars on a ribbon. The most attractive necklaces have antelope heads with horns turned up parallel with the woman's neck. The faces are rendered schematically, with thick eyelids and pupils of inlaid semiprecious stones. The hair has gentle waves and is parted in the middle. Some scholars identify these figures with the image of the goddess dhât-Himyam, while others associate it with women with religious functions.[23] This style, which is characteristic of Qatabanite regions in the final centuries B.C., underwent a profound change under external influence in the centuries that followed.

Sanctuaries of the Archaic Period

Recent archaeological exploration has allowed us to imagine with greater precision the original appearance of archaic santuaries. It might seem strange that these structures, which are among the oldest in South Arabia, could provide the best illustration of what temples may have looked like in ancient South Arabia, but their builders had already developed an impressive mastery of construction techniques. In fact, no great sanctuaries were built after the first century B.C., so we must rely on our imagination in trying to reconstruct the original appearance of these temples, which were set amidst the irrigated fields, no doubt shaded by trees, and surrounded by dense networks of canals. The priests and the faithful must all have recognized the perils as well as the benefits of locating their temples in the heart of the oasis, for the floods were not yet fully controlled, and their force could wipe out entire buildings. Siltation was also a chronic problem as alluvial deposits regularly raised the level of the fields around the temples. They attempted to solve this problem by raising the temples up whenever possible and surrounding them with protective walls. Another strategy was to build the temples on hillsides or within the towns. Since the temples were generally only one story high, they tended to blend in with other buildings built right up against them. The majority of these resembled fortresses, with high walls pierced by narrow openings; they seemed to be designed more to protect the privacy of those inside than to welcome crowds of pilgrims. The only entrance was through a single, bolted portal, a feature that suggests a desire to limit access.

One of the oldest sanctuaries in Jawf is that of ᶜAthtar dhū-Risaf at as-Sawdāʾ, a cube-shaped stone structure measuring some fifty meters on a side and lacking any exterior decoration.[24] A worshiper approaching from the west would encounter ten tall, trapezoidal stelae that bore no inscriptions or engravings of any kind. The traveler would enter first through a portal framed by two pillars covered with engraved patterns from top to bottom, with intertwined serpents, spears, crouching ibex, more serpents, more spears, then rows of walking ibex, and finally, long-stemmed plants. Two inscriptions report that this temple was built by a certain Abʾamar Sadiq in the eighth century B.C.

From this portal, a covered passageway led to a second, lower portal which was also decorated over its entire surface. Our visitor has now arrived in a small, paved courtyard surrounded by porticoes. He could sit on any one of a series of benches arranged amidst the pillars or could stand in the shade of the meticuluously joined monoliths that served as a roofing. He would certainly pause to admire the panels of the monoliths, which were completely covered with carvings of the same patterns as in the entry. Some visitors may have been able to read the great dedicatory inscriptions with the names of Sumhuyafaʾ, son of Labʾān, king of Nashshān, and his sons and brothers. The worshiper would then walk several steps and climb two stairs up to a platform covered by an immense lintel. Seven stone blocks arrayed in a semicircle provided seating; all were inscribed with the name of Labʾān and were apparently reserved for priests or members of an assembly. This was as far as a visitor could go before reaching a massive, blank caisson which may originally have been a tomb. One of the major features of this temple is that it did not contain any *cellae*.

It is impossible to know the number of objects which the faithful saw when visiting this temple, but there may have been many objects to look at in the eighth to fourth centuries B.C. One pilgrim left an incense altar at the base of the caisson; another installed an incense altar in a portico, with the following inscription: "[He] has offered this altar to ʿAthtar dhû-Risaf." A landowner made an offering of a large altar to the divinity in thanks for receiving lands which he put under cultivation. By all appearances, none of the faithful seem to have brought ceramic or stone vases as offerings. As to the vexing questions of what rites may have been performed in this sanctuary and what role may have been played by the women whose images are depicted on the pillars, no clear evidence has yet been found to provide an answer.

The architectural formula for this type of temple was widely used in Jawf around the eighth century B.C. A sanctuary to Matabnatyân in the village of Haram, not far from as-Sawdâʾ, was built on a similar plan.[25] Unfortunately, all that remains of this structure are the pillars and their massive architraves, which have been lying on the ground in recent times; their decorative engravings are even more lavish than those at as-Sawdâʾ. Small figures are framed by friezes depicting ibex with curled horns and plants with long branches bearing fruit which is being pecked at by birds. This unique hymn to the gods of fertility shows stunningly fresh ornamentation evoking the charms of the valley's gardens in ancient times. About ten kilometers to the west, outside the walls of Maʿîn, lie the majestic ruins of another fine temple built on a similar plan. It is surrounded by a mighty exterior wall with an enormous entrance on the western side leading to an open-air, porticoed courtyard. The design of the entrance shows Egyptian influences in its two portals, with the first leading through a covered passageway to the second, which is smaller. The most ancient pillars in the courtyard are covered with the same type of engravings of animals, plants, and human figures. The entry portal was apparently enlarged and renovated with decorated stones, and the newer pillars in the courtyard are inscribed with religious edicts.

Temples of Jawf and Hadramawt

In a new type of sanctuary that first appeared in Jawf around the sixth to fifth centuries B.C., architects abandoned the central courtyard and began building hypostyle courts entirely roofed over with stone slabs. The temple to the divinity Nakrah at Barâqish is the most accomplished example of its type.[26] There too, a mighty exterior wall has an enormous portico on the western side providing access to a small hypostyle court. Sixteen stone pillars supporting a roof of elegantly fitted stone slabs demarcate five aisles which were originally empty. Three long offertory tables decorated with ibex heads along their edges were later installed on the western side of the room (known as the "area of ritual feasts"); two of these were designated as the "autumn" and "spring" tables. The faithful would sit on stone benches as they partook of the sacred meals. To the east, visitors would take one step up to enter an elevated area oriented on a transverse axis; here the sacrificial victims were immolated, and the blood would be channelled out of the building through a system of drains. The innermost area of the sanctuary contained five *cellae* which originally held statues of divinities and were closed off by wooden doors.[27] The temple's entry portico was modified sometime around the third to second centuries B.C., near the end of the period of its use, and a two-story annex was built against the south wall. Numerous plaster icons of human heads have been found among the debris of this structure, as have several ceremonial vases decorated with animal figures and a variety of inscriptions. These icons confirm the importance of the cult of Nakrah, patron god of the Minaean state, and show that his adherents dedicated the temple's very pillars to the divinity.[28] The discovery of these texts also highlights the role of a certain Bâsil, son of Ma's, who installed two offertory tables, two stone pedestals in the hypostyle court, and a stone post outside the temple. Sadly, few details have emerged about the actual rites once performed in the temple.

Fortunately, though, some interesting evidence concerning the cult of Nakrah has been discovered at the sanctuary of Darb-as-Sabî, not far from Barâqish.[29] Aged, infirm, or dying people came here seeking cures or deliverance from suffering, as did women who had aborted a child or who were about to give birth. Others publicly confessed their sins or consulted oracles in the temple. This temple is a modest building with a stone roof and surrounded by a small open-air courtyard. In front, there is a tall stela inscribed with the following text:

The god Nakrah has been consulted by an oracle and has ordered that the boundaries of the sacred perimeter be established. If a dying person or a woman who has aborted or has delivered a stillborn child should ever enter within, he or she must make an offering of a bull with a double harness and a white kid-goat; if any man should ever molest a woman who has aborted or who is in labor, or any person who has been stricken with a mortal illness, that man is forbidden from taking refuge in this temple; finally, if a woman dies after aborting or after delivering a stillborn child, her relatives must make an offering of a billy goat and a ram.

The images gleaned from the different temples of the region of Barâqish suggest that Nakrah was a god of healing and confession as well as a "patron" god.

In Hadramawt, temples were built in towns or villages and on the high hillsides overlooking them. The architectural plans of these buildings were similar to those mentioned above, with large steps leading up to a platform containing one or more small, low structures with a hypostyle court.

Entering the temple of dhât-Himyam at Raybûn, the priest would climb a long stone stairway on his way to performing his religious duties.[30] He would pass through an enormous porch with two small rooms at the far end. The temple treasure was stored in the room on the right, behind a heavy door; a stairway to the left led up to a high terrace. Here the priest would find large jars from which he could draw water and stone altars upon which he might place beads of incense. Beyond, he could wander through a chamber supported by twenty-four wooden pillars lined with benches and an offertory table. Goats were sacrificed here, and the meat would be shared among the congregants; the victim's blood would run down a stone gutter that led outside. The priest would approach what was probably an altar in the center of the room: a wooden cube filled with pebbles and covered with fabrics. The priest would climb three steps to reach this altar and would address his prayers to the divinity or make a sermon to the gathered faithful. Among the offerings he would lay down at this altar were a small bronze mirror, a golden amulet adorned with blue glass, a bronze animal figurine, glass items, stone beads, and ceramic bowls with dedicatory inscriptions. The smoke of incense burning on an altar atop a pillar would waft over the worshipers and out through an opening in the roof.

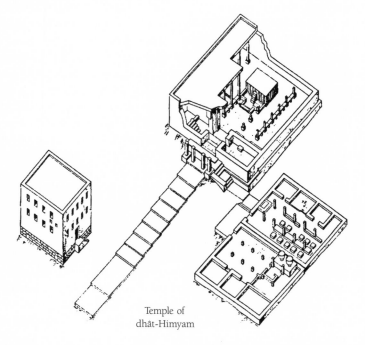

Temple of
dhāt-Himyam

A wood-framed structure found not far from this site originally contained an immense room with twenty-five wooden pillars; the room was later divided. The eastern part contained a raised wooden platform that held two large earthenware jars; offerings including an arrowhead, a bronze dagger, an incense altar, and various ceramic items were strewn about the floor. The western part of the room held a number of benches made of stone and unfired brick as well as a large hearth; fragments of large pots suggest this was a cooking area. Among the debris found in this site are several bone fragments of goats and ibex. Formal ceremonies were doubtless held in the eastern chamber, and ritual feasts would follow in the adjoining chamber to the west; the two chambers were laid out on a symmetrical plan. In another nearby sanctuary meticulously covered basins were presumably used for ceremonial ablutions. Beads of incense found in the cracks of the flooring stones were no doubt destined for nearby incense altars. These sites are among the best preserved of their kind in all of Hadramawt and strongly support the hypothesis that there existed a ritual association between temples and refectories in ancient South Arabia.

Recent archaeological digs in this region have provided a tantalizing glimpse of the original appearance of these ancient sanctuaries, which were all built with wood fames strengthened with unfired brick. Set within the framework of beams were limestone panels covering the exterior walls and often the interior walls. Their surfaces were covered with dedicatory inscriptions which were sometimes highlighted with red paint. Several statues graced the interior spaces of the sanctuaries, though few have been recovered. Among the figures were animals such as bulls, camels, cattle, and eagles (the image of Sayīn). As for the human figures, the pedestals of the statues mainly bore the names of well-off people such as Ilmahawu, lord of Raybûn.[31] It is unclear whether the image on the kiosk in the main aisle (referred to as an "altar" by excavators) depicts the god Sayīn; if so, this raised *adyton,* which is preceded by a series of steps, may be related to an Assyrian tradition that was well established in the Orient.[32]

In addition to statues, decorative elements including polychrome frescoes of humans, plants, and fish have been discovered on the walls of the hypostyle court of the temple of Rahban at Raybûn.[33] The altars were draped in fabric; weapons and other votive offerings were found leaning against the wall; large earthenware jars, libation tables, and baskets of incense cluttered the floor, which was covered with mats of palm fibers. This accumulation of objects in an interior space stands in stark contrast with the general austerity of the architecture.

Though these sanctuaries served a variety of functions, their underlying plans were generally similar. Their designs had several elements in common: an exterior of blank walls with a single side entrance, a propylaeum with several columns; and stelae and altars of similar design. While there was certainly a clear architectural evolution from the archaic temples of Jawf, with their central open-

air courtyard without *cellae,* to those of Hadramawt, with their hypostyle court and *cellae,* the two styles show profound regional differences. It is clear beyond a doubt that the Sabaeans gradually
abandoned the decorative lushness of the older style of sanctuary in
favor of the new model associated with the cult of Almaqah. Nonetheless it remains difficult to discern what influence this development may have had on the religious architecture of Hadramawt.

7. THE WORLD OF THE DEAD

The alabaster statuettes and the so-called eye stelae form the core of public and private collections; all come from the urban necropolises. The great majority of these are products of plunder or accidental discovery, and therefore it is only rarely possible to determine their exact origin. Archaeologists have been conducting digs in these tombs for many years, but they are often disappointed in their hopes of finding burial sites intact. Aside from the tombs of Hayd ibn ʿAqîl, the necropolis at Tamnaʿ, and the temple of Awwâm at Maʾrib, the architecture of burial sites remains largely unknown.

The evolution of the tombs of South Arabia is difficult to trace, in large part because the fragmented cultures of each state spawned various different types of burial sites. In general, however, it can be said that the world of the dead was kept separate from that of the living: no city had a necropolis within its confines. There are numerous examples of graves carved into cliffs surrounding the cities, as well as mausoleums, tower-tombs, and sepulchres carved right into the silt of the wadis. This variety of burial techniques suggests multiple conceptions of the beyond, probably with separate origins. One of the major difficulties faced by archaeologists is that many burial sites were recycled over the centuries, often more than once. Another problem is that the evidence excavated in these sites has not taught us much about ancient funerary rites. Even in the best of cases, the stelae with human figures rarely give even the name and geneaology of the deceased. There are no documents that mention any specific rites, only the construction and purchase of a given grave. And no literary texts exist to provide any description of the beyond or the fears that the South Arabian people may have had in the face of death.

The Heritage of the Past

The most common and most visible form of sepulchre on the edges of the desert was the round turret, but this form does not appear to have been specific to the South Arabian period. Instead it originated some time during the third to second millennia B.C. in the mountains of central Arabia. In the first millennium B.C., this type of round turret remained essentially indistinguishable from its Bronze Age predecessors.[1] These tombs were circular in construction, with a diameter of up to two meters, and ranged in height from about 0.7 to two meters. They all contained a central burial chamber built with slabs of stone laid edgewise and supporting a sloped ceiling with an opening to the outside; the walls were built of rough stone without mortar. Archaeologists have recently excavated several tombs of this type in the Ma'rib region, but the results have been unreliable since most of the tombs had already been plundered by looters. Still, some yielded useful evidence such as shells, fragments of necklaces, pieces of iron, and bone samples datable to the eighth to first centuries B.C.

Far from being isolated occurrences, these tombs have been found in fairly dense concentrations throughout the countryside. Dozens of such sites crown the ridges above Yalâ, Sirwâh, and Ma'rib, along with the main trails that connect them. In the region of Shabwa, the peaks overlooking the wadis ʿIrma and Jirdân are covered with hundreds of graves of this type, arrayed at regular intervals. Of the few that have been excavated, however, none has yet to yield material of any significance. In 1936, Saint-John Philby discovered hundreds of these graves on the summit of the escarpments of Ruwayk and ʿAlam, along the principal axes between Shabwa and Jawf.[2] A map of these sites shows how they run along the principal routes eastward from ʿIrma to Shabwa to Barâqish to upper Jawf, and southward from Sirwâh to Ma'rib to Barâqish. There is a clear connection between the geographical distribution of these burial sites and the caravans that followed these routes. This type of tomb was distinct from the kind known in the cities of South Arabia and belonged not only to a different time period but to a different culture.

Mummification of the dead seems to have been an equally ancient South Arabian tradition. The practice was known in Egypt as early as the third millennium B.C., and the people of South Arabia had the necessary materials in the form of aromatic plants, which they used for embalming the corpses of the dead, though it remains to be discovered exactly when this practice came into use in South Arabia. So-called mummies have been discovered in several different regions of Yemen, principally in the Highlands, Shibâm al-Ghirâs (northeast of Sana), Thula, Tawîla, and Mahwit. Turret tombs near Maʾrib have also yielded signs of mummification. In the two cavern-tombs of Shibâm, remains of bodies have been discovered with their viscera removed and replaced with woad; the bodies had been carefully wrapped in linen strips and then enclosed in animal hides stitched together.[3] Some clothing fragments were discovered, including ceremonial sandals with decorated thongs, other sandals for daily use, and pleated leather objects. A variety of objects had been placed around the bodies of the mummies, including miniature figures carved in wood, amulets, an iron spearhead, a leather shoulder bag, and what may have been a slingshot.[4] These tombs have been dated back to the middle of the first millennium B.C., but embalming is attested from at least the second millennium B.C. Within Yemen, the practice of mummification was confined to the mountainous regions; these rites were largely absent in the cities built around the wadis. In any case, the practice of mummification in Yemen seems to indicate that people in the remote mountainous regions were nonetheless exposed to the influence of Egyptian practices.

Cavern-Tombs

The cavern-tombs represent one of the most common burial practices in certain regions of ancient South Arabia, notably Hadramawt, where geography and geology lend themselves naturally to such a practice. The steep slopes of soft limestone which exist near the settlements are easy to cut into. Tombs of this type were first discovered at Huraydha in 1938 by the British archaeologist

Caton-Thomson.[5] She discovered a large, circular tomb buried nearly eight meters under the rock. Measuring more than eight meters in diameter, the tomb had a bench running completely around its interior. In the center some forty-two skulls were found scattered about, without their bodies; the heads belonged to adolescents between the ages of twelve and sixteen. This tomb was once thought to be the site of a ritual mass burial, but now the theory is that it is an ossuary, since no collective tomb could supply such a wide assortment of incomplete skeletons. The deceased, reduced to only their skulls, were probably committed to the earth by group or by family. The surrounding objects were mostly hemispheric bowls with tall bases, bell-shaped vases, and bowls with handles on the sides; inscribed stone pots, shells, stone beads, and other objects were also found. Caton-Thomson found another cavern-tomb nearby, which was also based on a circular plan, but only two bodies were found within, suggesting that the site had been looted at some point in the distant past. None of these tombs have yielded so much as a single statuette, but the objects that have been found indicate that the site probably dates back to the seventh to fifth centuries B.C.

Hundreds of similar tombs were cut into the hillsides above Raybûn. Among these are a group known as Raybûn-15, found near the temple of Mayfaʾân, which share several traits in common. These include smaller tombs which are nothing more than rectangular cavities with benches on both sides, and much larger ones with elevated niches on the sides. But of all these, only the tomb known as cavern-tomb 2 has allowed us to reconstruct funerary customs with any precision. It contained a dozen incense altars, millstones, all sorts of shells, fragments of bronze objects, stone carvings of human heads, stone beads, sharpening tools, a weight-stone, and an abundance of crockery—a rich trove that presents us with a fairly clear picture of the material culture of the prosperous populations of Hadramawt from the six to fourth centuries B.C.[6]

At Shabwa, the so-called hill of the dead overlooks the town from the north and northeast. The entrance, sometimes walling up several dozen tombs, is mainly visible along the sides of the hill facing the irrigated zone. Much of the site was looted long ago and is now used only for grain storage. A variety of types of tomb are represented here, including the simple underground cavity with a series of niches. So far only two have been opened up. The more interesting of the two, known as cavern-tomb 1, has an outer vestibule that had been meticulously framed with a compartmentalized façade of rectangular wooden panels which were carved with decorative sculptures and originally painted red.[7] Beyond this, there was a narrow wooden doorway and several steps down to the first underground chamber, which was divided into two parts, and then to a second chamber cut 2.6 meters into the rock below. Bones and broken jars found scattered within this related shaft suggest that they were thrown down in successive periods, perhaps to make room for new arrivals. This discovery lends strong credence to the theory that burial sites were used again and again during the South Arabian era. Unfortunately, this practice has hampered archaeologists' efforts to study the evolution of burial practices, since remains of the deceased were systematically discarded along with the objects that had been buried with them.

This way of carving out graves was also common in the Highlands. The tombs around Sana are easily located by a rectangular entrance set high enough to be out of reach of passersby. The best known series is at Shibâm al-Ghirâs, flanking the road to Ma'rib. It was here that the first so-called mummies were exhumed. To the east, similar tombs line the cliffs of Shibâm-Kawkabân, Hababa, and Tawîla. Not far from Dhamaar lies the tomb of Hirrân, a vast underground structure with several chambers all opening onto a central hall.[8] The great majority of these graves have been looted, but certain graves in the Mahwit region are awaiting excavation and thorough examination.[9]

Mausoleums

Some relatively impressive tombs have been discovered in the areas outside the metropolises of South Arabia, and the quality of the objects in these sites has long attracted the attention of travelers, not to mention looters. The necropolis of Tamnaᶜ, a vast burial complex comprising tombs, a temple, and a well, was built on the peak of Hayd Ibn ꜥAqîl just north of the city.[10] The mausoleums begin at the base of the hill and continue up the slope for nearly forty-five meters. The architecture is terraced, with entrance at a steep grade. Set side-by-side, they formed a great suite which was divided by a central hallway with steps. The mausoleums were all rectangular in shape and consisted of a central hallway with a series of four to eight connecting rooms along the sides. Each compartment was divided into at least three superposed loculi which opened into the central hall. The loculi were separated by slabs of schist supported by small blocks which projected from the inner surfaces of the walls. The vaults were 1.5 to 2 meters long, with just enough room for the deceased and their items; the opening was permanently sealed with a stone slab. These were family tombs not unlike those found in numerous regions of the Near East.

At the base of these tombs archaeologists have discovered an entire suite of buildings and a sanctuary. At the lowest point is a burial temple flanked by a deep pit into which families threw small funerary busts, incense altars, and other objects like those found in the graves. The presence of this pit is exceptional; the only other known example of such a pit is at Samhar, in Zafar. Climbing uphill from the temple, one next encounters a mausoleum with benches made of unfired brick, followed by a second temple of very modest dimensions with a *cella* preceded by a portico with six monolithic pillars. This was a burial sanctuary where the faithful came to perform rites connected to the cult of the dead. Among their offerings were statuettes with inscribed bases bearing texts that would begin, "This [object] was left by [so-and-so]."

The task of dating this vast burial complex is complicated; some scholars have argued that its oldest buildings and vases may go back to the seventh century B.C.,[11] while others note that most of the stelae and alabaster heads are from the first century B.C. to the first century A.D.

Outside of Tamnaꜥ, the most remarkable funerary monuments have been found at Maʾrib. The most outstanding example is surely the one built up against the wall of the temple of Awwâm. The site was excavated in 1951 and has since been entirely covered over with sand. The structure was about eight meters to a side, with a thick surrounding wall broken by a single doorway.[12] Inside is a burial chamber about four meters high with a ceiling of stone slabs supported by pillars with dentiled capitals. The sides are lined with three rows of meticulously constructed tombs, most of which are between 1.4 and 1.8 meters long, though some are only about 0.9 meters long (perhaps for children). The tombs were sealed with finely crafted stone slabs inscribed with the names of the deceased. About sixty of these tombs were stacked in tiers right to the ceiling. The mausoleum also contains a crypt carved into the rock. The names of two sovereigns appear on the enclosing stones, suggesting the possibility that this was a royal burial place.

About a hundred meters south of this mausoleum, American archaeologists have uncovered part of an extensive burial complex comprising one or more buildings with rows of adjacent burial chambers linked by a network of connecting passageways. These chambers measure from two to three meters to a side with walls up to six meters high and stacked with burial vaults. Though these were all looted long ago, perhaps in ancient times, they have nonetheless yielded objects and texts dating back to the eighth to seventh centuries B.C. Three other massive structures were discovered in 1997.[13] These well-built structures are veritable tower-tombs; the façade was plain with the exception of burial masks, some done in relief, others carved in the round. Some of the stone slabs that sealed the vaults are hollowed out in the center, with an alabaster funerary head set within and sealed with mortar. In these few towers, at least 166 people were buried along with their miniature incense altars, figurines, and crockery. Several ostraka mention the name of the deceased along with his or her lineage and tribal affiliation.

This type of funerary architecture has parallels in the Hellenistic or Greco-Roman east; the most accomplished and best-known parallels are the tower-tombs of Palmyra, whose chambers were packed from floor to ceiling with loculi.[14] These were family tombs which may have housed members of several generations while assuring the durability of individual graves. The most sumptuous of the towers, namely those of Jamblique and Elahbêl, are from the end of the first century A.D.; their predecessors date back as least as far as the first century B.C. While the earliest origins of the "houses of the dead" remain obscure, some historians have claimed that they were designed to resemble the houses of the living. There are not many significant examples to go by, however, other than a few massive and tall structures, and some scholars have concluded that the style of tower known in Palmyra is related to that of the mausoleums of western Syria. In South Arabia, the similarity between tower-houses and tower-tombs which apparently date back to the sixth or seventh century B.C. has opened up a fascinating new avenue of research. It is possible, moreover, that Assyria may have served as a way station in the diffusion of this type of monumental architecture into South Arabia.

Evidence on the cost of construction of this type of tomb is sparse. In Palmyra, a founding member of a family would typically erect a monument at his own expense and would proudly bequeath it to his successors. In Maʾrib, it is unknown whether associations were formed to cover the cost of construction or whether a single wealthy person would bear the cost of building a monument and then perhaps resell shares. Numerous surviving texts mention the acquisition of a quarter, third, or half a burial chamber: for example, a certain Abîʾamar acquired and built a quarter of his suite of three burial chambers; another person bought one level of loculi. Because of the high cost of building tower-tombs in ancient Maʾrib, it was probably common for several people to pool their resources in such ventures.

Images of the Dead

A variety of objects were left as offerings by families to accompany their dead; these items tended to be small, since tombs were generally narrow and cramped. Incense altars were common, and these were cube-shaped and never more than 12 centimeters high; among other typical offerings were bronze plates and statuettes, miniature ladles, small makeup boxes, and tiny ceramic or steatite vases. The body of the deceased was thus surrounded by objects from daily life, and presumably these were intended to accompany the dead in the afterlife. Another common object was the small stela, either entirely made of alabaster or consisting of a plate of alabaster inserted into a limestone base.[15]

The great majority of burial offerings were portraits. It has long been debated whether these images represented gods or the deceased, but it seems certain now that the names which frequently accompany these images are indeed those of the deceased. These objects show a stunning variety in appearance—a head with a long neck, mounted on an inscribed base; busts on pediments, statuettes of men in prayer; stelae in the shape of plates, probably designed to seal loculi—but these items are difficult to date with any precision. Long-necked heads mounted on inscribed cubes seem to have been common in the classical Sabaean and Qatabanite period. The Qatabanite regions have yielded numerous examples of alabaster statues mounted on pediments inscribed with the name of the deceased, and these are most likely from the classical period.[16] They are similarly rendered, with thickset figures, somewhat ungraceful proportions, and fixed traits, with "mechanical" poses; their clothing, if rendered at all, is reduced to a simple robe. The figures are identified by names like Labû, Hayw, Abîyada, ʿAmmîʾalî, and Ilîshara. Also commonly found at burial sites in Saba and Qatabân from the classical period is the niche with a burial mask, usually flat and rectangular in shape, with an alabaster head; the mask was sealed either in a limestone niche or in a slab of stone that was used to seal a loculus.

Numerous plaques with portraits have been found, and these are generally dated to the period between the first century B.C. and the first century A.D. These objects can be distinguished from their predecessors by a generally higher quality of execution, with more graceful rendering of clothing and more careful treatment of jewelry and arms. Notable among this series of items are the so-called goddess plaques presumably representing dedicants.[17] In these objects, the way the clothing drapes upon the breasts is similar to the so-called wet-drape of certain important statues in the Greco-Roman style. The plaque known (falsely) as "plaque to the young god" actually represents a certain Gawthʾîl son of ʿAsm, who is shown in profile wearing a flowing tunic and ornamental bracelet; he is armed with a dagger and long sword.

Incontestably the most remarkable among all known pieces are the alabaster heads with disproportionately large eyes inlaid with colored stones or glass. These figures have grooved eyebrows highlighted with paint or bitumen; the mouth is narrow, and a beard is often suggested by black stippling. The absence of the top of the head can be explained by the addition of hair that had been separately cast in mortar and painted; proof of this explanation, if any is needed, comes from numerous examples of intact heads which exist in private collections. The most celebrated example of these heads is known as Myriam (shown on the cover [of the French edition] of this book); she was discovered in 1950 in the necropolis of Hayd Ibn ʿAqîl. Her eyes are inlaid lapis lazuli held in place by a layer of bluish paste; presumably, earrings once dangled from her ears, and a necklace hung from two holes in the sides of her head. Her hair is made of plaster and falls down around her face in carefully arranged curls.

A Final Dwelling Place

An encouraging amount of evidence has become available for the ancient necropolises, and these objects—including numerous inscriptions and images, reliefs, stelae, busts, incense altars, and crockery—now await detailed analysis.

Burial sites contain plenty of crockery but so far there is no evidence of perishable items like food remnants that might have been left to accompany the deceased on the long journey to the afterlife. Archaeologists are thus forced to piece together the everyday environment of the deceased through close examination of the small personal artifacts that remain in the grave sites. The most common type of object is the stela inscribed with the name of the deceased; however, it is still unclear whether these objects were intended to portray the subject's image literally (as in the western Semitic peoples) or merely symbolically. The term that shows up most frequently, at least in Tamnaᶜ, is *mʾmr*, or "[final] dwelling place." The family's main concern was therefore likely to have been to honor the deceased by providing a durable place of burial, since the grave was the dead person's final place of residence, which he or she would never leave. That said, there is nothing in the inscriptions to suggest that any part of the human "soul" or "essence" (known as the personal *nefesh*) was capable of surviving in detachment from its earthly body. The *m³mr* was considered eternal, and there was no hope of any subsequent abode.

Burial of the Dead in the Silt

The available evidence suggests that mausoleums and other stone burial places were constructed by the well-off, while the poorest were generally interred beneath the alluvial deposits. Burial sites of this latter type have left few traces in the ground, though several have been excavated in Hadramawt. The largest known necropolis lies to the south of the town of Raybûn.[18] The most unusual tombs contain a series of shallow trenches arrayed along their entire length; the dead were placed in these graves, which were then covered with stone slabs. If a corpse was too tall for a particular grave, then the legs would be folded at the knees. The objects that have been exhumed from these grave sites—an iron dagger, shells, a leather water-skin, iron bracelets—bear witness to the humble status of their occupants.

Numerous graves of this type have been discovered in the Wadi Dura³, east of the Wadi Markha, and all of these were extremely modest. Bodies were generally laid directly in the ground, without a coffin, and accompanied by very few objects: a typical grave would contain two small pots, one alabaster, the other ceramic, placed near the head of the deceased. Tombs of more prosperous people contained more elaborate objects such as bronze ladles, fragments of metal swords, and vases with curved rims. In the necropolis of Hajar adh-Dhaybiyya, however, people of high social status were buried in simple graves without a coffin, with their weapons and tools of bronze, glass, and alabaster.[19] The graves were covered over with several dozen centimeters of silt. The graves would be reopened to accommodate other burials in a curious custom which seems to have been adopted by nomadic tribes rather than by the settled urban populations of South Arabia.

The Tombs of Camels

Camels played a major role in the economy of ancient South Arabia, but it is only in recent times that we have discovered tombs designed especially for them. The practice of burying camels is known to have existed in certain regions of the peninsula of Oman in the third millennium B.C., and this practice was known to have spread gradually along the coast of the Persian Gulf in the latter part of the first millennium B.C. There is now abundant evidence that camels acccompanied their masters even in death. This is surely one of the more peculiar funerary customs of South Arabia.

Approximately thirty camel graves are known, some at Raybûn and others on the high plateaus of Hadramawt on the sites of Balas and Baat. These mainly date to the final centuries B.C. and the first centuries A.D., and are the product of both nomadic and sedentary populations.[20] They contain complete skeletons which were laid to rest in either of two ways. Some lie on their side, with the legs folded up and the head and neck turned back; others are simply kneeling, with the neck always to the left. In a few rare cases, the head has been cut off and placed between the animal's legs. In some cases, the neck and pelvis are missing, perhaps removed for eating. In all cases, though, strenuous effort must have been required to dig such a large hole and put the animal in it.

It is surprising that some camels were intentionally decapitated before their death. Seven tombs at Raybûn include skeletons of camels with their heads cut off and separated from the body (or perhaps replaced with a stone). The animal was (presumably) led into the grave and forced to kneel, at which point its rear legs were hobbled, before the animal was decapitated. Ancient inscriptions are unfortunately mute on the details of this bloody ritual, so we are forced to examine the similar practices of Bedouin tribes in more recent times.[21] The Bedouins preferred camels to small livestock. The age and sex of the camel seems to have been unimportant, though they preferred white over black. Evidently without much attention to where the sacrifices were performed or to the formulas of the specific rites, the Bedouins simply turned the camel's head to face Mecca, cut its throat, and drained the blood into a receptacle for use in painting decorative motifs. Sacrifices of this kind took place throughout the year according to the rhythms of the agricultural seasons, feasts, pilgrimages, or other major events. Local divinities were invoked, as were supernatural spirits, astral divinities, and mythical figures. The symbolism of these sacrifices didn't focus on the deceased themselves: "The sacrifices for the dead were far from an expression of a true cult of the dead, but instead represented a continuation of the social obligations beyond the grave."[22] Unfortunately, no surviving text sheds light on this practice as it might have been conducted in the final centuries B.C. and first centuries A.D.

Men and their camels were sometimes joined in burial, either in the same burial site, in neighboring tombs, or perhaps within the same necropolis. In the first case, the dead person would be laid in the pit and his animal would be placed right on top of him.[23] The animal was considered part of his master's personal property and was therefore buried along with the other objects in the tomb. In the second case, the graves of camel and master lay side by side. Finally, in the case of the temple of Mayfaʾan, the graves of camels were situated at the base of the cavern-tombs, along the cliffs near the temple.[24] The objects found in these tombs, like those found in eastern Hadramawt, consist mainly of knives, razors, daggers, and spear tips—cutting implements useful for slaughtering the animal. These tools provide an indication of the social status of the deceased. In a context where camel graves were fairly rare, it appears that the social status of the deceased was measured by the number of camels that accompanied him in death.[25]

Later Burial Practices

The types of burial described above suggest a distinct evolution from the Sabaean and Qatabanite mausoleums, and attest to political and social changes in South Arabia over the course of its history.

From the second century B.C. on, nomadic populations of Arab origins progressively settled in the great wadis of South Arabia, and as these settlers gradually became more sedentary, they introduced new ways of life as well as different religious conceptions. This progression is clearly attested in numerous texts found in Jawf, and though the textual evidence is rarer in the wadis Bayhân, Markha, and Dura', changes in ancient burial practices provide an indicator of demographic changes in these regions. In the Highlands, the tribes played a growing role, and some eventually formed a new confederation centered around the tribe of Himyar. During the first century A.D., Saba remained under the protection of Himyar, a sign of the generally weakening influence of the tribes bordering the desert. South Arabia's exposure to influences from the coastal areas was a harbinger of the coming flood of Greco-Roman culture, and local artists readily adopted these new styles.

From the first century A.D. onward, burial customs reflected these new influences, especially those of the nomadic populations. These new arrivals did not built new mausoleums, but instead just reused existing ones; they did not carve new cavern-tombs in the limestone, but simply took over the ones they found. A new style of very simplified stela, commonly known as "eye stelae," is generally attributed to these relative latecomers; some were made of wood, generally from Jawf, but most were made of stone and came from the Wadi Bayhân.[26] Hayd Ibn ꜥAqîl, the necropolis of Tamnaꜥ, has yielded a large number of these small, oblong slabs of limestone in a prominent frame enclosing a carved image of two immense eyes with highly accentuated brows, a very long nose, and a tiny mouth. The nose and mouth disappear entirely to make room for the eyes in some cases. The northern Arab origins of many of these people is attested in the names of the dedicants, which differ significantly from those of the old Qatabanite tribes.[27] Curiously, none of these so-called eye stelae have been discovered in Shabwa or Hadramawt. The new Arab populations seem to have preferred interment. The burial sites of the Wadi Dura', where warrior chiefs were buried with their precious crockery and weapons, have been mentioned above. Examples of yet another type of grave, built out of a framework of stone slabs imbedded in the silt and fitted

with a paved floor, have been discovered in the Wadi Dura? (at
al-Huwaydar), the Wadi Markha (at Hajar Tâlib) near the edge of
the desert, and also near ad-Dâli? in the Highlands. The latter necropolis, which dates from the first century B.C., has yielded some
unusual evidence, particularly a group of votive offerings carved
out of alabaster or limestone in the shape of human arms, legs, feet,
and even female breasts. Stelae with human figures or with the
heads of bulls have also been discovered there. The most remarkable statuette, known as the Lady of ad-Dâli?, shows the slightly
stilted pose common to archaic statuary but with the addition of
necklaces and pendants which were in fashion at the time.[28] A burial temple can be found in almost every necropolis of this type, in
accordance with very ancient tradition.

The diffusion of these items, which are sometimes related to
burial rites, clearly coincides with the opening of South Arabia to
the Greco-Roman world. Some examples depict a seated figure or a
figure reclining on a ceremonial couch, surrounded by musicians
and perhaps servants or children. Architectural elements include
fluted columns (rather than the older pillars) surmounted with
acanthus (rather than dentiled) capitals supporting an arch; the
corners are covered with vine leaves or foliage. These elements, in
a flat and linear style, evoke Syrian models from the first and second centuries A.D., and indeed South Syria was the source of the
greatest possible variety of sculpture and ornamental stone carvings from that point onward.[29] The Greco-Roman Orient also offered new utensils designed for use in funeral banquets, from
bronze ladles to silver or bronze water-drawers, dishes with orna-
mented handles, bowls with handles in the shape of hands, and
incense shovels.[30] Without exception, every town produced local
copies with inscriptions, and every metropolis built its own banquet hall in the Greco-Roman style.[31] In the last centuries B.C., the
world of the dead was continually exposed to the new influences
from abroad, opening up new horizons of funerary practice.

8. TOWARD NEW HORIZONS

When the power of Rome supplanted that of the Seleucids in Syria and the Ptolemies in Egypt, one of the main goals of Roman leaders was to control the distant routes to the south. If Rome ultimately fell short of conquering the lands of frankincense, its leaders did manage to link the coasts of Hadramawt, whose immense horizons stretched from the Red Sea and the Strait of Bab al-Mandab all the way to the Indian Ocean as far as the island of Socotra. As profits from the caravan trade began to diminish, the states along the edges of the ancient caravan routes were drawn toward the Highlands, and particularly to the new federation known as Himyar. Under the pressure of Arab nomadic populations descending from the northeast, the kingdom of Saba began to move westward toward the central Highlands, where it created a new capital at Sana.

The Rise of Himyar

The mountainous regions of Yemen were not entirely isolated from the tide of history during South Arabia's archaic and classical periods. The Sabaeans were early participants in the onslaught upon these fertile regions; from around the seventh century B.C., large numbers of Sabaean colonists, soldiers, and minor officials began to settle in the region around the city of Sana and north all the way to Khamir. The cult of Almaqah was so well established in this region, which originally belonged to the Bâkil tribe, that the Temple at Alaw, above Shibâm-Kawkabân, bore the name of Awwâm—the same name as at Ma'rib. Bakîl may also have been considered a Sabaean tribe.[1] In the centuries that followed (a time that is better understood because of the large number of surviving inscriptions), the region saw a rise in power among original tribal alliances. The tribes of Sumʾay, to the north and northeast of Sana, gradually came together with those in Arhab and Nihim, and the resulting confederation created its own kings and political institutions, its own system of dating through eponyms, even its own gods, Taʾlab and Nawash. But like Bakîl, Sumʾay eventually came under Sabaean domination. Saba also exercised its influence over a host of minor tribes in the area of Sana, including the Ghaymân, the Simhân, and Fayshân, the latter being destined for a significant role in later history, as will be described below. The Sabaeans founded the city of Sana some time in the middle of the first century A.D. (local legends suggested an earlier date).

The territorial expansion of Saba was checked from the south by a loose confederation of tribes in the mountainous regions of Dhamar and Yarîm. This confederation was organized by several local leaders who were rivals for power amongst themselves; for reasons that are now obscure, the Himyarites, a modest tribe of Qatabanite origins, gradually emerged as the dominant tribe. It is not precisely known exactly where the Himyar tribe originated, or what its importance was in earlier times, but the tribe became increasingly cohesive over time. Their leaders were based at the fortress of Raydân in Zafar, several kilometers southeast of Yarîm.[2] Gradually there arose a regional power headed by the line known as "dhû-Raydân," or "of Raydan," which controlled the entire Dhamar Plain up to the Yaslah Pass. The new confederation differed from its archaic predecessor in that it was organized around allegiance to a common ruler, rather than the cult of a divinity (as in the cult of ʿAthtar). The territory was established as an independent principality some time around 110 B.C., and thereafter began a steady expansion westward into the mountains beyond their watershed, and northward, where it clashed with tribes that were still under Sabaean domination. The final break came in the final decades of the first century B.C., when the leaders of Raydân proclaimed themselves "kings of Saba and dhû-Raydân" rather than only dhû-Raydân. The simplest explanation for this change is that the Himyarite dynasty had by then succeeded in seizing the kingdom of Saba.

The factors behind the success of the Himyarites remain obscure. One clear advantage was their location in the heart of so-called Green Yemen, the prosperous land of the Dhamar Plain and its environs, where abundant rainfall (averaging more than 400 centimeters annually at Dhamar and more than 900 at Yarim) and fertile soil are capable of sustaining intensive agriculture and animal breeding.[3] The introduction of the horse some time in the first century A.D. doubtless had fateful consequences for the entire region.[4] The rapid development of cavalry units, first light-armored and later heavy cavalry, helped lead Himyar to decisive military success. Also, it has been suggested that Himyar's agricultural prosperity attracted populations from around the edges of the desert, where Arab incursions compounded the problem of diminishing productivity of ancient irrigated lands. However, this theory cannot be proved either by evidence of foundations of newer buildings or by the rapid expansion of pre-Himyarite villages.[5]

The power of Himyar was clearly due to a tightly organized tribal system that ensured the cohesion of the agricultural lands of small tribes (*sha'ab*) while providing extensive and well-maintained estates for the notables or chiefs (*qayls*), who had the right to impose taxes and levy troops from among their tenants. The *qayls* formed a separate, homogeneous social category and represented an entirely new force in tribal society. The social hierachy of the Highland tribes was highly adaptable and cohesive, in contrast with the vast states that rimmed the deserts below. Roman authors, who by this time had become fairly well informed observers, duly noted the rise of the Himyarites within this context. Pliny's statement that the Himyarites were very numerous was probably derived from information gathered during the first century B.C.[6] A later source refers to Zafar as a large metropolis whose sovereign, Charibaël, was the legitimate king of two tribes known as the Homerites (Himyarites) and the Sabaeans.[7] The balance of power had thus been reversed, with Saba reduced to a mere neighbor—a presitigious neighbor, to be sure, but one of secondary importance.

The Royal Tribe of Saba

Originally, the term Saba designated a community organized around the cult of Almaqah and only secondarily the territory it occupied in and around Maʾrib. With the expansion of Saba in the seventh century B.C., the term was replaced by the phrase "the descendants of Almaqah" and referred collectively to all of the groups who worshiped the god. As a unified community, Saba forged pacts of union which were celebrated principally at the sanctuaries of Jabal al-Lawdh. The sovereigns held the title of mukarrib. Over the course of the centuries, the name Saba began to denote the web of social groups governed by the kings of Maryab (Maʾrib); this entity became known collectively as "Saba and the tribes," a phrase which indicated the superiority of the royal tribe of Saba over all others.

    In the final centuries B.C., the nature of royal power at Saba underwent a transformation as it came to be defined less by belief in the gods and their rites, and more by personal allegiance to the king.[8] This gradual evolution seems to have been related to the emergence of the Highland tribes and the weakening of power among the old tribes that had long occupied the edges of the desert. This changing balance of power had the effect of further weakening the Sabaean royalty, and the status of the king fell roughly in line with that of the great tribal chiefs. An inscription dating from the early first century B.C. records that a king of Maryab referred to his subjects as "Saba and Fayshân." This inscription, though fragmentary, illustrates a changed political scenario in which the king's status had been effectively reduced to that of prince, and Saba had become merely one tribe among others. The king had authority over two tribes which in reality amounted to a single tribe. The Fayshân tribe were originally from the Sana plateau in the Highlands; they lived in Sana, in Shuʾûb to the north, and in Shibâm-Kawkabân.[9] It remains to be discovered exactly how these people, who began as a minor clan or perhaps a small tribe among the Sabaeans, achieved their rise to the top of the tribal hierarchy, but they eventually forged an alliance with Saba to form a single tribe. At the time of their union, "Saba" supposedly still referred to the

old Sabaean aristocracy from which the royal family was descended, while the members of the Fayshân tribe had been the king's
subjects.

Of the frequent changes in tribal composition toward the end of
the first century B.C., few were favorable to Saba. Three reasons can
be gleaned from the historical record: pressure from nomadic tribes
along the frontiers of the Sabaen domain; the Roman expedition of
26–25 B.C., which brought troops to the very gates of Ma'rib; and
the rising power of Hadramawt. Some scholars argue that these
circumstances caused Saba to retreat westward and seek protection in Himyar. Himyar was certainly a dominant power, and Saba
wound up in a position of dependence, allowing the Himyarite
sovereigns to lay claim to the royal title. The kings of "Saba and
dhû-Raydân," as they came to be known, now presided over the
traditional ceremonies in celebration of pacts of union at Jabal al-
Lawdh—a renewal of a traditional honor that certainly bolstered
their prestige. Ma'rib lost its privileged status as sole capital of Saba
after the city of Sana was also named a capital. A royal palace,
known as Ghumdân, was soon built in Sana, and its splendor must
have rivaled that of the old Salhîn castle at Ma'rib. Yemeni poets
sang its praises:

> Behold the proud Ghumdân, a sight for sore eyes; it rises twenty stories
> to the very roof of the sky; its towers are swathed in a turban of clouds.
> Its mantle is of marble, its belt is of alabaster, its brocade is of onyx.
> Behold its copper roof whose corners are decorated with eagles and
> lions. Its crowning treasure is a clepsydra that measures the day and
> the night.[10]

The Arrival of the Nomads

Groups of Arabic-speaking peoples commonly known as Arabs had
long inhabited the lands skirting the natural borders of the South
Arabian states; these neighbors had a long history of cooperation in
all sorts of pastoral, agricultural, and caravan-related activities. But
South Arabia's fertile oases and the wealth of its cities gradually

lured the nomads closer and closer to the heart of the South Arabia domain.

The oldest surviving texts concerning the Arab peoples date from about the sixth century B.C. and describe them as pastoral nomads, in distinction from the sedentary peoples who occupied the irrigated lands.[11] Since the Arabs generally remained apart and did not interfere in the daily or religious life of the cities, they were not seen as a menace. South Arabians seem to have made no distinction between the terms "nomad" and "Arab," and the latter essentially meant "shepherd". Saba maintained regular relations with only two Arab tribes, the Najrân and the Amîr. The military campaigns led by Karib'îl Watar against the Muha'mir and Amîr tribes, the main camel breeders of the Najrân region, were described in chapter two. Karib'îl Watar was reported to have captured large numbers of camels and cattle during these two campaigns, but despite his success, one of his successors saw fit to launch new expeditions against these particularly unruly tribes.[12] It was during this period that the history of cooperation between the South Arabian states and their neighbors finally deteriorated into outright conflict.

The tribes of the Jawf valley had always maintained friendly relations with their neighbors to the northwest, in large part because of their geographical proximity. Members of the tribes in Jawf had begun migrating northwest as early as the second century B.C., and presumably they settled initially in the eastern cities of Ma'în and Inabba', though archaeologists have found no traces of this migration. Curiously, it is the city of Haram, in the interior of this region, that has yielded the earliest evidence of such a migration. The great sanctuary to Matabnatyân was adapted to the cult of Halfân, at which point even its name was changed, to Arathat.[13] The earlier, Madhabian-speaking population of the city was evidently replaced, at least in part, by new arrivals who probably spoke a version of Arabic mixed with Sabaean. These Arabs brought with them the new divinities of Halfân and dhû-Samawî, who replaced the earlier gods. Finally, the king was replaced with a tribal assembly. These profound changes ushered in a new era of increased contacts with the nomadic world. After recovering Jawf, the Arabs slowly began to settle in Kaminahû (Kamna), Nashshân (al-Baydâ), and Manhiyat (Hizmat Abû Thawr). This settlement was achieved gradually and not without resistance; combat took the form of ongoing skirmishes rather than pitched battles.[14] In the region of Ma'rib, the Arabs also forged increasing contact with the Sabaeans, to the point where a sanctuary was reserved exclusively for their use within the capital. In the Qatabanite regions, comprising the area between the wadis Bayhân and Dura', there are several indications of slow infiltrations by these nomadic peoples. A superb bronze plaque found at Tamna^c and dating back to the first century B.C. bears a dedicatory inscription by the Qatabanites to the god dhû-Samawî, a divinity associated with the Arab Amîr tribe; requesting the god's protection of a camel whose image is represented in the center of the plaque. The existence of such an artifact suggests that these two populations had united around the same cult.[15] Certain settlements consisting of small houses arranged in circular formation have also been attributed to these immigrant populations: ceramics found at these sites date from the first century B.C. to the first century A.D.

A curious parallel to this ancient migration can be found in certain valleys of Yemen in modern times. The arrival of nonnative populations has been felt in the Wadi Markha around the site of Hajar Yahirr, the ancient capital of Awsân, which until 1975 had remained virtually uninhabited, with a single well irrigating an orchard in the area around Dhât al-Jar. Slowly but surely, so-called Bedouin setters began arriving in this area with their goats and camels. At first they lived in simple tents, but soon they began fencing them off with barbed wire and transforming their dwellings into huts built out of fallen branches, wooden planks, and corrugated steel. Within the next ten years, about a dozen wells were sunk, and the newcomers began planting alfalfa and legumes. The appropriation of this originally desolate land culminated in the construction of more solid homes and small shops. Needless to say, the settlement caused problems with other tribes in the region—problems which persist to this day.

After successfully infiltrating the valleys of Yemen, the Arabs began to settle in the Highlands during the first century A.D. The older tribes, including the Hashîd and the Yusram, who had long inhabited the area north of Sana, were experiencing increasing pressure along their borders. The wave of migrant Arabs gathered force until the Sabaean state was menaced from all sides; the result was a proliferation of hostile encounters between Arabs and South Arabians. There is evidence of several attempts at mediation during this period, including one instance in which a king of Saba led a successful effort to recruit auxiliary troops of nomads who had sought refuge in the desert or in Jawf. But by the second century the entire region was embroiled in conflict, and the outcome was not always favorable to the South Arabians. Certain states adopted a strategy of enrolling Arabs as auxiliaries whenever possible—a strategy similar to the Roman army's use of cavalry units including the famous Palmyrian archers. Some South Arabian states even deployed Arab auxiliaries in internal conflicts. This use of Arabs in warfare had the effect of gradually introducing Arabs to the customs of South Arabian society.

The Roman Army in South Arabia

The Roman expedition into South Arabia of 26–25 B.C. took place within troubled circumstances. In the aftermath of the Battle of Actium (31 B.C.), in which the emperor Augustus had taken possession of Egypt, he conceived a plan to extend Roman domination into the Red Sea and reconnoiter its farthest shores. His mission to explore Arabia Felix was founded on a desire to end the monopoly the people of this remote country had long exercised over the trade in aromatic products. To this end Augustus mustered two legions—some ten thousand troops—and contingents from Judea and Nabataea, and placed them all under the command of Aelius Gallus, prefect of Egypt.

In 26 B.C., the contingent crossed the Red Sea and landed at Leukê Kômê (probably the ancient name for modern-day Qarna or al-Wajh), about 300 kilometers south of Petra.[16] Having encountered difficulties at sea, the army of Aelius Gallus rested at Leukê Kômê for the summer and winter of 25 B.C. before moving southward past Yathrîb (Medina) to the area around Mecca. After six months they arrived at the threshold of the South Arabian domain. Strabo described the trip in detail:

> He spent fifty days, arriving at the city of the Negrani [Najrân] and at a country which was both peaceable and fertile. Now the king had fled and the city was seized at the first onset; and from there he arrived at the river [Wadi Madhâb] in six days. Here the barbarians joined battle with the Romans, and about ten thousand of them fell, but only two Romans; for they used their weapons in an inexperienced manner, being utterly unfit for war, using bows and spears and swords and slings, though most of them used a double-edged axe; and immediately afterwards he took the city called Asca [Nashq], which had been forsaken by its king; and thence he went to a city called Athrula [Yathill = Barâqish]; and, having mastered it without a struggle, he placed a garrison in it, arranged for supplies of grain and dates for his march, advanced to a city called Marsiaba [Maʾrib], which belonged to the tribe of the Rhammanitae, who were subject to Ilasarus [Ilîsharah]. Now he assaulted and besieged this city for six days, but for want of water desisted. He was indeed only a two days' journey from the country that produced aromatics, as informed by his captives, but he had used up six months' time on his marches because of bad guidance, and he realized the fact when he turned back, when at last he had learned the plot against him and had gone back by other roads; for on the ninth day he arrived at Negrana, where the battle had taken place . . . and thence, at least, marching through a peaceful country . . . and then through a desert country, which had only a few watering places, as far as a village called Egra [and its port city of Leukê Kômê]. This village is in the territory of Obodas; and it is situated on the sea. On his return he accomplished the whole journey within sixty days, although he had used up six months in his first journey. . . . This expedition did not profit us to a great extent in our knowledge of those regions, but still it made a slight contribution. But the man who was responsible for this failure, I mean Syllaeus, paid the penalty at Rome, since, although he pretended friendship, he was convicted, in addition to his rascality in this matter, of other offences too, and was beheaded.[17]

(A scapegoat was required, and Syllaeus, the organizer of the expedition, fit the bill.) Pliny's version is much briefer:

Aelius Gallus, a member of the Order of Knights, is the only person who has hitherto carried the arms of Rome into this country; for Gaius Caesar son of Augustus only had a glimpse of Arabia. Gallus destroyed the following towns not named by the authors who have written previously—Negrana, Nestus, Nesca [Nashq], Magasus, Caminicus [Kaminahû], Labaetia; as well as Maʾrib above mentioned, which measure six miles around, and also Caripeta [Hinû az-Zurayr, near Harîb], which was the farthest point he reached.[18]

This was certainly the southernmost point ever attained by Roman troops. The emperor Augustus tersely celebrated the achievement as follows: "In Arabia the army advanced into the territories of the Sabaei to the town of Mariba."[19]

Without going into this campaign in detail, certain facts should nonetheless be clarified. The Romans unquestionably had at their disposal a superior army of skilled tacticians and forces trained to fight on open terrain; they were experienced in siege tactics, and no adversary was their equal in military terms. Najrân was defended by nomads who were, at best, inexpert in the art of war, and Barâqish was partially abandoned. Maʾrib, with its 4.5 kilometers of defensive walls, was more difficult to take, and the Roman army, weakened by their long journey and by illnesses, lifted their siege after six days. The absence of the Sabaean king from Maʾrib remains somewhat enigmatic, as does the presence of the Rhammanites, who have been identified with the Aryumân tribe. It is possible that the Himyarites may have dominated Saba and that the king resided at Zafar. In any event, it is clear that the Sabaean kingdom was seriously weakened by the time of the Roman invasion.

South Arabian texts are silent on the subject of the Roman expedition, despite the fact that the Roman army stayed for several months in certain cities such as Barâqish. Some soldiers, including a certain Cornelius Publius Eques, apparently died there and were buried in the necropolis southwest of the city.[20] Some of these soldiers must have been on somewhat neighborly terms with the locals, at least to the point of being able to get supplies; others must have left behind tools or other objects that were subsequently copied by local artisans; and surely some became familiar with local customs and the organization of the caravans. Ultimately, the main outcome of the Roman expedition was an increase in knowledge about the region, as is clear from an attempt to create a "full assessment" intended principally for use in governing back at Rome.[21] Strabo, the first writer to respond systematically to the need for geographical information, was conscientious about listing city names and describing the natural resources of different areas, the weapons used by the inhabitants, and the critical role of the Red Sea in regional commerce.

New Horizons beyond the Sea

Strabo's account makes it clear that the real goal of Augustus' expedition was to gain control of the Strait of Bab al-Mandab, where "the Arabian Gulf, which separates the Arabians from the Troglodytes, is extremely narrow. Accordingly he [Augustus] planned either to compel the Arabs to be Rome's allies or to conquer their territory outright."[22] Aelius Gallus wasted a lot of time building a naval fleet whose first mission was to transport troops to Leukê Kômê. This may have been the same fleet that tried to strike against Aden. Unfortunately the details of Augustus' actions in this arena are still poorly understood.

This political situation nonetheless was the result of a long development in maritime trade in the Red Sea. Sailors had been venturing into these waters for more than a century, and ships had long used the famous Strait of Bab al-Mandab in journeys between Egypt and India. But the Arabs had always served as essential intermediaries, for it was necessary to transship merchandise at Aden since boats from India could not go all the way to Egypt. Around 177 B.C., a sailor named Eudoxus of Cyzicus made his first voyage with the aid of two sea pilots, an Indian and a Greek named Hippalos. They set sail from the southern Red Sea and continued through the Strait of Bab al-Mandab into the Gulf of Aden; they then left the coast for Cape Guardafui (on the Somalian coast) and thence directly to India, where they made landfall at Barygaza (Broach, on the Gulf of Cambay). On the Red Sea, they made use of currents and prevailing winds from the north during the month of July; on their return in January, the winter winds blew them back home. Emboldened by the success of this first expedition, Eudoxus went on to lead two more trips between 117 and 109 B.C.[23] Sailors soon mastered these shifting seasonal winds, and regular contact developed within the next several decades. Strabo credited the Ptolemies with building flotillas of as many as twenty ships which crossed the Strait every year and pressed on toward India by way of Cape Guardafui, which came to be known as the "incense cape."[24] Strabo also credited Augustus with ordering a hundred ships to set sail for India from Myos Hormos (Abu Sha'ar?) in the course of the mission of Aelius Gallus.[25] The total number of ships plying these waters had thus increased sixfold from the time of the first Roman occupation of Egypt, and subsequently increased under the emperor Tiberius. These boats, laden with cargoes of Arretine ceramics, would have stopped first at one of India's northern ports and then moved southward along the coast, finally rounding the subcontinent's southernmost point to reach the region of Pondicherry.[26] They would return with precious stones, aromatic products, spices, and textiles.

It is clear from surviving evidence that the South Arabian states were unable to prevent Roman Egypt from conducting trade directly with India. It is known that the Sabaeans never had control of the seas and that none of the South Arabian states had a naval fleet. Although the Himyarite confederation had access to the ports of Muza, Okêlis, and probably Aden, near the Strait of Bab al-Mandab, they nonetheless failed to muster a naval blockade or any kind of punitive expedition. No doubt Rome profited substantially from maritime commerce in the region, to the detriment of their Sabaean rivals. In any case, monopolistic control of land routes in the aromatic spice trade was the key to the national fortunes of the caravan kingdoms, regardless of how they rated its importance.

Times had changed since the glory days of the seventh to third centuries B.C. The collapse of Ma'în by the first century B.C. was due in large part to incursions by Arab nomads who were apparently less appreciative of the economic significance of the caravan trade in the area. The city of Barâqish, which had long served as a point of origin for trips north, lost its economic importance by the time Roman troops arrived there. The kingdoms of Saba and Qatabân were certainly hit with an economic recession as well. The city of Tamnaᶜ, which in the first century B.C. was a brilliant artistic center, was irrevocably affected in the first century A.D. Court life and the principal cults of Tamnaᶜ had been transferred to dhû-Ghaylum (Hajar bin Hamid), a smaller city some ten kilometers inland. And Saba, deprived of its main source of revenue, ceased altogether its large-scale construction projects.

Only Hadramawt was able to benefit from the changing geopolitical situation. Toward the end of the first century B.C., Hadramawt seized Saʾkalân (modern-day Zufar). The inhabitants of Shabwa migrated some 800 kilometers east to found the new settlement of Samhar (modern-day Khôr Rûri) on the coast of the Indian Ocean. By extending its domination to the forests of frankincense trees, Hadramawt became the foremost producer of aromatic plants. It became the only state to have a flotilla of reed-ships, and soon thereafter it had organized a network of collection and coastal navigation from Khôr Rûri to Qanaʾ, with regular caravan connections to Shabwa. Finally, Hadramawt's control of the island of Socotra provided a critical port of call for boats heading toward India, thus ensuring control of a vast maritime empire. On the land routes, Hadramawt maintained relations with Maᶜîn, but the latter's decline led the Hadramitic people to send caravans directly north as far as Najrân; and the intermediary role of Qatabân was also negligible. Thus, by the early first century A.D., the regional influence of Hadramawt had increased to the point where one of its kings assumed the title of mukarrib, a clear indication of his nation's supremacy in South Arabia.[27] He founded the city of Khôr Rûri, may have intervened militarily in Jawf, and minted large bronze coins, inaugurating a long period of prosperity for Hadramawt.

The Periplus of the Red Sea

The *Periplus of the Red Sea,* a strange document from the middle of the first century A.D., reveals the extent of the new commercial horizons of this era. The work, by an anonymous author, is presented as a sort of manual for Roman merchants and contains all the information that might be useful for commercial travelers on the Red Sea and the Indian Ocean: itineraries, names of principal ports, types of merchandise available, business opportunities, and names of local chiefs and sovereigns.[28]

The *Periplus* begins by listing the four major port cities on the Arabian coast, namely Muza (Mauza, south of modern-day Makhâ), Okêlis (modern-day Shaikh Saîd), Arabia Felix (Aden) and Qana˒ (modern-day Bir Alî). The first two cities belonged to the kings of Saba and dhû-Raydân: the so-called Charibaël was none other than Karib˒îl, king of the Homerites (Himyarites); Sapahar was the capital of Zafar. There is no mention of the rulers of Aden in the *Periplus,* and it is uncertain whether the Qatabanites still held it by this time. In its description of the maritime trade, the text specifies that Qana˒ belonged to Eleazos (˒îl˓azz in South Arabian), the king of Hadramawt:

> Beyond the projecting headland is another port of trade on the coast, Qana˒, belonging to the kingdom of Eleazos, the frankincense-bearing land; near it are two barren islands, one called Orneôn ["of the birds"] and the other Trullas, 120 stades offshore from Qana˒. Above it inland lies the metropolis of Sabautha [Shabwa], which is also the residence of the king. All the frankincense grown in the land is brought into Qana˒, as if to a warehouse, by camel as well as by rafts of a local type made of leathern bags, and by boats. It also carries on a trade with the ports across the water—Barygaza, Skythia, Omana [Oman]—and with its neighbor, Persis. [Shabwa's] imports from Egypt are: wheat, limited quantity, and wine, just as to Muza; also as to Muza, Arab clothing, either with common adornment or no adornment or of printed fabric, in rather large quantities; copper; tin; coral; storax; and the rest of the items that go to Muza. Also, for the king, embossed silverware and money (?), rather large quantities, plus horses and statuary and fine-quality clothing with no adornment.[29]

In exchange, Qana˒ exported frankincense and aloe. The ancient site of Qana˒ still retains traces of the blocks of frankincense that were stowed in palm-leaf baskets for shipment: these were kept in large storerooms that were partially carved into the rock and covered with a roof.[30] These buildings were clustered in a group at the base of the fortress of Corbeau, a rocky peak which is difficult to get to, but which had houses, four reservoirs, and possibly a lighthouse on its summit. Russian archaeologists have uncovered numerous items including fragments of amphoras that were originally filled with wine from Rhodes or Italy, sigillated ceramic items, and Nabataean bowls, which tend to suggest that the commercial horizons of Qana' in the first century A.D. stretched all the way from the western Mediterranean to India.[31]

The *Periplus* refers to Socotra, the island facing Qana', as the island of Dioscuridês:

> Though very large, it is barren and also damp, with rivers, crocodiles, a great many vipers, and huge lizards, so huge that people eat the flesh and melt down the fat to use in the place of oil. The island bears no farm products, neither vines nor grain. . . . The island yields tortoise shell, the genuine, the land, and the light-colored, in great quantity and distinguished by rather large shields, and also the oversize mountain variety with an extremely thick shell, of which the parts over the belly, whichever are useful, do not take [sc. regular] cutting; besides, they are rather tawny. On the other hand, whatever can be used for small boxes, small plaques, small disks, and similar items gets cut up completely. The so-called Indian cinnabar is found there; it is collected as an exudation from the trees. The island is subject to the aforementioned king of the frankincense-bearing land. . . . Trade with it used to be carried on by some of the shippers from Muza and also by those sailing out of Limyrikê and Barygaza who by chance put in at it; these would exchange rice, grain, cotton cloth, and female slaves, which found a market because of a shortage there, for big cargoes of tortoise shell.[32]

The *Periplus* describes the newly acquired Hadramitic territory of Zufar as a mountainous region that is foggy and not easily accessible:

> The frankincense-bearing trees are neither very large nor tall; they give off frankincense in congealed form on the bark, just as some of the trees we have in Egypt exude gum. The frankincense is handled by royal slaves and convicts. For the districts are terribly unhealthy, harm-

ful to those sailing by and absolutely fatal to those working there—who, moreover, die off easily because of the lack of nourishment.[33]

The *Periplus* is a trove of information about ancient geography, ports, and maritime activity in the mid-first century A.D., particularly the thirty-year period up to 70 A.D., the probable date of its first publication.[34] Indeed, the Periplus is the prime source of evidence on commercial relations in the region during this period, since other available sources are sparse and widely scattered. On the Eyptian coast of the Red Sea at Leukos Limên (the port closest to Koptos, on the Nile), evidence has been found of a Himyarite merchant and a trader from Aden who were engaged in the wine trade between 57 and 70 A.D. At Alexandria, which had monopoly control of all Red Sea traffic, it is likely that South Arabians were engaged in shipping along with Syrians and Indians. And the presence of one or more merchants from Hadramawt is attested on the island of Delos. Overall, it is clear that the commercial horizons of South Arabia began to expand significantly in this period, and an influx of foreign cultural influences naturally followed.

A Hybrid Art

Large-scale commerce in the region had the effect of increasing cultural ties between Egypt, Syria, and South Arabia. Caravans and trading ships not only carried merchants but also artists and their creations. Along with everyday utensils that were apparently imported into South Arabia from Alexandria and Italy there came items with cult associations—serving dishes, platters, plates, and ladles made of bronze—as well as bronze statuettes of ephebes, warriors, and other human and animal figures.[35] It is possible that molds for statues circulated in South Arabia, as they did in other parts of the ancient world, though so far none have been discovered in South Arabia. The simplest items were reproduced in local foundries, while more complicated products imply the importation of skilled artisans from abroad. It is likely that itinerant artists settled in the larger centers of production, for instance Maʾrib,

Tamna^c, and Shabwa. Their less accomplished counterparts (whose existence can be deduced from items of inferior quality) perhaps made their way from the eastern provinces of the Roman Empire, though with lower financial prospects.

The most familiar designs are vines and clusters of grapes, which adorn a large number of objects and monuments. These were apparently the most prominent motifs adopted by artists from the first century B.C. on. The more intricate designs, such as those depicting grapevines with animals emerging through the leaves, were often poorly executed. This was also the case with the Greco-Roman architectural elements such as fluted columns, Corinthian capitals, and arches, as well as the Greek friezes and overhanging scrolls, which increased in popularity during the first and second centuries A.D.

The most complex artworks suggest that foreign and local artists were working in a similar style beginning around the first half of the first century A.D. Among the most significant works dating from this period are the famous cherub plaques overhanging the lions of Tamna^c; art historians conjecture that these sculptures were executed in situ by local technicians working from imported molds.[36] Another object found nearby, the statue of the seated "Bar^ɔat Lady," was executed in an entirely different style; the fine treatment of a close-fitting drapery suggests a Syrian influence.[37] The thrust of the surviving evidence suggests that the conservative artistic traditions of Arabia Felix were permeated by outside influences in the early years of the new millennium, and that these foreign styles, though adopted only timidly at first, gradually took hold over the following three centuries.

CONCLUSION

When the princes of the Himyarite confederation proclaimed themselves the "kings of Saba and dhū-Raydân," the end was at hand for one of South Arabia's most celebrated kingdoms. Saba didn't disappear for good, however. In fact, it later recovered some of its independence in the second century A.D., when its rulers reverted to the simple title "king of Saba." And for two centuries the sanctuary of Awwâm in Ma'rib continued to draw large numbers of pilgrims who came to dedicate statues. But power had shifted elsewhere, to the high plateaus of the Yemen. The tribes of Bakîl and Samî' had already begun shaping the landscape of the regions of Sana and Himyar, including the southern regions of Radman and Khawlan. Their social hierarchy, with great noble families and notables who headed the clans and their factions, would endure for centuries. These military aristocracies descended from the great tribes of the mountains now held real power, at the expense of the traditional dynasties. Three noblemen from the Hashîd tribes succeeded to the throne of Saba. These ascendant tribes actually looked back to Sabaean tradition as a model and sought legitimacy by claiming to perpetuate the heritage of Saba.

Saba had played a central role in the formation of South Arabian civilization. The Sabaean language is attested as early as the eighth century B.C., and was presumably spoken even earlier; its use continued long after the fall of the Sabaean kingdom in 275 A.D. The Himyarites, as heirs of Saba, left inscriptions in Sabaean, though they spoke other dialects. Sabaean was the favored language of the political and religious elites, whose scribes always used the large letters which had been perfected centuries earlier. Sabaean remained in use until the fourth or fifth centuries A.D., and the latest known documents using the South Arabian alphabet were created after the appearance of Islam.[1] By that time, however, the national language of Saba had, after some fifteen centuries of active use, been replaced by Arabic script.

Saba, initially a small group of tribes unified by the cult of Almaqah, expanded gradually until it comprised a large population of subjects under the authority of the king of Maʾrib. The cult of Almaqah remained a strong unifying force in South Arabia until the arrival of the great monotheistic religions. Numerous sanctuaries stood atop the mountains northwest of Sana right up until the final fall of the Sabaean kingdom, and Almaqah continued to be worshiped thereafter, though as a specialized cult. In the third century A.D., the heirs of Saba gave Almaqah the title of Lord, and worshipers at the temple of Awwâm at Maʾrib continued to make offerings to Almaqah; it was not until the end of the fourth century A.D. that the sanctuary was finally abandoned. The decline of the Sabaean religion corresponded roughly with the diffusion of the monotheistic religions.

The name of Saba came to reflect the institutional prestige of royalty who reigned for a millennium and who had dominated all of South Arabia from the time of the earliest mukarribs. It is hardly surprising that the Himyarite rulers adopted the title of "king of Saba and dhû-Raydân," even though they came from the mountains. Saba conferred legitimacy, even if only symbolically. Himyar's adoption of the royal palace derives from a similar tradition. Just as Salhîn played an important but nonessential role for Saba, the castle of Raydân was not just a royal residence but a symbol of the master's authority to all those who were his subjects. Himyarite coinage bore the emblem of Raydân. By the fourth century A.D., Saba was just a name, but it remained the most prestigious of royal titles.

Can the hydraulic works of Saba be seen as a model for subsequent engineering and organization? Surely not, for other states had also developed similar irrigation techniques. But Sabaeans were the first to make explicit the interrelationship of human collective, cult, and irrigated lands. This formulation had a profound effect on political thinking for the entire era of Sabaean influence. Moroever, the Maʾrib oasis came to be seen as a model of prosperity and technical innovation. After all, it was there that large-scale masonry waterworks made their first appearance.[2]

The greatest oasis in South Arabia was an early victim of its own success. Ongoing siltation spurred a continuing search for higher points of water supply. The so-called dike, which was certainly a major work of art in and of itself, can also be seen as the outgrowth of a technical crisis in ancient irrigation, and the Himyarites introduced no important innovations after they became masters of Maᵓrib. Indeed, no other state was able to engineer a solution to the problem of siltation, beyond certain desperate measures that essentially amounted to digging out the fields.[3]

Saba also stood for a style of artistic expression. We do not know (and will probably never learn) the origins of certain construction techniques in Saba, or, for that matter, the variety of artistic forms that preceded those of Saba. But it is reasonable to surmise that Saba, during the course of its expansion, gradually imposed its own artistic norms throughout Arabia. Saba's goal may well have been to eclipse the various local styles of the regions it came to dominate. The artistic formulas perfected by the Sabaeans proliferated so widely that it is difficult to distinguish between archaic alabaster heads and the more classical examples, or between Sabaean figures and Qatabanite copies. The Himyarites seem to have entirely lacked an artistic tradition of their own; the best they could do was copy Sabaean models. There was no ancient building, palace, temple, or tomb in Himyar that did not borrow from Sabaean or Qatabanite formulas, and construction techniques were similarly dependent on those of their ancestors. The porticoes of the sanctuaries all have slender monolithic pillars surmounted by a dentilled motif. The opening of South Arabia to influences from the Greco-Roman world was certainly a major event which considerably enriched the artistic vocabulary of local artisans in the so-called minor arts, but in architecture the result was often merely cosmetic, without any effect on underlying architectural techniques.

The memory of Saba was not totally lost after the advent of Islam. Certain writers made mention of Himyarite tribes which proclaimed their descent form Sabaean ancestors. For al-Hasân al-Hamdâni, a prolific tenth-century writer, Maᵓrib would always remain the "city of Saba," the fifth-century-B.C. marvel of Yemen, and the surviving traces of the dike and two gardens were an undying testament to the splendor of the ancient capital and the technical mastery of its inhabitants. "If the kings of Sirwâh and Ma'rib can disappear," he added, "who can hope for lasting security in this world?"[4]

GLOSSARY

Archaic period: A period spanning roughly the eighth century B.C. in South Arabia, corresponding to the early mukarribs of Saba and the inscriptions known as Graphic A. This period was followed by the classical period.

Aromatic spice: Plant substance used medicinally, as a seasoning, as a perfume, or as an aphrodisiac.

Balm: Aromatic preparation made from odiferous resins and used as healing ointment.

Classical period: A period spanning roughly the seventh and sixth centuries B.C. in South Arabia, corresponding to the great mukarribs of Saba and the inscriptions known as Graphic B. The period that followed, from the fifth through the first centuries B.C., was known as the period of the kings of Saba.

Dentils: A series of small, rectangular indentations forming a decorative molding pattern. The term *pseudo-bondstone* refers to a cross section of a wooden beam.

Eponym: One for whom another person or a thing is named.

Hadramawt: The valley which runs parallel to the coast of the Indian Ocean down to Sayhout; the name also applies in a wider sense to the regions north and south of this valley. In the South Arabian era, Hadramawt was a kingdom with its capital at Shabwa.

Highlands: The mountainous region of northern Yemen, where the altitude ranges from 1,000 to 2,500 meters above sea level.

Ibex: A species of wild goat (*Capra ibex*) distinguished by large re-curved horns transversely ridged in front; the South Arabian variety is known as *Capra ibex nubiana*. These relatively tame animals were hunted in all regions of Yemen in ancient times and are still hunted today.

Jawf: A vast tectonic depression 100 kilometers northeast of Sana. The Wadi Jawf, formed by the confluence of the Wadi Madhâb with the wadis Khârid and Majzir, flows east-southeast toward the Hadramawt valley.

Loculus: A small burial chamber. In the mausoleums at Tamnaᶜ and Maʾrib, loculi were stacked in layers and sealed with stones bearing decorative portraits of the deceased.

Lowlands: Territory surrounding the Ramlat as-Sabʾatayn desert in Yemen, where the altitude ranges from 600 to 1,000 meters above sea level.

Maᶜîn: A small kingdom which arose in the central Jawf valley in the early seventh century B.C. and collapsed circa 120–110 B.C. Its two main cities, Maᶜîn (modern-day Qarnaw) and Yathill (modern-day Barâqish), were devoted principally to serving the caravan trade.

Maʾrib: Capital of the kingdom of Saba. Originally called Maryab (*Mryb*), it came to be known as Maʾrib by the end of the second century B.C.; the name is now used to designate the ancient city and archaeological site as well as its small modern-day counterpart on the Wadi Dhana.

Mukarrib: Title of the early sovereigns of South Arabia. Though later rulers employed the title of king, the title of mukarrib remained associated with an authority which had once extended throughout South Arabia. In late antiquity, several kingdoms sought to reclaim the title's former prestige.

Myrrh: An aromatic gum resin from the *Commiphora simplicifolia* tree.

Pact of union: A ceremony that marked the unification of various tribes connected with Saba but not associated with the cult of Almaqah. The pacts were celebrated with ritual banquets held principally in the temples of Jabal al-Lawdh.

Palm petiole: The petiole is properly the slender stem that supports the foliage leaf, but the term is also used to designate the entire stalk including the leaflets.

Qatabân: Name of the tribe and kingdom that grew up around the Wadi Bayhân (south of Maʾrib), whose capital was Tamnaᶜ. Attested from the seventh century B.C., the kingdom collapsed by circa 175 A.D.

Ritual confession: A public ceremony in which a person confesses and repents his or her sins; in ancient South Arabia, such offenses were often related to purity. Declarations of guilt and repentance were engraved on bronze tablets and put on public display in the temples.

Rockrose: A Mediterranean shrub (genus *Cistus*) which secretes gum-labdanum, a viscous oleoresin with medicinal and pharmaceutical applications and also used in perfumery.

Socotra: An island off the coast of Hadramawt about 400 kilometers from the coastal city of Râs Fartak. Socotra has an area of 3,650 square kilometers; its highest elevation is 1,500 meters above sea level.

Storax: A fragrant balsam from the bark of the *Liquidambar orientalis* tree (an Asian tree of the witch hazel family) used as an expectorant and sometimes in perfumery; any of the trees or shrubs of the family Styracaceae (genus *Styrax*).

Thurifer: A person who carries a censer in a religious ceremony.

Unguent: A mixture of fats and perfume applied to the skin as a soothing or healing salve and often used in massage.

Wadi: A temporary course of water in arid regions (from the plural form of the Arabic word *wed*).

NOTES

Introduction

1. Agatharchides of Cnidos, writer of the second century B.C. (in *Geographi Graeci Minores,* ed. C. Müller).

2. "Gate of Tears" is a translation of Bab al-Mandab, the name of the strait at the southern end of the Red Sea.

3. Volkoff 1971 and Bonnet 1985.

4. For the iconography of the Queen of Sheba, see Daum 1988.

5. Passages from the Koran are from M. H. Shakir's translation in *The Qurʾan* (Elmhurst, N.Y.: Tahrike Tarsile Qurʾan, Inc., 1997).

6. Faure 1987.

7. Pirenne 1958.

8. Phillips 1955.

9. Two volumes have already appeared on the excavations at Shabwa (Pirenne 1990 and Breton 1992a), and the third is in press (Breton, *Fouilles de Shabwa, III, Architecture civile et religieuse*).

1. The Gardens of Saba

1. Agatharchides, in *Geographi Graeci Minores,* ed. C. Müller, para. 99 (quoted in Pirenne 1961, p. 82).

2. Kessel 1932, pp. 3–4.

3. *Surface Water Resources, Final Report,* vols. 1–3, High Water Council, Sana, 1992.

4. De Maigret 1990; see also Wilkinson, Edens, and Gibson 1997.

5. Information communicated by B. Vogt, whom the author wishes to thank here.

6. Schmidt 1987, pp. 179–84.

7. Flood observed April 12, 1990, in the Wadi Bayhân; see B. Coque-Delhuille, "Le milieu naturel de la région de Bayhân," in *Une vallée antique du Yémen: le wâdi Bayhân* (forthcoming).

8. Gentelle 1991 (in Breton 1992a), pp. 5–55.

9. ABADY 1986 and Schmidt 1987.

10. Gentelle 1992, pp. 42–43.

11. Schaloske 1995, pp. 162–64.

12. For these sites, see Schaloske 1995, plates 1, 8, 10, 11, etc.

13. See the plan in J. Schmidt, "Zweiter vorläufiger Bericht über die Ausgrabungen und Forschungen des DAI . . . " ABADY 3 (1986–87), plan of the Hauptverteiler (in appendix).

14. The text of this stela can be found at CIH 541.

15. Inscriptions CIH 622 and 623: Yasrân is the name for the southern oasis and Abyan the northern oasis.

16. Cf. Forthcoming article in *Syria* by P. Gentelle and J.-Cl. Roux.

17. Pliny, *Nat.* 8.28–29.

18. Levkovskaya and Filatenko 1992.

19. Pliny, *Nat.* 24.107–8.

20. Hepper and Wood 1979, pp. 65–71.

21. Breton 1994a, pp. 89–92.

22. Phillips 1955.

23. Bowen 1958, pp. 215–68.

24. B. Vogt, *Barʾân (aujourdʾhui ʿArsh Bilqîs), temple dʾAlmaqah*, in Institut du Monde Arabe 1997, 140–41.

25. Pirenne 1984, entries 569–89; more recently, Robin 1996, entries 1091–96 and 1147–51.

2. The Caravan Kingdoms

1. Ryckmans 1994. See also J. Ryckmans, "Pétioles de palmes et bâtonnets inscrits: Un type nouveau de documents du Yémen antique," Académie Royale de Belgique, 1993.

2. Robin 1996, entry 1216.

3. See chapter one, "The Gardens of Saba."

4. Robin 1996, entries 1091–92 and 1095–96.

5. In addition to the lists of eponyms, see the texts catalogued as Jamme 2848 and CIH 610.

6. Robin 1996, entries 1150–53.

7. De Maigret 1988, pp. 21–44.

8. Inscriptions RES 3945 and 3946.

9. Breton 1994b, 41–47. The waters of the Wadi Markha dissipate far to the north, not far from Shabwa, where they join the underground course of the Wadi Hadramawt.

10. Robin 1996, entries 1121–23.

11. B. Vogt, "Sabr: Une ville de la fin du seconde millénaire dans l'arrière-pays d'Aden," in Institut du Monde Arabe 1997, 47–48.

12. Translated from C. Robin's French version.

13. Inscription RES 3946.

14. See Anfray 1990, 17–63.

15. Eph'al 1982, p. 42, n. 117.

16. Pirenne 1956.

17. Van Beek 1969.

18. Strabo 16.4.2. (All translations of Strabo are from the Loeb Classical Library edition.)

19. Today this port is well known as a haven for sailors. See Henri de Monfried, *Les Secrets de la mer Rouge* (Paris 1932), especially the first chapter.

20. Pliny, *Nat.* 12.64.

21. One of these sovereigns erected a large stone ibex statue in the temple of Sayîn at Hurayda (see Institut de Monde Arabe 1997, p. 102).

22. Breton 1987.

23. Gentelle 1991, pp. 5–55.

24. Badre 1992.

3. Fragrances of Arabia

1. Herodotus 3.107, 3.113. (Passages from Herodotus are from the translation by David Grene.)

2. Herodotus 3.107, 3.110, 3.111.

3. Theophrastus, *Nat. Hist.* 12.70. (Translation is from Loeb Classical Library edition, 9.4.2–6.)

4. Agatharchides, in *Geographi Graeci Minores,* ed. C. Müller.

5. Pliny, *Nat.* 12.70.

6. The rue is a strong-scented perennial woody herb with yellow flowers.

7. Theophrastus, *Nat. Hist.* 9.4.4–5.

8. Strabo 16.4.4.

9. Exodus 30:22–25, 33.

10. See Faure 1987 and Détienne 1972. (The myth is charmingly recounted in Book 10 of Ovid's *Metamorphoses.*)

11. Retsö 1991, p. 198.

12. Animal sacrifices were banned outside the city of Jerusalem in 610 B.C., along with the burning of animal fats on altars.

13. Monod 1979; see also Monod and Bel 1996, pp. 100–102.

14. *Boswellia sacra* does not grow near Shabwa, where myrrh flourishes, but the common species of frankincense may be found in this area.

15. Bent 1990.

16. Pliny, *Nat.* 12.58–59.

17. Pliny, *Nat.* 12.59–60.

18. Bent 1900, pp. 252–53.

19. Thomas 1932, p. 122.

20. Faure 1987, p. 294.

21. Pliny, *Nat.* 12.74–76.

22. Faure 1987, pp. 291–93.

23. Pliny, *Nat.* 12.89–92. (For one version of the legend, cf. Herodotus 3.107.)

24. Simeone-Senelle 1994, pp. 9–11.

25. Simeone-Senelle 1994, pp. 12–14.

26. Faure 1987, pp. 299–301; cf. Herodotus 3.107.

27. Groom 1981, pp. 160–61.

28. Pliny, *Nat.* 12.82; also at 12.93.

29. J.-F. Breton, "Le site de Shabwa," in Breton 1992a, pp. 61–66.

30. Pliny, *Nat.* 12.63–64.

31. Pliny, *Nat.* 9.4–6.

32. We learn from Pliny (*Nat.* 12.63–64) that frankincense "can only be exported through the country of the Gebbanitae." There is no doubt that after the disintegration of Qatabān in the second century, merchants turned to the direct route from Shabwa to Najrān. But is also possible that Pliny confused the Qatabanites with the Minaeans.

33. Philby 1939, p. 358.

34. Pliny, *Nat.* 12.65.

35. Pliny states that cassia grown in the horn of Africa was shipped to Arabia and then re-exported.

36. A pound equals 327 grams.

37. Pliny, *Nat.* 12.84.

38. Lammens 1924, p. 274.

39. From a French translation by C. Robin, in Robin 1991, pp. 59–62.

40. J.-F. Salles, "La circumnavigation de l'arabie dans l'Antiquité classique," in Salles 1988, vol. 1, pp. 79–86.

41. Ibid., pp. 86–91.

42. Arrian, *Anabasis* 7.21.1.

43. Pliny, *Nat.* 12.62.

44. Faure 1987, p. 197, citing Pouilloux 1960, no. 37.

45. This thesis is presented by J. Rougé in "La navigation en mer Erythrée dans l'Antiquité," in Faure 1987, p. 68.

46. Pliny, *Nat.* 12.87–88.

4. Cities and Villages

1. One example is the area at the base of the Jabal an-Nisiyîn, west of Bayhân.

2. Breton 1994a, pp. 17–19.

3. Ibid., pp. 95–97.

4. J.-L. Bessac uses the term *Lesbian* to describe this type of joint (*Fouilles de Shabwa III,* in press).

5. De Maigret and Robin 1993, p. 430.

6. See chapter three, "Fragrances of Arabia."

7. Pliny, *Nat.* 6.153–55.

8. Hamilton 1942, p. 116.

9. Beeston 1971a, pp. 26–28.

10. J.-F. Breton, "Le site et la ville de Shabwa," in Breton 1992a, pp. 59–66.

11. C. Darles, "L'architecture civile à Shabwa," in Breton 1992a, p. 83.

12. Strabo 16.4.2–3.

13. J. Seigne, "Le château royal de Shabwa: Architecture, techniques de construction, et restitutions," in Breton 1992a, pp. 113–31; and J.-F. Breton, "Le château royal de Shabwa: Notes d'histoire," in Breton 1992a, pp. 209–29.

14. J.-F. Breton and C. Darles, "Le Grand Temple," in *Fouilles de Shabwa III* (in press).

15. Breton and Darles 1980.

16. Texts from the Yemen Highlands.

17. Doe and Serjeant 1975, pp. 1–23 (with plates I–VIII) and pp. 276–95 (with plates I–III).

18. Breton 1997.

19. Pirenne 1990, pp. 72–73.

20. Bonnenfant 1996, p. 104; example: Bayt G., p. 208, fig. 9, and p. 209.

21. From a French translation by C. Robin.

22. Bonnenfant 1996, pp. 145–53; example: house of Bayt az-Zubayrî, pp. 249–60.

23. Mauger 1996: houses of Bilad Qahtan, Bani Bishr, etc.

24. Institut du Monde Arabe 1997, p. 202.

25. Agatharchides, in *Geographi Graeci Minores,* ed. C. Müller, p. 100.

26. Text dating from the fifth century A.D.

27. Text dating from the first century A.D.

28. Institut du Monde Arabe 1997, p. 202.

29. Breton, Darles, Robin, and Swauger 1997.

30. Breton 1991.

31. Breton, McMahon, and Warburton 1997.

32. De Maigret 1988, pp. 10–20.

33. Breton 1997, pp. 92–100.

34. Caton-Thomson 1944, pp. 139–43.

35. R. Audouin, "Al-ʿOqm (sur la zone IR3)," in Breton 1992a, pp. 55–59.

36. Breton and Darles 1994.

37. Breton 1997, pp. 69–89. See also J.-F. Breton, B. Coque-Delhuille, P. Gentelle, and J.-C. Arramond, *Une vallée du Yémen antique: Le wâdi Bayhân* (in press).

5. Economy and Society

1. For Hadramawt, see Serjeant 1962.

2. Robin 1996, entry 1194.

3. Robin 1982a.

4. Robin 1979, p. 157.

5. Preissler 1984.

6. Texts cited in Avanzini 1991–93, 61:159–60.

7. Robin 1988.

8. Avanzini 1991–93, 61:160.

9. Strabo 16.4.25.

10. J. Chelhod, "L'évolution du système de parenté au Yémen," in Chelhod 1984–85, p. 108.

11. A. F. L. Beeston, "Women in Sabaʾ," in Bidwell and Smith 1983, pp. 7–13.

12. Avanzini 1991–93, 61:160.

13. Ryckmans, Müller, and Abdallah 1994 (text, YM 11726).

14. Text, Jamme 619.

15. Levkovskaya and Filatenko 1992.

16. Ryckmans, Müller, and Abdallah 1994 (text, YM 11729).

17. Pliny, *Nat.* 13.34–35.

18. Lankester Harding 1964, pl. 52; Bâfaqîh 1978.

19. Lundin 1987.

20. Wild olives were present on the high plateaus.

21. Goblot 1979, pp. 105–6.

22. See translation by Y. Abdallah, *Ein altsüdarabischer Vertragstext von den neuentdeckten Inschriften auf Holz, Arabia Felix, Beiträge zur Sprache und Kultur . . .*, 1994, pp. 1–12; and in *Archéologia* 271 (September 1991):52. See also Ryckmans 1993.

23. J. Pirenne, "La juridiction de l'eau en Arabie du Sud antique d'après les inscriptions," in Pirenne 1982, vol. 2: *Aménagements hydrauliques: Etat et législation,* pp. 84–86.

24. Beeston 1971b.

25. Cf. Roux 1996.

26. Ryckmans, Müller, and Abdallah 1994, texts 13 (YM 11743) and 12 (YM 11730).

27. Ibid., text 15 (11738).

28. J. Ryckmans kindly provided the French translation of this text before its publication in PSAS (1997).

29. See J.-C. Bassac, *Techniques de construction, de gravure, d'ornementation en pierre dans le Jawf (Yémen)* and *Le Travail de la pierre à Shabwa,* in J.-F. Breton, *Fouilles de Shabwa III* (in press).

30. Breton 1994a, pp. 158–59.

31. Ryckmans, Müller, and Abdallah 1994, pp. 43–44.

32. Ibid., pp. 63–65.

33. Strabo 16.1.27; Ashurbanipal: Pritchard 1955, p. 298 (cited in Briant 1982, p. 127).

34. Herodotus 3.113.

35. Retsö 1991, pp. 205–9.

36. Strabo 16.4.18 (later echoed by Diodorus Siculus).

6. The Gods and Their Temples

1. On South Arabian religion in general, see Ryckmans 1989, as well as the entry by Ryckmans under "Arabian Religions, Middle East-

ern Religions" in the *Encyclopaedia Britannica* (1992 edition, pp. 115–19 and bibliography on p. 128); see also Bron 1995.

2. The importation of statuettes of the Greco-Roman gods does not necessarily imply their religious "incorporation" by the South Arabians.

3. Nielsen 1922 and Nielsen 1942.

4. Robin 1982b, pp. 49–50 and p. 54, fig. 3.

5. See chapter one.

6. Schmidt 1982a.

7. Robin 1996, entries 1160–61.

8. Ryckmans 1989, p. 164.

9. Theophrastus, *Nat. Hist.,* 9.4.5; Pliny, *Nat.* 12.62.

10. See chapter four.

11. Robin 1996, entries 1163–34.

12. Breton 1995, pp. 45–49.

13. De Maigret and Robin 1993, p. 480.

14. Pirenne 1990, pp. 75–76 (text RES 2693 in the British Museum).

15. Ryckmans 1945; see also Ryckmans 1972.

16. Schmidt 1982b.

17. Robin and Breton 1982.

18. Robin 1996, entry 1180–81.

19. Garbini [n.d.]; De Maigret 1988, pp. 21–41.

20. All sorts of hypotheses have been offered about the uses of this oval space; it is certainly conceivable that it contained ritual installations, benches, or numerous inscribed stelae.

21. Breton 1992b, pp. 439–41.

22. This tendency was a commonplace in the iconography of Mesopotamia dating back to the reliefs of Ur-Nanshé around 2250 B.C.; the influence of Mesopotamian art spread widely but came relatively late to South Arabia.

23. Pirenne 1962 and 1965; Institut du Monde Arabe 1997, p. 164.

24. Breton, Arramond, and Robine 1990; see also Breton 1992b.

25. Breton 1998.

26. De Maigret and Robin 1993, pp. 432–58.

27. If these divine figures did exist, the question remains whether they were hidden (as in the Holy of Holies in the Temple of Jerusalem) or open to the view of worshipers.

28. De Maigret and Robin 1993, pp. 471–75.

29. Robin and Ryckmans 1988; the first part of this study was published as Robin, Breton, and Ryckmans 1981.

30. Sedov and Bâtayi 1994.

31. Ibid., p. 188.

32. Will 1959, pp. 136–45, and plates 36–39.

33. See Audouin, "Sculptures et peintures du château royal de Shabwa," in Breton 1992a; for the frescoes of Qaryat al-Fau, see Al-Ansary 1981.

7. The World of the Dead

1. A. De Maigret, "Les Pratiques funéraires," in Institut du Monde Arabe 1997, p. 165–66.

2. Philby 1939, pp. 373–79.

3. Two of these so-called mummies were excavated at Shimab al-Ghirâs and are now in the museum of the University of Sana.

4. Abd al-Halîm 1995.

5. Caton-Thomson 1944, plates 23–43.

6. "Raybûn 15 Cemetery (1985–1986 Excavations)," in Sedov and Griaznevich 1996, pp. 117–43.

7. J.-C. Roux, "La tombe-caverne 1 de Shabwa," in Breton 1992a.

8. Von Wissman and Rathjens 1932, pp. 159–66.

9. Research is being led by Michel Garcia and Madiha Rashâd.

10. Cleveland 1965.

11. Phillips 1955, pp. 163–64.

12. Albright 1958, pp. 215–39 and plates 182–88.

13. *Antik Welt* 5 (1997):429–30.

14. Will 1949a, Will 1949b. More recently, Sartre 1989, pp. 423–47.

15. Cleveland 1965, plates 70–74 (pediments with stelae), and plates 75–86 (pediments only).

16. Institut du Monde Arabe 1997, pp. 152–57 and 171–73.

17. Dedicants or deceased? The archaeological context does not allow us to decide conclusively.

18. "Ground Cemetery in the Wâdî Naʾam (Raybûn 17)," in Sedov 1996 and Griaznevich, pp. 143–58 and plates 108–31.

19. Breton and Bâfaqîh 1993.

20. Vogt 1994.

21. Henninger 1981a and 1981b.

22. Henninger 1981b, p. 200.

23. "Ground Cemetery in the Wâdî *Naʾam* (Raybûn 17)," in Sedov and Griaznevich 1996, plate 113.

24. Necropolis of Raybûn 15.

25. Vogt 1994, pp. 286–87.

26. Rathjens 1955.

27. Alî Aqîl 1984 lists 159 stelae.

28. See Institut du Monde Arabe 1997, pp. 168–70.

29. Will 1989.

30. S. Tassinari, "Propos sur la vaisselle de bronze," in Breton and Bâfaqîh 1993, pp. 49–50 and plates 11, 13, 14, and 26–28.

31. This is probably the best interpretation of Building 74 at Shabwa.

8. *Toward New Horizons*

1. Robin 1982b, pp. 45–46 and 48–67.

2. Robin 1984, or, more recently, Tindel 1994.

3. Rainfall figures are ten-year averages (1978–88) at Yarim with a maximum of 1717 millimeters in 1981. The average at the Sumara Pass was approximately 630 millimeters.

4. Ryckmans 1963.

5. Wilkinson, Edens, and Gibson 1997.

6. Pliny, *Nat.* 6.32.

7. *Periplus of the Red Sea* 23 (in Casson 1989).

8. Robin 1996, entries 1099–1102.

9. The village of Shuʾûb has since been incorporated within the larger metropolis of Sana; entry into Shuʾûb was through the fortified gate with the same name.

10. From the tenth-century Yemeni writer al-Hasân al-Hamdâni. See Faris 1938, p. 15.

11. Robin 1991a, p. 72.

12. Inscription RES 3943.

13. Robin 1992.

14. Institut du Monde Arabe 1997, p. 185.

15. Ibid., p. 184.

16. P.-L. Gatier and J.-F. Salles, "L'emplacement de Leuké Komé," appendix to "Aux frontières méridionales du domaine nabatéen," in Salles 1988, pp. 186–87.

17. Strabo 16.4.24. (Cited in Pirenne 1961, pp. 94–96.)

18. Pliny, *Nat.* 6.160. (Cited in Pirenne 1961, p. 61.)

19. *Res Gestae Divi Augusti* 26; cited in Gagé 1950, pp. 130–31.

20. Costa 1977; for another, more recent, view, see Bowersock 1983, pp. 148–53.

21. Nicolet 1988, pp. 86–95 and 98–99.

22. Strabo 16.4.22.

23. Desanges 1978, pp. 155–73; J. Rougé, "La navigation en mer Erythrée dans l'Antiquité," in Salles 1998, pp. 67–74.

24. Strabo 2.5.12 and 17.1.13.

25. The identification of the port of Myos Hormos remains uncertain; see S. E. Sidebotham, "The Red Sea and the Arabian-Indian Trade," in Fahd 1987, pp. 204–5.

26. The findings from excavations of Virampatnam-Arikamedu (near Pondicherry) were published by J. M. Casal in 1949. See also Sidebotham 1986, pp. 13–47.

27. Robin 1994.

28. Casson 1989 is an authoritative edition of the Greek text with English translation and commentary.

29. *Periplus of the Red Sea* 27–28 (cf. Pirenne 1961 and Dagron 1997, p. 19). Passages from the *Periplus* cited here are from Lionel Casson's translation (from the original Greek) in Casson 1989.

30. Sedov 1992.

31. Sedov 1994, pp. 11–35.

32. *Periplus* 30–31.

33. *Periplus* 29.

34. Robin 1991b.

35. Segall 1955.

36. B. Segall, "The Lion-Riders from Timnaʾ," in Albright 1958, pp. 155–78.

37. Will 1989, p. 277; he dates the statue to the first century A.D.

Conclusion

1. Robin 1991–93, pp. 134–35.

2. Schaloske 1995, pp. 162–65.

3. Work of this type was carried out on some of the outlying irrigated areas around Shabwa.

4. Faris 1938, pp. 34–36 and 67–68.

REFERENCES

Abbreviations

AAE   *Journal of Arabian Archaeology and Epigraphy*

ABADY   *Archäologische Berichte aus dem Yemen* (German Archaeological Institute, Sana)

BSOAS   *Bulletin of the School of Oriental and African Studies* (London University)

CNRS   Centre National de Recherche Scientifique (Paris)

CRAIBL   *Comptes-rendu de l'Académie des inscriptions et belles-lettres*

IsMEO   Istituto Italiano per il Medio ed Estremo Oriente, Reports and Memoirs

MUSJ   *Mélanges de la faculté orientale* (Université Saint-Joseph)

PSAS   *Proceedings of the Seminar for Arabian Studies* (London)

REMM   *Revue du monde musulman et de la Méditerranée*

Works

ABADY. 1986. *Antike Technologie, die Sabäische Wasserwirtschaft von Mârib.* ABADY, vol. 3. Mainz: Philipp von Zabern.

Abd al-Halîm, N. D. 1995. "The Mummies of Shibâm al-Ghirâs (Sanaʾa District)." *al-Iklîl* 23.

Al-Ansary, A. 1981. *Qaryat al-Fau: A Portrait of Pre-Islamic Civilization in Saudi Arabia.* Riyadh: University of Riyadh Press.

Al-Ansary, A., ed. 1979. *Studies in the History of Arabia,* vol. 2: *Sources for the History of Arabia.* Riyadh: University of Riyadh Press.

Albright, F. P. 1958. "Excavations at Mârib, Yemen." *Archaeological Discoveries in South Arabia.* Baltimore.

Alî Aqîl, A. 1984. "Les stèles funéraires de Yémen antique." Unpublished dissertation. Paris.

Anfray, F. 1990. *Les anciens Ethiopiens*. Paris.

Avanzini, A. 1991–93. "Remarques sur le "matriarcat" en Arabie du Sud." *L'Arabie antique de Karib'îl à Mahomet*. REMM 61.

Badre, L. 1992. "Le sondage Stratigraphique de Shabwa." In Breton 1992a, pp. 229–314.

Bâfaqîh, M. A. 1978. "The Enigmatic Rock Drawings of Yatûf in wâdî Girdân: Notes and Observations." PSAS 8: 5–14.

Beeston, A. F. L. 1971a. "Functional Significance of the Old South Arabian 'Town'." PSAS (1971): 26–28.

Beeston, A. F. L. 1971b. "Qahtan: Studies in Old South Arabian Epigraphy." *The Labakh Texts (With Addenda to the "Mercantile Code of Qataban")*, fasc. 2. London.

Beeston, A. F. L. 1983. "Women in Saba." In Bidwell and Smith 1983, pp. 7–13.

Bent, T. 1900. *Southern Arabia*. London.

Bidwell, R. L., and G. R. Smith. 1983. *Arabian and Islamic Studies: Articles Presented to R. B. Serjeant*. London: Longman.

Bonnenfant, G. 1996. *Sanaa: Architecture domestique et societé*. CNRS.

Bonnet, J. 1985. *La reine de Saba⁾ et sa légende*. Roanne.

Bowen, R. LeBaron, ed. 1958. *Archaeological Discoveries in South Arabia*. Publications of the American Foundation for the Study of Man, vol. 2. Baltimore: The Johns Hopkins University Press.

Bowersock, G. W. 1983. *Roman Arabia*. Cambridge: Harvard University Press.

Breton, J.-F. 1987. "Shabwa, capitale antique du Hadramawt." *Journal Asiatique* 275: 14–15.

Breton, J.-F. 1991. "A propos de Najrân." *Etudes sud-arabiques* 59–84. Louvain.

Breton, J.-F. 1992b. "Le sanctuaire de ᶜAthtar dhû-Risaf d'as-Sawdâ." CRAIBL: 429–49.

Breton, J.-F. 1994a. *Les fortifications d'Arabie méridionale du VIIe siècle au Ier siècle avant notre ère*. ABADY, vol. 8. Mainz: Philipp von Zabern.

Breton, J.-F. 1994b. "Hajar Yahirr, capitale de ᶜAwsân?" *Raydân* 6: 41–47.

Breton, J.-F. 1995. "Les représentations humaines en Arabie préislamique." *L'Image dans le monde arabe*. Paris: CRNS.

Breton, J.-F. 1997. "L'architecture domestique en Arabie Méridionale du huitième siècle avant J.C. au premier siècle après J.C." Doctoral thesis, University of Paris-I.

Breton, J.-F. 1998. "Temples of Maʿîn et du Jawf (Yémen): État de la question." *Syria.*

Breton, J.-F. and C. Darles. 1980. "Shibâm." *Storia della città,* vol. 14. Milan.

Breton, J.-F. and C. Darles. 1994. "Hajar Surbân 1 et 2: Villages du Jabal an-Nisiyîn." *Arabia Felix* (1994): 46–62.

Breton, J.-F., A. McMahon, and D. Warburton. 1997. "Two Seasons at Hajar am-Dhaybiyya (Yemen)." AAE 8: 1–22.

Breton, J.-F., and M. A. Bâfaqîh. 1993. *Trésors du wâdî Duraʾ (République du Yémen): Fouille franco-yéménite de sauvetage de la nécropole de Hajar adh-Dhaybiyya.* Paris.

Breton, J.-F., C. Darles, C. Robin, and J. L. Swauger. 1997. "Le grand monument dit T T 1 de Tamnaᶜ: Architecture et identification." *Syria* (1997): 1–40.

Breton, J.-F., ed. 1992a. *Fouilles de Shabwa II: Rapports préliminaires.* First published in *Syria* 68(1991). Paris: Geuthner.

Breton, J.-F., ed. In press. *Fouilles de Shabwa III: Architecture civile et religieuse.* Paris: Geuthner.

Breton, J.-F., J.-C. Arramond, and G. Robine. 1990. *Le temple de ᶜAthtar d'as-Sawdâʾ.* Paris.

Breton, J.-F., R. Audouin, L. Badre, and J. Seigne. 1982. *Le Wâdî Hadramawt: Prospections, 1978–1979.* Beirut.

Briant, P. 1982. *Etats et pasteurs au Moyen-Orient.* Paris.

Bron, F. 1995. "Los dioses y el culto de los Arabes preislamicos." *Mitologia y religion del Oriente Antiguos,* pp. 412–47. Barcelona: AUSA.

Casson, L. 1989. *The "Periplus Maris Erythraei": Text with Introduction, Translation, and Commentary.* Princeton University Press.

Caton-Thomson, G. 1944. *The Tombs and Moon-Temple of Hureidha (Hadhramawt).* Report of the Research Committee, Number 13. London: Society of the Antiquaries of London.

Chelhod, J. 1984–85. *L'Arabie du Sud: Histoire et civilisation.* 3 vols. Paris: Maisonneuve.

Cleveland, R. L. 1965. *An Ancient South Arabian Necropolis, Objects from the Second Campaign (1951) in the Timnaᶜ Cemetery.* Publications of the American Foundation for the Study of Man, vol. 4. Baltimore: The Johns Hopkins University Press.

Costa, P. 1977. "A Latin-Greek Inscription from the Jawf of the Yemen." PSAS 7: 69–72.

Dagron, C. 1997. "La mer Erythrée, escales d'une découverte." *Saba*ʾ, vols. 3 and 4.

Daum, W. 1984. *Yemen: 3,000 Years of Art and Civilization in Arabia Felix*. Frankfurt am Main: Innsbruck. English Translation of *Jemen: 3000 Jahre Kunst und Kultur des glücklichen Arabien*, by the same publisher.

Daum, W. 1988. *Die Königin von Saba*ʾ: *Kunst, Legende und Archäologie zwischen Morgenland und Abenland*. Zurich: Belser.

De Maigret, A. 1988. *The Sabaean Archaeological Complex in the Wâdî Yalâ (Eastern Hawlân at-Tiyâl, Yemen Arab Republic): A Preliminary Report*. Rome: IsMEO.

De Maigret, A. 1990. *The Bronze Age Culture of Khawlân at-Tiyâl and al-Hadâ (Republic of Yemen): A First General Report*. Rome: IsMEO.

De Maigret, A., and C. Robin. 1993. "Le temple de Nakrah à Yathill (aujourdʾhui Barâqish)." CRAIBL.

Desanges, J. 1978. *Recherches sur l'activité des Méditerranéens aux confins de l'Afrique*. Collection de l'École Française de Rome.

Détienne, M. 1972. *Les jardins d'Adonis*. Paris.

Doe, B. 1978. *Southern Arabia*. London: Thames and Hudson.

Doe, B. 1983. *Monuments of South Arabia*. Cambridge.

Doe, B., and R. B. Serjeant. 1975. "A Fortified Tower-House in Wâdî Jirdân (Wâhidî Sultanate)." BSOAS: 38.

Ephᶜal, I. 1982. *The Ancient Arabs: Nomads on the Borders of the Fertile Crescent, 9th–5th [Century] B.C*. Jerusalem: The Hebrew University, Leiden-Brill.

Fahd, T., ed. 1987. *L'Arabie préislamique et son environnement historique et culturel*. Université de Sciences Humaines de Strasbourg. Proceedings of a colloquium, June 24–27, 1987.

Faris, N. A. 1938. "The Antiquities of South Arabia, Being a Translation." *Princeton Oriental Texts*, vol. 3. Princeton.

Faure, P. 1987. *Parfums et aromates de l'Antiquité*. Paris: Fayard.

Gagé, J. 1950. *Res gestae divi Augusti*. Paris: Publications de la Faculté des Lettres de l'Université de Strasbourg.

Garbini, G. [n.d.]. *The Inscriptions of Sh*ʾ*ib al-ᶜAql, Al-Gafnah, and Yalâ/ ad-Durayb*.

Garcia, M.-A., and M. Rachad. 1997. *L'art des origines de Yémen*. Paris: Le Seuil.

Gentelle, P. 1991. "Les Irrigations antiques de Shabwa." *Syria* 68. Reprinted in Breton 1992a.

Glanzmann, W. D., ed. 1987. *Site Reconnaissance in the Yemen Arab Republic, 1984: The Stratigraphic Probe at Hajar ar-Rayhani.* Washington, D. C.

Goblot, H. 1979. *Les Qanats: Une technique d'acquisition de l'eau.* Paris.

Groom, N. 1981. *Frankincense and Myrrh: A Study of the Arabian Incense Trade.* London: Longman.

Hamilton, R. A. B. 1942. "Six Weeks in Shabwa." *The Geographic Journal.*

Hellfritz, H. 1936. *Le pays sans ombre: Au royaume de Saba: Yemen et Hadramaout.* Paris.

Henninger, J. 1981a. "Das Opfer in den altsüdarabischen Hochkulturen." *Orbis Biblicus et Orientalis* 40: 204–53. Reprint. Freiburg.

Henninger, J. 1981b. "Le Sacrifice chez les Arabes." *Orbis Biblicus et Orientalis* 40: 189–203. Reprint. Freiburg.

Hepper, F. N., and J. R. I. Wood. 1979. "Were There Forests in the Yemen?" PSAS 9.

Herodotus, 1987. *The History.* Translated by David Grene. University of Chicago Press.

Institut du Monde Arabe. 1997. *Yémen, au pays de la reine de Saba'.* Paris: Flammarion. Exhibition catalog.

Jamme, A. 1962. *Sabaean Inscriptions from the Mahram Bilqis (Mârib).* Publications of the American Foundation for the Study of Man, vol. 3. Baltimore: The Johns Hopkins University Press.

Kessel, J. 1932. *Fortune carrée.* Paris.

Krencker, D. 1913. *Deutsche Aksum Expedition.* 4 vols. Berlin.

Lammens, P. H. 1924. *La Mecque à la veille de l'Hégire.* MUSJ, vol. 9, fasc. 3. Beirut.

Lankester Harding, G. 1964. *Archaeology in the Aden Protectorates.* London.

Levkovskaya, G. M., and A. A. Filatenko. 1992. "Palaeobotanical and Palynological Studies in South Arabia." *Review of Palaeobotany and Palynology* 73: 241–57.

Lundin, A. 1987. "Le décret de Hadaqan sur l'exploitation de la terre." *Palestinskij Sbornik,* vol. 29.

Mauger, T. 1996. *Tableaux d'Arabie.* Paris.

Monod, T. 1979. "Les arbres à encens (*Boswellia sacra,* Flückiger, 1867) dans l'Hadramaout (Yémen du Sud)." *Bulletin du Muséum d'histoire naturelle,* 4th series, vol. 1, section B3, pp. 131–69.

Monod, T., and J.-M. Bel. 1996. *Botanique au pays d'encens.* Brussels.

Nebes, N. 1994. *Arabia Felix: Beiträge zur sprache und Kultur des voris-lamischen Arabien.* Festschrift Walter W. Müller zum 60. Geburstag. Wiesbaden: Harrassowitz Verlag.

Nicolet, C. 1988. *L'inventaire du monde: Géographie et politique aux origines de l'Empire romain.* Paris: Fayard.

Nielsen, D. 1922. *Der dreieinige Gott in religionshistorischer Beleuchtung,* vol. 1: "Die drei Göttlichen Personnen." Copenhagen.

Nielsen, D. 1942. *Der dreieinige Gott in religionshistorischer Beleuchtung,* vol. 2: "Die Drei Naturgottheiten." Copenhagen.

Nou, J.-L. 1990. *Mémoires d'Euphrate et d'Arabies.* Photographs. Paris: Hatier.

Philby, H. St.-J. 1939. *Sheba's Daughters.* London.

Philby, H. St.-J. 1981. *The Queen of Sheba.* London: Quartet Books.

Phillips, W. 1955. *Qatabân and Sheba: Exploring Ancient Kingdoms of the Biblical Spice Routes of Arabia.* London: Victor Gollancz. (French translation by G. Rives was published as *Qatabân et Saba,* Paris, 1956.)

Pirenne, J. 1954. *La Grèce et Saba.* Paris.

Pirenne, J. 1956. *Paléographie des inscriptions sud-arabes: Contribution à la chronologie et à l'histoire de l'Arabie du Sud antique,* vol. 1. Brussels.

Pirenne, J. 1958. *A la découverte de l'Arabie: Cinq siècles de science et d'aventure.* Paris: L'aventure du passé.

Pirenne, J. 1961. *Le royaume sud-arabe de Qatabân et sa datation d'après l'archéologie et les sources classiques jusqu'au "Périple de la mer Erythrée."* Bibliothèque du Muséon, University of Louvain.

Pirenne, J. 1962 and 1965. *Notes d'archéologie sud-arabe,* vols. 3 & 4.

Pirenne, J. 1982. *L'homme et l'eau en Méditerranée et au Proche-Orient.* 2 vols. Lyon.

Pirenne, J. 1984. "La lecture des rochers inscrits et l'histoire de l'Arabie du Sud antique." *Biblioteca Orientalis* 61: 569–89.

Pirenne, J. 1990. *Les témoins inscrits de la région de Shabwa et l'histoire.* Paris: Geuthner.

Potts, D. T., ed. 1988. *Araby the Blest: Studies in Arabian Archaeology.* The Carsten Niebuhr Institute of Ancient Near Eastern Studies, University of Copenhagen.

Pouilloux, J. 1960. *Choix d'inscriptions grecques.* Paris.

Preissler, H. 1984. "Abhängigkeitsverhältnissein Südarabien im mittel-sabäischer Zeit (1. Jh. v. u. Z.–4.Jh. u. Z.)." *Ethnogr. Archäol. Zeitung.* 25: 73–83. Leipzig.

Pritchard, J. 1955. *Ancient Near-Eastern Texts Relating to the Old Testament.* Princeton.

Rathjens, C. 1955. "Sabaeica, Bericht über die archäologischen Ergebnisse seiner zweiten, dritten, und vierten Reise nach Südarabien." *Die unlocalisierten Funde,* part 2, photos 245–50, pp. 219–20.

Retsö, J. 1991. "The Domestication of the Camel and the Establishment of the Frankincense Road from South Arabia." *Orientalia Suecana* 60: 198.

Robin, C. 1979. "La cité et l'organization sociale à Maʿîn: L'example de Ytl (aujourd'hui Barâqiš)." Second International Symposium on Studies of the History of Arabia. Pre-Islamic Arabia (Departments of History and Arachaeology. Faculty of Arts, University of Riyadh), 1399/1979.

Robin, C. 1982a. "Esquisse d'une histoire de l'organisation tribale en Arabie due Sud antique." *La Péninsule Arabe aujourd'hui* (1982): 19–20. CNRS.

Robin, C. 1982b. *Les Hautes-Terres du Nord-Yémen avant l'Islam.* 2 vols. Istanbul: Publications de l'Institut Historique-Archéologique Néerlandais de Stamboul.

Robin, C. 1984. "Aux origines de l'Etat himyarite: Himyar et dhû-Raydân." *Arabian Studies in Honor of Mahmoud Ghul.* Wiesbaden. Symposium at Yarmouk University, December 8–11, 1984.

Robin, C. 1988. "Two Inscriptions from Qaryat al-Faw mentioning Women, Araby the Blest." *Studies in Arabaian Archaeology* (1988): 172–74. Copenhagen.

Robin, C. 1991–93. "Les écritures avant l'Islam." REMM 61: 134–35.

Robin, C. 1991a. "La pénétration des Arabes nomades au Yémen." REMM 61: 72.

Robin, C. 1991b. "L'Arabie du Sud et la date du 'Périple de la mer Erythrée' (Nouvelles données)." *Journal asiatique* 279: 1–31.

Robin, C. 1992. *Inventaire des inscriptions sud-arabiques,* vol. 1: *Innabaʾ, Haram, al-Kâfir, Kamna et al-Harâshîf.* Paris: Académie des Inscriptions et Belles-Lettres–IsMEO.

Robin, C. 1994. "Yashurʾîl Yuharʾish mukarrib du Hadramawt." *Raydân* 6: 101–11 and plate 48 (p.192).

Robin, C. 1996. "Sheba dans les inscriptions d'Arabie du Sud." *Dictionnaire de la Bible,* Supplement. Paris: Letouzey.

Robin, C., and J.-F. Breton. 1982. "Le sanctuaire préislamique du Gabal al-Lawd (Nord-Yémen)." CRAIBL: 621–27.

Robin, C., and J. Ryckmans. 1981. "Le sanctuaire minéen de Nakrah à Darb as-Sabî (environ de Barâqish): Rapport préliminaire (second partie)." *Raydân* 5: 91–159.

Robin, C., ed. 1991. "L'Arabie antique de Karibʾîl jusquʾà Mahomet: Nouvelles données sur l'histoire des Arabes grâce aux inscriptions." *Revue de monde musulman et de la Méditerranée* 61(1991–3). Edisud.

Robin, C., J.-F. Breton, and J. Ryckmans. 1981. "Le sanctuaire minéen de Nakrah à Darb as-Sabî (environ de Barâqish): Rapport préliminaire." *Raydân* 4: 249–61 and plates 1–10.

Roux, J.-C. 1996. *Fouilles archéologiques des ouvrages hydrauliques.* Roussillon: DRAC du Languedoc.

Ryckmans, J. 1945. "La confession publique des péchés en Arabie méridionale préislamique." *Le muséon* 58: 1–14. Louvain.

Ryckmans, J. 1963. "L'apparition du cheval en Arabie ancienne." *Ex Oriente Lux* 17: 211–26.

Ryckmans, J. 1972. "Les confessions publiques sabéens: Le code sud-arabe de pureté rituelle." *Annali dell'Isituto Orientale di Napoli* 32: 1–15. Naples.

Ryckmans, J. 1989. "Le panthéon de l'Arabie du Sud préislamique: Etat des problèmes et brève synthèse." *Revue d'histoire des religions* 206: 151–69. Paris.

Ryckmans, J. 1993. "Pétioles de palmes et bâtonnets inscrits: Un type nouveau de documents du Yémen antique." *Bulletin de la classe des lettres.* Académie Royale de Belgique.

Ryckmans, J., W. W. Müller, and Y. Abdallah. 1994. *Textes du Yémen antique inscrits sur bois.* Louvain-le-Neuve: Institut Orientaliste.

Salles, J.-F., ed. 1988. *L'Arabie et ses mers bordières.* Lyon: Travaux de la Maison de l'Orient, vol. 16.

Sartre, A. 1989. "Architecture funéraire de la Syrie." *Archéologie et histoire de Syrie,* vol 2. Saarbrücken.

Sartre, M. 1991. *L'Orient romain: Provinces et sociétés provinciales en Méditerranée orientale d'Auguste aux Sévères (31 av. J.-C.–235 ap. J.-C.).* Paris: Le Seuil.

Schaloske, M. 1995. *Untersuchungen der sabäischen Bewässerungsanlagen in Marib.* ABADY, vol. 7. Mainz: Philipp von Zabern.

Schmidt, J. 1982a. "Tempel und Heiligtum von al-Masâgid." ABADY, vol. 1, pp. 135–43 and plate 56. Mainz: Philipp von Zabern.

Schmidt, J. 1982b. "Mârib: Erster vorläufiger Bericht." ABADY, vol. 1, pp. 73–77. Mainz: Philipp von Zabern.

Schmidt, J. 1987. *Der Tempel des Waddum dhû-Masmaʾim.* ABADY, vol. 4. Mainz: Philipp von Zabern.

Sedov, A. V., and Griaznevich, eds. 1996. *Raybûn Settlement (1983– 1987 Excavations).* Preliminary Reports of the Soviet-Yemeni Joint Complex Expedition, vol. 2 (in Russian). Moscow.

Sedov, A. S. 1992. "New Archaeological and Epigraphical Material from Qanaʾ (South Arabia)." AAE 3.2: 110–38 and fig. 4.

Sedov, A. S. 1994. "Qanaʾ (Yemen) and the Indian Ocean: The Archaeological Evidence, Tradition, and Archaeology." *Early Maritime Contacts in the Indian Ocean.* Proceedings of the International Seminar, New Delhi.

Sedov, A. S., and Bâtayi. 1994. "Temples of Ancient Hadramawt." PSAS 24: 183–96.

Segall, B. 1955. "Sculpture from Arabia Felix: The Hellenistic Period." *American Journal of Archaeology* 599: 207–14 and plates 62–65.

Segall, B. 1958. "The Lion-Riders of Timnaᶜ." In Albright 1958, pp. 155–78.

Serjeant, R. B. 1962. "Haram and Hawtah, the Sacred Enclaves in Arabia." *Mélanges Taha Husain.* Cairo. Republished in Serjeant 1981.

Serjeant, R. B. 1976. *South Arabian Hunt.* London: Luzac.

Serjeant, R. B. 1981. *Studies in Arabian History and Civilisation.* London: Variorum Reprints.

Serjeant, R. B., and R. Lewcock. 1983. *Sanaʾa, an Arabian Islamic City.* London: World of Islam Festival Trust.

Sidebotham, S. E. 1986. *Roman Economic Policy in the Erythra Thalassa, 30 B.C.–A.D. 217.* London: Leiden Brill.

Simeone-Senelle, M.-C. 1994. "Suqutra: Parfums, sucs, et résines." *Sabaʾ,* vol. 2.

Starck, F. 1992. *La route de l'encense: Un voyage dans l'Hadramaout.* Paris: Payot.

Thomas, B. 1932. *Arabia Felix.* London.

Tindel, R. D. 1994. "The Rise of the Himyar and the Origins of Modern Yemen." *Arabia Felix* (1994): 273–79.

Van Beek, G. 1969. *Hajar ibn-Humayd: Investigations at a Pre-Islamic Site in South Arabia.* Publications of the American Foundation for the Study of Man, vol. 5. Baltimore: The Johns Hopkins University Press.

Vogt, B. 1994. "Death, Resurrection, and the Camel." *Arabia Felix* (1994): 279–90.

Volkoff, O. V. 1985. *D'où vient la reine de Saba?*. Cairo: IFAO.

Von Wissman, H., and C. Rathjens. 1932. "Vorislamische Altertümer." *Rathjens-v. Wissmanche Süderabien-Riese,* vol. 2.

Von Wissmann, H. 1982. *Die Geschichte von Saba? II: Das Grossreich der Sabäer bis zu seinem Ende im frühen 4 Jht v. Chr.* Österreichischen Akademie der Wissenschaften, Philiosophische-historiche Klasse, Sitzungsberichte, vol. 402. Herausgegeben von W. W. Müller.

Wilkinson, T. J., C. Edens, and M. Gibson. 1997. "The Archaeology of the Yemen High Plains: A Preliminary Chronology." AAE 8(1997): 99–142.

Will, E. 1949a. "La tour funéraire de Palmyre." *Syria* 26 (fasc.1–2): 87–116 and plates 5 and 6.

Will, E. 1949b. "La tour funéraire de Syrie et les monuments apparentés." *Syria* 26 (fasc. 3–4): 258–313 and plates 13 and 14.

Will, E. 1959. "L'adyton dans le temple syrien à l'époque impériale." *Études d'archéologie classique,* vol. 2: "Annales de l'Est," report 22. University of Nancy.

Will, E. 1989. "De la Syrie au Yémen: Problèmes des relations dans le domaine de l'art." *L'Arabie préislamique et son environnement historique et culturel,* pp. 271–81. Université de Sciences Humaines de Strasbourg. Proceedings of a colloquium.

INDEX

Abraha (king of Yemen), 20

Abyan, 186n.15

Actium, battle of, 166

Aden, 7

Aelius Gallus (prefect of Egypt), as
commander, 166–67, 168,
169, 170

Agatharchides: on aromatics, 55; on
houses, 86; on Maʾrib, 22; and
maritime routes, 73; on Saba, 9

agriculture: in Awsân, 34; and barter
system, 106, 107; cities' dependence on, 108–9; collectivity of, 93, 108; decline of, 108–
9; and fields, 1; on
floodplains, 11–12; history of,
103; inscriptions about, 105;
in Maʾrib, 20–21, 93; and
money, 106–7; in Qatabân, 44,
105–7; in Saba, 40, 41; in
Shabwa, 47–48; and sover-
eigns, 105, 106; and tribes,
94–95, 105; and Yadaʾab
Dhubyân, 105

ahl, defined, 95

Alexander the Great (king of Mace-
donia), 6, 72, 73

Almaqah (god): and Awwâm, 25; and
bulls, 127; importance of, 117,
120, 178; inscriptions about,
120; pilgrimages to honor,
132; and Saba, 32, 117, 119–
20, 159, 162; in Shabwa, 48;

and Shams, 120; temples to,
13, 120

aloe, 62, 172. *See also* aromatics

American Foundation for the Study of
Man, 7

ʿAmm (god), 121–22

Amran rifts, 12

animals: images of, 124–27, 134–35,
136, 138, 141; importance of,
104; raising of, 103–5

Arabia Deserta, 2

Arabia Felix: agriculture in, 49; Arabia Deserta compared to, 2; archaeological digs in, 7–8; and
Assyrians, 2; decadence and inertia in, 1–2; deforestation of,
82; disappearance of, 1; geography and topography of, 1, 2, 8,
9–11, 12–13, 48–49; and Hebrews, 2; incense trade in, 50–
51; irrigation in, 49; location
of, 1; origins of name, 1; and
Phoenicians, 2; population of,
75–76; trade in, 2, 49–51;
unity of, 29, 49–50; wealth of,
2. *See also specific headings*

Arabic, 29

Arabs: defined, 116, 164; gods of,
164; inscriptions about, 165;
and Jawf, 164; and Kaminahû,
164; and Karibʾîl Watar, 164;
and Maʿîn, 170; and Manhiyat,
164–65; and Maʾrib, 165; and

Arabs: (cont'd)
 Nashshân, 164; as nomads,
 116, 164; origins of, 163–64;
 and Qatabân, 165; and Romans, 166–69; and Saba, 164,
 165–66
Araby the Blest. *See* Arabia Felix
archaic period, of Greek literature, 5–6
architecture: Greco-Roman influence
 on, 175, 179; of temples, 137–
 38, 139, *140* (figure), 141–42;
 of tombs, 157
Aristotle, 62
Arnaud, Théodore, 7
aromatics: Agatharchides on, 55; and
 Augustus, 166; and caravan
 kingdoms, 29; in Greek literature, 5–6; Herodotus on, 53–
 54; Theophrastus of Eresos on,
 54; trade in, 50–51. *See also*
 cassia; *costus;* dragon's blood;
 frankincense; gum-labdanum;
 incense; myrrh; rue; saffron;
 storax
ʿArsh Bilqîs, 25–26
art, 141, 174–75, 179. *See also*
 specific headings
Assyrians: and aromatics, 2, 5; art of,
 141; tombs of, 150
ʿAthtar (god): banquets for, 130, 131;
 characteristics of, 126; and
 floods, 27; hunts dedicated to,
 132; and Saba, 32, 132; in
 Shabwa, 48; supremacy of,
 117, 119, 131; temples of, 136
ʿAthtar dhû-Dhibân (god), 27
ʿAthtar dhû-Qabd (god), 48
ʿAthtar dhû-Risaf, 136
Augustus (Roman emperor): and
 aromatics, 6, 166; and Bab
 al-Mandab Strait, 169; growth
 of empire of, 166; Strabo on,
 170
Awsân: agriculture in, 34, 35; capital

of, 34; history of, 34; location
 of, 29; prosperity of, 34; and
 Saba, 34, 36, 40; sovereigns of,
 34–35
Awwâm: and Almaqah, 25; importance of, 177; purposes of,
 120; and tombs, 148–49

Bab al-Mandab, 169, 185n.2 (Introduction)
Bâkil tribe, 159, 177
banquets, ritual, 130–31, 157
Barʾân, 120
Barâqish, 76, 77–78, 171
Barʾat Lady, 175
Bardey, Alfred and Pierre, 7
Barîra, 47
barter system, 106–7
al-Baydâʾ. *See* Nashshân
Bedouins: and farmhouses, 91; gods
 of, 118; and Hajar Yahir, 165;
 women among, 99
beekeepers, 102–3
Bent, Theodore, 58, 60
Bilqîs, 5. *See also* ʿArsh Bilqîs; Mahram Bilqîs
Botta, Paul-Emile, 7
bronze-casters, 112, 113
bulls, 124–25, 127
burial practices. *See* tombs

camels: in caravans, 69, 104, 115–
 16; and dhât-Himyam, 127;
 and dhû-Samâwî, 127; domestication of, 51; images of, 127–
 28; importance of, 104, 114;
 inscriptions about, 104; sacrifices of, 154–55; and Sayîn,
 127; Strabo on, 115; tombs of,
 154–55; as transportation, 2,
 51; in wars, 114–15
caravan kingdoms, 29. *See also*
 Awsân; Hadramawt; Qatabân;
 Saba

caravans: camels used in, 69, 104, 115–16; decline of, 159; guides for, 69–70; inscriptions about, 70–71; and nomads, 70; organization of, 69–71; raids on, 70; routes of, 6, 66–68; Strabo on, 69

carpenters, 110–11

cassia: origins of word, 5; Pliny on, 62, 188n.35; price of, 68; and Sappho, 5, 57; species of, 61; trade in, 68, 188n.35; uses of, 61–62; and Vespasian, 63. *See also* aromatics

Caton-Thomson, Gertrude, 7, 145–46

cavalry, 161

cereal crops, 101

ceremonies and pacts, of federations, 131–32

cherub plaques, 175

Christians, 4

cinnamon. *See* cassia

cities, 79, 107–9. *See also specific cities*

clans, 95

coins. *See* money

commerce. *See* trade

confessions, ritual, 128–30

construction projects: artisans involved in, 109–12; in Nashshân, 35; in Qatabân, 179; in Saba, 171, 179; and sovereigns, 34. *See also specific headings*

costus, 63

cults, 29, 32

ad-Dâliʾ, Lady of, 157

dams, 19. *See also* irrigation

Danes, 7

Darius the Great (king of Persia), 71–72

date palms, 1, 21, 102

datha, defined, 11

dead, hill of the, 146–47. *See also* tombs

dedications, offerings, and sacrifices: banning of, 188n.12; of camels, 154–55; metaphorical nature of, 127–28; purposes of, 103, 151, 152–53; in tombs, 150–53, 155, 157; types of, 136–37, 150–52, 153, 155, 157

deforestation, 21–22, 82

Dhamar Alî Watar (king of Saba and dhû-Raydân), 131–32

dhât-Himyam (goddess): and camels, 127; characteristics of, 134–35; temple of, 139–41, *140* (figure)

dhû-Samâwî (god), 127, 132, 164

dikes, 19–20, 179. *See also* irrigation

divinities. *See* gods and goddesses

donkeys, 12

dragon's blood, 62–63. *See also* aromatics

eagles, 125

Egyptians, 145

embalming, 145, 147, 193n.3. *See also* tombs

Epigraphic South Arabian (language): history of, 8, 29–30; inscriptions in, 31–32

eponyms, lists of: defined, 27; priests in, 126–27; and Saba, 32, 93

Ethiopia, 39–40

Eudoxus of Cyzicus, 169–70

Evangelists, 3

farmhouses, 90–91

Fayshân tribe, 162, 194n.9

federations, ceremonies and pacts of, 131–32

fields, 1. *See also* agriculture

flash floods. *See* floods

floodplains, 11–12

floods: and ʿAthtar dhû-Dhibân, 27; characteristics of, 14–18; and

floods: (*cont'd*)
irrigation, 15–16, 18, 19–20,
21; and Maʾrib, 13–18, 19–20,
21; and peasants, 100; and
temples, 135. *See also* monsoons
forests, 21–22, 82
fortifications: of Barāqish, 77–78;
characteristics of, 77, 189n.4;
history of, 76–78; houses as,
83–84, 89, 91; and inscriptions, 77, 78; of Maʿîn, 78,
111; of Maʾrib, 22–24, 76; of
Nashshân, 77; purposes of,
76; of as-Sawdâʾ, 111; of
Shabwa, 76, 78; of Tamnaʿ,
76; and villages, 89
fragrances. *See* aromatics
frankincense: and Assyrians, 2, 5;
Bent on, 58, 60; characteristics
of, 57–58; effects of, 1; and
Hadramawt, 2, 38, 64, 171;
harvesting of, 58–60; and
Hatshepsut, 71; and Hebrews,
2, 5; and Herodotus, 6; location of plants, 6, 58, 188n.14;
and Maʿîn, 45–46; Monod on,
58, 59; and Nero, 63–64; and
Phoenicians, 2; Pliny on, 58–
59, 60, 63–64, 65–66, 67, 68;
price of, 68; and Qanaʾ, 172–
73; in Qatabân, 45, 56; rue
compared to, 55, 187n.6; and
Saba, 2–3, 40–41; and Sappho,
5, 57; species of, 57–58; Strabo
on, 56; and Theophrastus, 6;
trade in, 60–61, 63, 64–67,
68, 188n.32; uses of, 5, 57,
115; at Wadd dhû-Masmaʾim,
13. *See also* aromatics
funerals. *See* tombs

Garden of Earthly Delights (Hohenbourg), 4

Gate of Tears, 169, 185n.2 (Introduction)
Ghumdân, 163
Glaser, Eduard, 7
goddess plaques: characteristics of,
134–35, 151, 193n.17;
defined, 134; Greco-Roman
style of, 151
gods and goddesses: dedications and
sacrifices to, 127–28; of
Greeks and Romans, 118,
192n.2; in Hadramawt, 122;
images of, 123, 132–35, 138,
141, 192n.27; inscriptions
about, 117–18; in Maʿîn, 121;
pilgrimages to honor, 132,
192n.20; in Qatabân, 121–22,
135; in Saba, 119–21. *See also*
specific gods and goddesses
gold mines, 1
grapes, 101
graves. *See* tombs
Greeks: architecture of, 175, 179; banquet halls of, 157; gods of,
118, 192n.2; literature of, 5–6;
and myrrh, 56–57; tombs of,
149–50, 157
Green Yemen, 11, 161, 194n.3. *See*
also Yemen
gum-labdanum, 61, 68. *See also* aromatics

Hadramawt: aromatics in, 2, 38, 56,
64, 171; gods in, 122; growth
of, 171; location of, 29, 46–
47; and Maʿîn, 46, 171; and
Qatabân, 47; and Saba, 47,
163; and Socotra, 171; and
sovereigns, 171; temples in,
139–42; tombs in, 145; trade
by, 171. *See also* caravan kingdoms
Hadrami, 31
Hajar Ibn Humayd, 7

Hajar Yahir, 16, 34, 165
Halévy, Joseph, 7
Halfân (god), 164
al-Hamdâni, al-Hasân, 179–80
Happy Arabia. *See* Arabia Felix
al-Haraja, 18
Haram, 126
haram, defined, 94
Hashîd tribes, 177
Hatshepsut (queen of Egypt), 71
Hawbas (god), 121
Hayd Ibn ʿAqîl, 7, 156
Hebrews: and aromatics, 2, 5; and
    Queen of Sheba, 3–4
Herodotus: on aromatics, 6, 53–54,
    63; on sheep and shepherds,
    114
hill of the dead, 146–47. *See also*
    tombs
Himyar, 6
Himyar tribe, 156, 160–61, 163
honey, 102
hoopoe, 3–4
horses, 104–5, 161
houses: Agatharchides on, 86; charac-
    teristics of, 12; decoration of,
    85–86; on floodplains, 12; as
    fortifications, 83–84, 89, 91;
    inscriptions in, 83, 84, 85, 87–
    88; purposes of, 86–88; in
    Shabwa, 80–88; Strabo on, 80;
    temples compared to, 88; tombs
    compared to, 150; as towers,
    80, 82–85, 91, 150; wood
    used in, 82; Woolley on, 79
hunts, ritual, 132
al-Huqqa, 7
al-Huraydha, 7
hydraulic works. *See* waterworks

ibex, 124, 132
incense, 63–64. *See also* aromatics
Indian Ocean, 73
inscriptions: about agriculture, 105;

about animals, 104; about
Arabs, 165; about banquets,
130; at Barâqish, 78; about
barter system, 107; about caravans, 70–71; confessions as,
128–29; contents of, 30; in
Epigraphic South Arabian, 31–
32; about federation ceremonies, 131; and fortifications,
77, 78; about gods and goddesses, 117–18, 120, 121; history of, 29; in houses, 83, 84,
85, 87–88; about irrigation,
100–101, 106; and Karibʾîl
Watar, 34, 38; at Maʾrib, 22,
24, 25, 26, 27; at Nashshân,
77; about priests, 126; in Qatabân, 165; and Saba, 43, 162;
in Sabaean, 31–32, 177; at
Shabwa, 83; in temples, 136,
138–39, 141; in tombs, 148,
152–53, 157; about water-
works, 101; about and by
women, 98
irrigation: and floods, 15–16, 18, 19–
20, 21; and Hajar Yahir, 16;
history of, 49; inscriptions
about, 100–101, 106; and
peasants, 100–101; and Raybûn, 16; and Saba, 27; and
Shabwa, 16; and Tamnaʿ, 16;
and taxation, 126; of temple
properties, 126; and Yadaʾab
Dhubyân, 105. *See also* dikes
istisqâ, defined, 132

Jabal Balaq, 13, 19
Jawf: and Arabs, 164; cities of, 75;
    and Saba, 36; temples in, 124,
    126, 132–34, 137–39, 141–
    42; tribes in, 164

Kaminahû, 76, 164
Karibʾîl Watar (king of Saba): and

Karibʾil Watar: (cont'd)
    Arabs, 164; banquets of, 131;
    and Barāqish, 78; construction
    projects of, 38; and inscrip-
    tions, 34, 38; and Saba, 131;
    and Sumhuyafaʾ, 37; and
    trade, 34; and Warawʾil, 38;
    wars of, 34, 35–39, 40, 41,
    43, 164; and Yadʾil, 47
kharaf, defined, 11
kings and queens. See sovereigns
Kirwan (god), 132
Kuhâl (god), 123

Lady of ad-Dâliᶜ, 157
Livy, 63
locust trees, 21–22

Madhabian (language), 31
Mahram Bilqîs, 17, 24–25
Maᶜîn: and Arab nomads, 170; decline
    of, 170, 171; fortifications of,
    78, 111; and frankincense, 45–
    46; gods in, 121; and Hadra-
    mawt, 46, 171; size of, 45, 76;
    temples at, 134; Wadd in, 121
Maᶜîn tribe, 95
Manhiyat, 164–65
Maʾrib: aerial photographs of, 19;
    Agatharchides on, 22; agricul-
    ture in, 20–21, 93; and Arabs,
    165; and Arnaud, 7; buildings
    in, 24–26; as capital city, 22,
    33, 163; characteristics of, 13–
    14, 22; deforestation of, 21–
    22; dike in, 19–20; floods in,
    13–18, 19–20, 21; fortification
    of, 22–24, 76; al-Hamdâni on,
    179–80; importance of, 22,
    33; inscriptions at, 22, 24, 25,
    26, 27; location of, 33; quar-
    ries of, 26; and Saba, 162; and
    siltation, 16–18; size of, 76;
    tombs at, 26–27, 148–49,

    150; Wadi Dhana compared
    to, 13–14; waterworks in, 15–
    16, 17, 18, 19–20, 23 (figure)
maritime routes, 71–73. See also cara-
    vans
marketplaces, 107–8
marriage, 98–100
mausoleums, 148. See also tombs
Mesopotamia, art of, 134, 192n.22
Minaean (language), 31
monarchs. See sovereigns
money, 106–7
Monod, Théodore, 58, 59
monsoons, 11. See also floods
moon, images of, 125
mountains, 1, 9–10, 11
mukarrib, defined, 33. See also sover-
    eigns
mummification, 145, 147, 193n.3.
    See also tombs
Muslims, 4–5
Myriam (alabaster head), 152
myrrh: and Assyrians, 5; and Awsân,
    35; characteristics of, 1, 55–
    56; and Greeks, 56–57; in
    Hadramawt, 56; and Hebrews,
    5; history of, 5, 55; location of
    plants, 188n.14; Pliny on, 55,
    65–66; price of, 68; Sappho
    on, 5, 57; Strabo on, 56; trade
    in, 63, 64, 65–66; uses of, 5,
    56. See also aromatics

Nakrah (god), 138–39
Nashshân: and Arabs, 164; construc-
    tion projects in, 35, 77, 126;
    destruction of, 37; fortification
    of, 77; inscriptions at, 77; pros-
    perity of, 35; and Saba, 35,
    36–37; temples in, 126
Nawash (god), 160
Nearchus, 72
Nero (Roman emperor), 63–64
nobility. See sovereigns

nomads: Arabs as, 116, 164; and cara-
    vans, 70; defined, 116; as in-
    fluential group, 156; and
    Maʿīn, 170; and Saba, 159,
    163; Strabo on, 114; tombs of,
    156

offerings. See dedications, offerings,
    and sacrifices
olives, 103, 191n.20
oracles, 128. See also priests

pacts and ceremonies, of federations,
    131–32
palms, date, 1, 21, 102
Palmyra, 149–50
peasants: as beekeepers, 102–3; cereal
    crops grown by, 101; and irri-
    gation, 100–101; in social life,
    100–103; taxation of, 106
perfumes. See aromatics
Periplus of the Red Sea (Anonymous),
    171–74
Philby, Saint-John, 144
Phoenician (language), 29–30
Phoenicians, 2
pilgrimages, 132, 192n.20
plateaus, 10, 11–12
Pliny (the Elder): on Alexander the
    Great, 72; on Arabia Felix, 2;
    on aromatics, 55, 58–59, 60,
    61, 62–64, 65–66, 67, 68,
    188nn.32, 35; on date palms,
    21, 102; on Himyarite tribe,
    161; on maritime routes, 73;
    on Qatabân, 45; on Roman-
    Arab war, 167–68; on Sayîn,
    122; on trade, 68–69, 73
Pliny the Younger, 1
portraits, 151–52
priests, 126–28
Ptolemies, 170

Qanaʾ, 172–73

al-Qarn, 13
Qatabân: agriculture in, 44, 105–7;
    and Arabs, 165; capital of, 44;
    construction projects in, 179;
    decline of, 171; and frankin-
    cense, 45, 56; gods and god-
    desses in, 121–22, 132, 135;
    growth of, 44–45; and Hadra-
    mawt, 47; hunts in, 132; in-
    scriptions in, 165; location of,
    29; marketplaces in, 107–8;
    Pliny on, 45; and Saba, 43–44;
    sovereigns in, 33; Strabo on,
    44–45; temples in, 124; water-
    works in, 44. See also caravan
    kingdoms
Qatabanian (language), 31
quarries, 26, 109–10
Queen of Sheba, 3–5, 41–43
queens. See Queen of Sheba; sovereigns

Rahban (god), 141
Ramlat as-Sabʾatayn, 10
Rathjens, Carl, 7
Raybûn, 16, 146
Raydân, 178
Raydân tribes, 160–61
Rimbaud, Arthur, 7
Romans: and Arabs, 166–69; architec-
    ture of, 175, 179; and Bab al-
    Mandab, 169; banquet halls
    of, 157; explorations of, 6;
    gods of, 118, 192n.2; and in-
    cense, 63–64; and Saba, 2,
    163; tombs of, 149–50, 157;
    and trade, 159
rue, 55, 187n.6

Saʾad family, 95
Saba: Agatharchides on, 9; agriculture
    in, 40, 41; and Arabs, 164,
    165–66; and art, 179; and
    Awsân, 34, 36, 40; capital of,
    22, 33, 163; construction

Saba: (cont'd)
    projects in, 171, 179; decline
        of, 43–44, 161, 162, 163,
        168, 171; demographics of,
        41; and Dhamar Alî Watar,
        131–32; and eponyms list, 32,
        93; and Ethiopians, 39; federa-
        tion pacts of, 131; and frankin-
        cense, 2–3, 40–41; gods in,
        32, 117, 119–21, 132, 159,
        162; growth of, 39, 41, 160,
        177; and Hadramawt, 47, 163;
        hunts in, 132; importance of,
        50, 178–79; and inscriptions,
        43, 162; and irrigation, 27;
        and Jawf, 36; and Karib'îl
        Watar, 131; location of, 2–3,
        29; and Ma'rib, 162; and
        Nashshân, 35, 36–37; and no-
        mads, 159, 163; origins of, 2,
        93, 131, 162; prosperity of,
        40; and Qatabân, 43–44; and
        Romans, 163; sovereigns of,
        32–34, 162–63, 168, 177; tem-
        ples in, 124, 126; tombs in,
        50; and tribes, 156, 160, 162,
        163, 177; unity of, 32–33, 40;
        and waterworks, 179. See also
        caravan kingdoms
Saba and dhû-Raydân, kings of, 163,
    178
Sabaean (language): characteristics of,
        31; in Ethiopia, 39–40; growth
        of, 39, 50; history of, 30–31,
        32, 177; importance of, 39–
        40, 50, 177–78; inscriptions
        in, 31–32, 177; in Shabwa, 48
Sabaeans, 1, 2
sacrifices. See dedications, offerings,
    and sacrifices
saffron, 5, 57. See also aromatics
Salhîn Palace, 24
saltworks, 80
Samî (god), 123

Samî' tribe, 177
Samsara, defined, 13
Sana, 159, 160, 163
sanctuaries. See temples
Sappho, 5, 57
as-Sawdâ', 111, 133–34
Sayîn (god), 122, 127, 132
sayl, defined, 14
scribes, 112–13
sculptors, 111–12
Scylax, 71
sea routes, 71–73. See also caravans
Seleucus (king of Seleucid Empire), 72
sexual offenses, 130
Shabwa: agriculture in, 47–48; and
        Barîra, 47; characteristics of,
        79–82; excavation of, 7; forti-
        fication of, 76, 78; gods in, 48;
        houses in, 80–88; importance
        of, 65; inscriptions in, 83; and
        irrigation, 16; location of, 47;
        Sabaean used in, 48; saltworks
        in, 80; and siltation, 195n.3;
        and trade, 47; waterworks
        in, 48
Shams (goddess), 120, 132
Shaqîr Palace, 80–81
Sheba. See Queen of Sheba; Saba
sheep and shepherds, 114
Shibâm al-Ghirâs, 147
shipping. See maritime routes; trade
silt and siltation: and al-Haraja, 18;
        and Mahram Bilqîs, 17; and
        Ma'rib, 16–18; remedies for,
        179; and temples, 17, 135;
        tombs in, 153–54, 156–57
Sirwâh, 7, 13
slaves, 97
social life: characteristics of, 93–94;
        nobility and sovereigns in, 96,
        97; organization of, 95–97;
        peasants in, 100–103; slaves
        in, 97; women in, 97–100
Socotra, 62, 171

Solomon (biblical figure), 3, 4–5, 41–43
South Arabia. *See* Arabia Felix
sovereigns: and agriculture, 105, 106;
        of Awsân, 34–35; in caravan
        kingdoms, 29; construction
        projects of, 34; duties of, 97,
        123; and Hadramawt, 171;
        and hunts, 132; of Saba, 32–
        34, 132, 162–63, 168, 177; in
        social life, 96, 97; and Tamnaᶜ,
        108
spices. *See* aromatics
stelae, 156, 157
stonecutters, 110
storax, 63. *See also* aromatics
Strabo: on aromatics, 56; on Augus-
        tus, 170; on beekeeping, 103;
        on camels, 115; on caravans,
        69; on houses, 80; on nomads,
        114; on Ptolemies, 170; on
        Qatabân, 44–45; on Roman-
        Arab war, 167, 169; on
        women, 98–99
Sulaiman, 3, 4–5, 41–43
Sumʾay tribes, 160
Sumhuyafaʾ (king of Nashshân), 37
Syria, 150, 157

Taʾlab (god), 160
Tamnaᶜ: as capital city, 44; decline of,
        171; fortification of, 76; and ir-
        rigation, 16; necropolis of,
        147–48; and sovereigns, 108
taxation, 106, 126
temples: to Almaqah, 13, 120; animal
        images in, 124–25, 127–28,
        134–35, 136, 138, 141; archi-
        tecture of, 137–38, 139, *140*
        (figure), 141–42; to Awwâm,
        148–49; contents of, 136–37;
        of dhât-Himyam, 139–41,
        140; and floods, 135; god and
        goddess images in, 132–35,
        138, 141, 192n.27; in Hadra-

mawt, 139–42; in Haram,
        126; history of, 125–26;
        houses compared to, 88; hu-
        man images in, 132–35, 137;
        inscriptions in, 141; and irriga-
        tion, 126; in Jawf, 124, 126,
        133–34, 137–39, 141–42; lo-
        cation of, 135–36, 139; in
        Maᶜîn, 134; moon images in,
        125; in Nashshân, 126; priests
        of, 126–27; in Qatabân, 124;
        of Rahban, 141; in Saba, 124,
        126; at as-Sawdâʾ, 133–34; to
        Sayîn, 122; and siltation, 135;
        of Wadd dhû-Masmaʾim, 13;
        and wealth of builders, 126
Theophrastus of Eresos, 6, 54, 122
thorn, Arabian, 21
Tiberius (Roman emperor), 170
Tihâma, 10
tombs: architecture of, 157; and ban-
        quets, 157; of camels, 154–55;
        and Caton-Thomson, 145–46;
        contents of, 144, 145–47,
        148, 149, 150–52, 153, 155;
        and demographic changes,
        156–57; houses compared to,
        150; human images in, 151–
        52, 157; influences on, 50,
        149–50, 157; inscriptions in,
        148, 152–53, 157; living
        world compared to, 143; loca-
        tion of, 26–27, 50, 143, 145–
        47, 148–50, 153–54, 156–57;
        of nomads, 156; offerings left
        in, 150–53, 155, 157; and
        Philby, 144; of poor persons,
        153–54; reuse of, 147, 154,
        156; types of, 144. *See also*
        mausoleums; mummification
towers: houses as, 80, 82–85, 91,
        150; tombs as, 149–50
trade: in aromatics, 60–61, 63–67,
        68, 166, 188nn.32, 35; and

trade: (cont'd)
    Barîra, 47; in cities, 107–8;
    and Hadramawt, 171; history
    of, 2, 49–50; and Indian
    Ocean, 73; and Karibʾîl Watar,
    34; and Periplus of the Red Sea,
    171–74; Pliny on, 68–69, 73;
    and Romans, 159; and
    Shabwa, 47; and Tiberius, 170
tribes: and agriculture, 94–95, 105;
    characteristics of, 94–96; and
    clans, 95; confederation of, 97,
    105, 159–60; duties of, 97;
    and gods and goddesses, 160;
    importance of, 156; in Jawf,
    164; organization of, 95–97
"two gardens": See Saba; Sabaeans

valleys, 12–13
Vespasian (Roman emperor), 63
villages, 12, 88–90

Wadd (god), 121
Wadd dhû-Masmaʾim, 13
Wadi Dhana, 12–14
Wadi Dura, 153, 156
walls. See fortifications
Warawʾîl (king of Qatabân), 38
wars: between Arabs and Romans,

166–69; camels used in, 114–
    15; and cities, 109; horses
    used in, 104–5; of Karibʾîl
    Watar, 34, 35–39, 40, 41, 43,
    164
water masters, 18, 101
waterworks: construction of, 48; in-
    scriptions about, 101; of
    Karibʾîl Watar, 38; in Maʾrib,
    15–16, 17, 18, 19–20, 23
    (figure); and peasants, 101; in
    Qatabân, 44; in Saba, 179; in
    Shabwa, 48
Wissmann, Hermann von, 7
women: autonomy of, 97–98; among
    Bedouins, 99; confessions of,
    129; images of, 134–35, 137;
    inscriptions about and by, 98;
    sexual offenses of, 130; in so-
    cial life, 97–100; Strabo on,
    98–99
Woolley, Leonard, 79

Yadaʾab Dhubyân, 105
Yaʾdîl (king of Hadramawt), 47
Yasrân, 186n.15
Yathîʾamar Bayân (king of Saba),
    33–34
Yemen, 7–8, 11. See also Green Yemen